IT

SEEMS

LIKE

YESTERDAY

Also by H. V. Kaltenborn

We Look at the World
Kaltenborn Edits the News
I Broadcast the Crisis
Kaltenborn Edits the War News
Europe Now
Fifty Fabulous Years

IT

SEEMS

LIKE

YESTERDAY

H. V. KALTENBORN

G. P. PUTNAM'S SONS NEW YORK

70242

To my four Kaltenborn grandsons, Kurt, Karl, Konrad, and Kristian, who are all old enough to enjoy the pictures, if not the text.

Preface

The inspiration for this book, like that for many others, came from the publisher. He had enjoyed my television program "It Seems Like Yesterday" and suggested that the combination of script and picture, as used on television, might provide much of the raw material for a book.

Having just canceled my radio and television programs to enjoy the first real rest of a long life, I was not eager to take up a new task. But when told that there would be no deadline and that the publisher would furnish competent research assistance, I capitulated. After all, it was a challenge, and as an old newspaperman, I took it on.

In my more than threescore years of reporting, traveling, and interviewing I have accumulated and preserved a huge mass of material. As a broadcaster I am conscious of the words from I Corinthians 24.9—"So likewise ye, except ye utter by the tongue words easy to be understood, how shall it be known what is spoken? For ye shall speak into the Air!"

So I rather liked the idea that some of this material might have enough value to be printed in a book. No matter how well you may know a situation intellectually, when you can actually be on the spot and meet the men who make history face to face, the impressions you receive are much more vivid.

I have had the good fortune to play an active part in each one of the four foreign wars the United States has fought during the past sixty years. I have broadcast spoken editorials since 1922. If years of experience in expounding current history by pen and voice have any value this book should reflect it. I have personally witnessed or currently reported and analyzed all the historic events here recalled by text and pictures. Which does not mean that my evaluations and conclusions are necessarily correct. Certainly, some of my most widely heard prophecies were completely mistaken. Yet I have always tried to report the facts honestly and to interpret them as fairly as is possible for an editor who has developed a vigorous point of view.

And since this is a book that requires personal reminiscence, the inclusion of what I said about events on the very day they happened may help make your remembrance more vivid, so that to you also they "will seem like yesterday."

I was surprised to learn how much of the necessary text could be provided from my accumulated editorials, articles, radio and television scripts. A newspaperman hardly expects anything he writes or speaks to be used years later in a book.

I am under particular obligation to Frank A. Wrensch for his patient and efficient cooperation in wading through a library full of Kaltenborn radio and TV scripts, topic cards, books, and articles and for relieving me of much tedious research work incident to organizing the text.

Most of the work of collecting and organizing the illustrations was done by Frances Orkin and the Putnam organization.

But I will be satisfied if my readers will enjoy leafing through this book to recall and perhaps gain a new perspective on some of the sixty years of eventful history which carried the United States from provincialism to world leadership.

H. V. K.

8

Contents

IT
SEEMS
LIKE
YESTERDAY

1.

William Jennings Bryan— 1896 Campaign

"You shall not press down upon the brow of labor this crown of thorns, you shall not crucify mankind upon a cross of gold." Such were the dramatic, challenging words uttered by William Jennings Bryan at the Democratic convention of 1896. They won for him the Democratic nomination for president at this Chicago convention. This eloquent address by the man then known as the Boy Orator of the Platte has gone down in history as the "Cross of Gold" speech.

The big issues of the 1896 campaign were William Jennings Bryan and free silver. The Democrats had drafted a platform which called for the free and unlimited coinage of silver at the 16 to 1 ratio. It condemned high protective tariffs, trusts, and monopolies as well as the use of injunctions against labor. The Great Commoner, as Bryan came to be known, was running against William McKinley, lawyer, former Republican congressman, former governor of Ohio. McKinley was backed and promoted by Marcus A. Hanna, the Cleveland millionaire, who was always cartooned with the dollar sign. The Republican platform upheld the single gold standard, advocated a high protective tariff, and a strong foreign policy. But the dominant issue of the campaign was the money question. The Republican campaign cry was "Elect McKinley, the Advance Agent of Prosperity."

McKinley was also called the "Full Dinner Pail" candidate and as a boy I can remember parades and rallies where the marchers carried tin dinner pails to emphasize the campaign slogan. Like most youngsters of the Middle West, I was wild for Bryan. A Democratic friend suggested I make speeches in German on free silver to the German farmers of Lincoln County, Wisconsin, where I lived. He hinted that there would be free railroad passes for me if Bryan won. In those days, the un-

William Jennings Bryan delivered the "Cross of Gold" speech at the Democratic convention in 1896.

UNDERWOOD & UNDERWOOD

Free silver was the issue in the 1896 election. This cartoon by W. A. Rogers shows Bryan preparing to halve a silver dollar resting on the neck of a workingman.

regulated railroads bribed politicians of both parties with free rides and expected favorable legislation in return.

I studied the Democratic campaign book, *Coin's Financial School,* which was the bible of the silver advocates, and did my best to make German farmers understand the free coinage of silver at the rate of 16 to 1. I didn't understand it myself, but Lincoln County was the only county in Wisconsin that went

Democratic. When I was offered a pass on the famous Milwaukee Railroad, my father wouldn't let me take it. But I proudly wore a blue ribbon which bore the legend: LINCOLN, THE BANNER COUNTY, *16 to 1*. Back in 1896, young Vachel Lindsay, the American poet, was just as enthusiastic about Bryan as I was and just as ignorant about the real issues of the political campaign. But he captured the spirit of the day in a poem which started off,

> I brag and chant Bryan, Bryan, Bryan
> Candidate for President who sketched a silver zion
> In a coat like a deacon, in a black Stetson hat
> He scourged the elephant plutocrat
> Prairie avenger, mountain lion
> Bryan, Bryan, Bryan, Bryan!

Bryan began a new era of political campaigning in this country. He carried the silver issue to every doubtful state, traveling about 18,000 miles and making 600 speeches. He was a great crusader, the champion of the common man. His campaign technique of going straight to the people with the issue was something new. It eventually set the pattern that Franklin Delano Roosevelt used so successfully in his Fireside Chats and that gave Harry Truman the victory in 1948. Now, sixty years after Bryan's inauguration of a new cam-

In the twilight of his career, Bryan (*left*) faced Clarence Darrow (*right*) in the historic courtroom struggle that took place during the famous Scopes "Monkey Trial" in 1925.

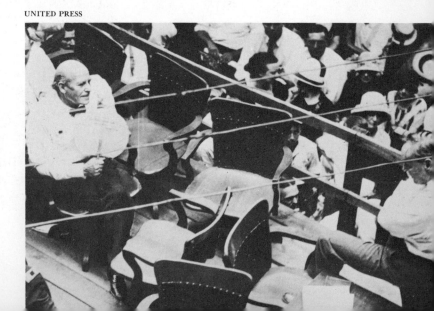

paign tactic, all candidates go straight to the people by means of radio and television.

Although Bryan was defeated in the 1896 election, he was renominated in 1900 and 1908. He became the undisputed leader of the Democratic party and held that prerogative until after 1912. His is a political record few men have ever achieved. In 1900 he was the Democratic nominee against McKinley who, in that campaign, had Theodore Roosevelt as his running mate. Free silver was again the big issue—that and the fight against the trusts and the "imperialism" of the American policy in the Philippines. Bryan tried again a third time, eight years later, but was once more unsuccessful.

My own devotion to Bryan lasted until some time after his Spanish War service. In 1897, I bicycled the 100 miles from Merrill, Wisconsin, to Marinette, Wisconsin, to hear Bryan speak at a Chautauqua meeting.

At the Baltimore convention, in 1912, as the leader of his party, Bryan secured the nomination of another great liberal, Woodrow Wilson. As a reward he became Secretary of State in Wilson's first cabinet, but lasted only from 1913 to 1915. He was fundamentally a pacifist and adhered to a strict neutrality policy when war broke out in Europe in 1914. Because of his difference with Wilson over the President's stern protest to Germany on the *Lusitania* sinking, he resigned his post.

After his break with Wilson, Bryan's political prestige declined. The booming voice of the Lion of the West was heard less and less. The world had changed; we had engaged in a European war, and few people listened to Bryan's "anti-imperialist" views. Ever the fighter, Bryan came into national prominence for the last time in 1925. He participated as prosecuting attorney in the famous Scopes evolution trial in Dayton, Tennessee. In this notable court battle, Bryan, who was a funda-

mentalist in religion and often allowed his heart to dominate his brain, was matched against Clarence Darrow and Dudley Field Malone, the able defense attorneys for the young teacher who was guilty of teaching evolution. Darrow and Malone were ruthless in their handling of Bryan at the trial, so much so that Bryan's health became impaired. He died in Dayton on July 26, 1925. Echoes of the trial and the withering blows aimed at Bryan were heard again in the tremendously successful Broadway play *Inherit the Wind*. The play was based on the Scopes trial record and held closely to the facts, using many quotations from the actual trial. We should have many more such plays based on some of the many dramatic personal conflicts in American history.

2.

The Spanish-American War

In 1895 a savage revolt broke out in Cuba due largely to Spain's unenlightened colonial policy. The iron-fisted island rule of the pure-blooded Spaniards was based almost entirely upon slavery. Only Puerto Rico and Cuba remained of Spain's once vast and proud American empire. The Cuban Nationalists were united under the insurrection leader, Maximo Gomez, who was regarded in this country as a minor George Washington. In their rebellion against Spanish rule, the Nationalists had the sympathy and tried to enlist the support of the United States Government. They had the support of the American public, which had been reading lurid accounts of Spanish atrocities.

15

President McKinley, like President Cleveland before him, sought to avoid official United States intervention. Considerable American money was invested in Cuba, and this helped the pressure for action against Spain. President McKinley did obtain some concessions. Spain offered autonomy to Cuba and promised to relax some of the harsh reprisals against Cuban natives.

McKinley was considerably hampered in his opposition to intervention. Public hysteria fed by the sensational Hearst press demanded action. Newspaper correspondents flocked to Cuba to report on the revolt. They sent back lurid stories for the unthinking public. William Randolph Hearst's New York *Journal* clamored for war. Hearst was in the midst of a circulation war with Joseph Pulitzer's New York *World*. He used the Cuban crisis to build circulation.

On February 15, 1898, the United States battleship *Maine,* which McKinley had sent into Cuban waters to protect American interests, blew up in Havana harbor. Although there was no evidence that Spain was responsible for the explosion public opinion was deeply stirred. Reluctantly, McKinley yielded to the clamor of press and public for war. He recommended intervention. With 100,000 other Americans, I volunteered for military service, determined to do my bit to free "poor little Cuba" and "avenge the *Maine.*"

McKinley's own Assistant Secretary of the Navy, Theodore Roosevelt, who liked nothing better than a good fight, exuded a belligerence that helped bring on the war. At one point he referred to his chief as having "no more backbone than a chocolate éclair."

This unnecessary war was declared in April 1898, despite the fact that Spain had finally agreed to do everything we asked. Roosevelt resigned his government post and organized the Rough Riders, a cavalry regiment composed largely of ex-cowboys, college athletes, and adventurers. Their recklessness gained fame at the Battle of San Juan Hill. Actually, this was one of the most pointless, stupid engagements of the Spanish-American conflict, which John Hay, then Secretary of State, called "a splendid little war." From a military point of view, the only really important and creditable clash at arms was the Battle of Manila Bay. In this decisive victory Admiral Dewey completely routed major units of the Spanish navy. The ambitious and publicity-conscious Theodore Roosevelt successfully capitalized on his heroic but impudent Spanish-American War exploits when he sought and won the nomination and election as governor of New York State in 1898.

This "splendid little war" was as unneces-

William Randolph Hearst's New York *Journal* ran the "Maine Extra"—February 17, 1898.

TORPEDO HOLE DISCOVERED IN THE BATTLE SHIP MAINE.

Teddy Roosevelt's Rough Riders and their famous, futile charge at the battle of San Juan Hill.

H. V. Kaltenborn (*second from right*) was a sergeant in the Spanish-American War.

sary as it was epoch-making in United States history. It demonstrated to the world that the United States had abandoned her traditional policy of isolation. For better or worse, we had become a world power. The sphere of our political and economic interests had expanded across the Caribbean and the Pacific. By the Treaty of Paris of December 10, 1898, we obtained Puerto Rico, Guam, and the Philippines, and forced Spain to give up Cuba.

We had awakened to the fact that we could play a major role in world affairs. But it was to take the American public a long time to become "world-minded." The necessary two-thirds vote in the Senate to ratify the Treaty of Paris was delayed by the strong "anti-imperialist" element led by William Jennings Bryan. Nowadays, his followers would be called "isolationists." When the Senate was deadlocked over the Treaty, Bryan finally advocated ratification so he could use the "imperialist" theme in the 1900 campaign. It did him no good. The Hawaiian Islands also became a territory of the United States in that year.

As first sergeant of Company F, Fourth Wis-

Admiral Dewey crushed the Spanish fleet at the Battle of Manila Bay. This bit of verse commemorating the victory appeared in the New York *Sun* in 1898.

> *Oh, dewey was the morning*
> *Upon that first of May;*
> *And Dewey was the Admiral*
> *Upon Manila Bay.*
> *And dewey were the Regent's eyes*
> *Those royal eyes of blue,*
> *And do we feel discouraged?*
> *I do not think we do!*

17

consin Volunteer Infantry, and as correspondent for the Milwaukee *Journal*, the Merrill (Wisconsin) *Advocate,* and the Lincoln County *Anzeiger,* I got to know the weaknesses of our military establishment. Some of our equipment and much of our training routine dated back to the Civil War. Grafting contractors cheated on our supplies and our food. Investigations got under way only when the war was over. Battle casualties were a small fraction of those due to illness. We were fortunate in being opposed by an enemy even less prepared than we were to wage a real war. And we learned enough so that when war came again in 1917 we did not send into conflict men as poorly prepared and equipped as they were in 1898.

3.

Marconi Sends His First
Transatlantic Radio Message—1901

It was on December 12, 1901, that the young Italian inventor and physicist, Guglielmo Marconi, stood on the shore near St. John's, Newfoundland, listening for sounds to come through space. He was only twenty-seven and had already spent considerable time and money to develop wireless communication. He had delved deeply into the behavior of electromagnetic waves. A few years earlier he had established communication across the English Channel and he himself had sent by wireless the story of yacht races off Cowes.

On that wintry December day in 1901 he was concerned with an unprecedented experiment—that of receiving a sound hurled

through the air across the ocean. He had sent up a kite with a 400-foot antenna which he connected with his crude receiving apparatus. At noon that day he hoped by this means to pick from the air three dots, the letter "S," which was to be sent to him from a big spark station at Poldhu on the southwest tip of England in Cornwall. This was then the most powerful station in the world.

Scientists and mathematicians had ridiculed the young Italian inventor. They insisted that a message could never be sent across the sea by wireless because of the earth's curvature. Marconi persisted, built his apparatus, made his arrangements, and waited. At a prearranged time the electric signal, the three dots, fluttered across 2,000 miles of broad, curving ocean. The sounds hit the slender copper antenna on his kite, and Marconi received his message. The first international broadcast had been sent and received. The young Italian inventor had pointed the way and opened a new era in communications. The world had shrunk.

Thirty-six years later wireless waves from all the continents and all the oceans hurtled through space in tribute to the man who put them there. The long, invisible wireless impulses projecting into the infinite from tall steel masts were the living monument to the great Italian who died in Rome in 1937. In 1909 he shared the Nobel Prize for Physics and he was honored by the King of Italy when, in 1919, he appointed Marconi as a delegate to the Peace Conference in Versailles.

Many pioneers have joined in the development of communication to bring it to the high point it has reached today. Slowly and patiently, sometimes by accident, but largely through labored research and invention by such men as Dr. Lee De Forest, who patented the three-electrode vacuum tube, Ernst F. W. Alexanderson, Reginald A. Fessenden, and

Guglielmo Marconi at the receiving set at St. John's, Newfoundland, where he received the first transatlantic wireless signal on December 12, 1901.

many others, long-distance communication without wires developed from what Marconi first achieved on that eventful day in 1901.

The first commercial radio broadcast was made in this country in 1920 by the Westinghouse Station in East Pittsburgh. That same year Station KDKA won national fame and a permanent place in radio history by broadcasting the results of the Harding-Cox election. In 1929 Marconi himself made his first transatlantic talk for broadcasting. The next year we were able to listen to our then Secretary of State, Henry L. Stimson, King George V of England, and Prime Minister Ramsay MacDonald. They all spoke from the Naval Limitations Conference in London.

When I broadcast the Munich Crisis over the Columbia network for twenty hectic days and nights in 1938, it was the first time an entire sequence of critical international developments had been covered every step of the way by transocean and transcontinental radio.

Aside from what radio has brought to millions in culture, education, and enjoyment —the Metropolitan Opera Association celebrated its twenty-fifth anniversary of Saturday-afternoon opera broadcasts in March of 1956—I feel that radio has made two fundamental contributions. First, it has made our

Marconi's floating wireless laboratory, where he carried out many of his early experiments in wireless telegraphy.

RIGHT: The first important radio news broadcast, reporting the Harding-Cox election returns, came from station KDKA in Pittsburgh, November 2, 1920.

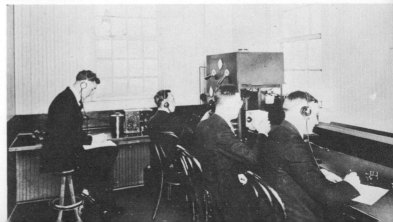

Modern electronics have created the broadcasting complexity of this present-day television studio.

H. V. Kaltenborn
during the Munich Crisis in 1938.

people government conscious, and it has made them speech conscious. Radio has probably done more to develop the knowledge of good English on the part of millions of Americans than anything else. This important contribution to popular education is often forgotten. Broadcasting has also helped eliminate the provincial aspects of American speech, which may be a mixed blessing.

As for radio making people more government conscious, I am convinced that thanks to radio and television, women, young people —and, men too, for that matter—have taken a much larger interest in government affairs.

It has made us all—young and old—familiar with government problems and personalities. It has given us a greater interest in the news of all the world. It is only due to radio and television that our people have in so little time learned to accept and support the larger role that the United States has come to play in world affairs. Our people need still more understanding of the world-wide struggle between communism and democracy and how fate has decreed that our young country must lead, direct, and support the forces of freedom.

Here are a few statistics. Television is still growing too rapidly to make today's figures (September, 1956) of some 500 television stations and 37,000,000 television homes more than temporarily important. As of August, 1956, there were nearly 2,669 standard broadcasting stations in the United States and possessions with over 100 permits for new construction.

As of the same date there were in this country some 50,000,000 homes with radios and there were 50,000,000 secondary sets in homes. Also, 35,000,000 radios were being used in automobiles. What an opportunity to bring to every American not only what we would like to hear, but also what we ought to know! We can still stand in reverent wonder and repeat the Morse message of a century ago: "What God hath wrought!"

20

4.

Henry Ford—1903

The year 1903 saw the beginning of what may have been the last important example of unlimited family and private enterprise. Henry Ford created a great empire by working with his hands and brain. For a long time he ran it as he pleased and with outstanding success. He began building his first two-cylinder car in a woodshed while working as an engineer for the Detroit Consolidated Edison Company. He met Thomas Edison and talked with him about his motorcar idea. Edison told him, "You're on the right track, young man—don't let anybody throw you off."

Ford then built the famous racing car 999, got Barney Oldfield to drive it, won prizes, and thus advertised the name of Henry Ford. His career and his business were soon on their way to fame and fortune.

The first transcontinental automobile trip was made in 1903 by Dr. H. Nelson Jackson and Sewall K. Crocker. It stimulated considerable interest in the revolutionary motor vehicle. Henry Ford began collecting money to start his own business. From various sources he got together $28,000. This was the original investment which he built into a billion-dollar enterprise.

In 1909 Ford launched his Model T with this announcement: "I will build a motorcar for the great multitudes. It will be family size, made of the best materials by the best workmen. But it will be so low priced that no man making a good salary will be unable to own one."

To anyone who has met Ford that pronouncement typifies the man. It is the essence of his philosophy of large-scale, low-cost production which brought him such outstanding business success. When I visited Henry Ford in Detroit, I found that this mild-mannered man, lean, wiry, and active, was at once simple and shrewd. He didn't like meeting newsmen because he was shy and sensitive. He had heard and enjoyed my broadcasts and for that reason was willing to give me a little of his own time. He escorted me through his research department at Dearborn, Michigan, and explained the importance of research in building motorcars.

Then he took me for a ride in a new Ford car not yet on the market, showed me his experimental farm where he was growing soy beans as a base for plastics. He pointed with pride to a new type of Ford tractor which he called the most important unit on which he was working at that time. When he was finally called away by one of his associates, he turned me over to his Swedish expert Johannson, who had developed block gauges which could measure up to one millionth of an inch. Ford

Henry Ford in his first car.

FORD

FORD

Ford Motor Company advertisement, 1912.

Barney Oldfield and Ford's famous Car 999.

FORD

didn't need such precision to build automobiles, but he had put Johannson on the pay roll because he was an engineering genius who deserved support. The Johannson gauges were soon in demand by the builders of airplanes and precision machinery. Henry Ford believed all machines should be used to full capacity to avoid social waste.

The immortal Model T first came out in two models—the coupé and the roadster, and you could buy it in any color so long as it was black. In the next nineteen years Ford made 15,000,000 cars. The Model T changed the nation's folkways and before World War I every second car on the road was a Ford. "Watch the Fords go by" became a valuable slogan. Not a thing of beauty, the old Ford rode high, could withstand rough going on dirt roads, and rarely failed. It was often compared to a mule, a camel, or a bull terrier.

The parts of the Model T were simple, interchangeable, and inexpensive. Ford reduced the cost of his cars by freezing the design and by quantity production. The price in the early days fell from $1,200 to $295. If today car models were less numerous and were changed less frequently, cars would be much cheaper.

Ford became a world figure and at one time he was suggested for president of the United States. The late Will Rogers proposed as the Ford campaign slogan, "Elect me and I'll change the front end." The Model T was produced until 1927. Then the competition of Dodge and Chevrolet forced the change to the Model A. Everything stopped for a while at the Ford plant and people predicted that Henry Ford would go broke because of the heavy costs involved in making this change. He didn't.

Henry Ford's inherent individualism and independence were demonstrated in another way. In 1914 he created a sensation by raising the minimum wage from $2.35 to $5.00 a day. No one forced him to do it. He simply believed wages should be kept high and prices low to enable workers to buy Ford cars and other luxuries. In 1929, after the stock market crash, he raised the minimum wage in his plants to $7.00 a day. In his attitude toward his workers he was paternal and sentimental. He set up his own social department and tried to influence the personal habits of his workers. They refused to accept the code of living he recommended. He hated the experts and preferred letting a novice try the impossible. Sometimes it worked.

Labor relations became a tragic failure in Henry Ford's plants. He was bitterly opposed to labor unions. When the Wagner Labor Relations Act transferred power from industry to labor, Ford was a beaten man. The unions wanted to slow down his machines. When union organizers tried to organize his employees, Ford used his private police force to oust them from his plants. Ford was even brought up before the Labor Relations Board for fighting the union organizers. In 1941 he finally signed a full contract with the C.I.O. United Auto Workers. But he could not understand why, after that concession, the union did not come over to his side. The defeat of his efforts to keep out the union was a severe blow. He never again had the same interest in the Ford plants.

Ford was a realist with more than a touch of sentiment. His fads and fancies often got him into difficulties. In 1914 he chartered the *Oskar II* as a peace ship. It sailed to Europe on December 4, carrying a strange assortment of quarrelsome cranks and pacifists to "get the boys out of the trenches by Christmas." He got the idea from a stout woman pacifist from Budapest who told him that all the belligerents wanted to stop fighting but didn't know how. She proposed a world-wide strike against war. Ford repudiated this idea, but since it was right to stop war, he thought it could be done with the peace ship. Most of the *Oskar II* passengers went along for the ride. Their continued bickering on the ocean journey discouraged Ford, who returned home and abandoned his worthy but wholly impractical undertaking.

Ford's anti-Semitism also got him into trouble. He made thoughtless public statements about Jews which he was finally forced to retract, much to the satisfaction of the many Ford dealers whose business had suffered. On more than one occasion he gave foolish interviews on public issues he knew nothing about. When the Chicago *Tribune* called him an ignoramus, he sued the newspaper. On the stand at the Mt. Clements trial Ford did show considerable ignorance, chiefly about elemental facts of American history. Even so, he won his suit and collected six cents in damages.

One of the industrial giant's hobbies was an effort to re-create the America of his youth. He built Greenfield Village, and bought old inns, such as the Wayside Inn at Sudbury, Massachusetts. The village and the inns were completely restored and refurnished in the authentic manner. He hired old-time fiddlers and revived old-fashioned square dancing.

In 1936 he made it possible for his family to found the Ford Foundation. Its purpose is to devote its large resources to programs for peace, education, the behavioral sciences, democratic institutions, and economic stability. Nine years after Henry Ford's death in 1947 the Ford Foundation sold a portion of its Ford Motor Company holdings. They were listed on the New York Stock Exchange. The prestige of the Ford name sold out the issue at $62.50 a share, but this soon dropped around ten points in a more realistic market appraisal. The vast industrial empire started

23

by Henry Ford in 1903 and guarded so zealously for many years as a family holding is now shared by thousands of investors.

The genius of Henry Ford created the assembly line. He revolutionized industry and vastly increased industrial production. More than any other single individual, he helped promote the high standard of living we enjoy today.

5.

The United States Becomes a World Power

From 1899 to 1906, the years following the Spanish-American War, the United States participated significantly in foreign affairs. Our intervention came on three widely separated fronts: the Boxer Rebellion took our troops to China, the Panama Canal increased our world power, and our leadership in ending the Russo-Japanese War raised our prestige. Thus our participation was military, economic, and diplomatic. Each intervention was a foreign-policy development that logically followed our victory in the war with Spain.

The Boxer Rebellion

The first turn-of-the-century event that called for a definite foreign-policy stand was the Chinese Boxer Rebellion. Although this was of brief duration—it lasted from June 13 through August 14, 1900—American troops were sent into action in the Orient. This up-

24

rising was a direct result of the imperialist encroachments by European powers in China. It was launched by a Chinese secret society called "Righteous Harmonious Fists"—hence Boxers. The European powers were engaged in a mad scramble to divide the still-somnolent Chinese Empire into spheres of influence. This went on even though Secretary of State John Hay's Open-Door Policy, framed to provide equal opportunity for all powers in China, had been accepted by the major powers.

The Boxers were volunteer Chinese militiamen organized to block what they rightly considered to be the predatory designs of the foreigners. Supported by the wily Empress Dowager Tzu Hsi, they savagely insulted, attacked, and killed foreigners. In Peking, nationals of European powers and the United States locked themselves behind the walls of their legations.

One of the Empress Dowager's Boxers.

NATIONAL ARCHIVES

Together with France, Germany, Great Britain, Italy, Austria, Russia, and Japan, the United States formed an expeditionary force which fought its way to Peking and eventually relieved the besieged legations. The United States had organized a contingent of 15,000 troops to fight the Boxers, but only 5,000 arrived in time to participate in the capture of Peking. It was the United States Marines who guarded the American legation when the Boxers attacked, while the United States Sixth Cavalry, under General Chaffee, took part in the actual relief.

A major international factor of the Boxer Rebellion was that it gave Russia, despite opposition by other powers, the opportunity to occupy Manchuria with 100,000 troops. It was the demand for the evacuation of these troops that became a key issue in the Far East and a contributing cause of the Russo-Japanese War.

United States Secretary of State John Hay took the Boxer Rebellion as a good opportunity to reaffirm the Open-Door Policy. He sent a circular letter to the various powers having interests in China, stating it to be the policy of the United States "to seek a solution which may bring about permanent safety and peace to China, preserve Chinese territorial and administrative entity . . . and safeguard for the world the principle of equal and impartial trade with all parts of the Chinese Empire."

Once the Boxer uprising was put down, China had to pay an enormous indemnity. The United States as a friendly gesture reduced the amount due her by one half and in 1924 remitted the unpaid balance. About $18,000,000 of the United States share of the indemnity was devoted to the education of Chinese students in America.

The Boxer Rebellion and the Protocol of

A contemporary cartoon pictures the willingness of the United States to use force to maintain and reaffirm the Open-Door Policy in China.

American troops move into Peking—1900.

September 1901 which set up the indemnity led to our permanent interest in China and Chinese affairs. In China, these events gave rise to the feeling that the United States was a moral ally.

Panama Canal

Early in the new century shrewd diplomatic maneuvering and dramatic intervention on the Panama Canal issue marked our further advance in world power, for the completion of the Panama Canal in 1914 gave the United States a great military and economic advantage just as World War I began.

For many years the French, the British, and the United States had been interested in building a canal across Nicaragua or Panama to join the Atlantic and the Pacific. The French De Lesseps Panama venture of the 80's ended in bankruptcy. The British were only half-heartedly interested in going along with the United States on digging a canal. In 1900 Secretary of State Hay negotiated the first Hay-Pauncefote Treaty between Great Britain and the United States by which England was to renounce her right to joint construction and ownership of an Isthmian Canal. This treaty was rejected by Great Britain.

On November 18, 1901, the second Hay-Pauncefote Treaty was successfully negotiated. This gave the United States the sole right of construction, maintenance, and control of a canal between the two oceans. With the ratification of this treaty, Congress still faced the choice between a canal across Panama (then a province of Colombia) or a sea-level canal in Nicaragua. The Nicaraguan route utilized existing lakes and rivers while the Panama route would require locks. After price dickering for the franchises and holdings of the New Panama Canal Company, successor to the defunct De Lesseps venture, Congress decided upon the Panama route.

Then came more diplomatic maneuvering. Secretary of State Hay successfully negotiated the Hay-Herran Treaty between the United States and Colombia. This provided for the acquisition by the United States of the same zone for a canal the Colombian Government had granted to the French years before. But Colombia failed to ratify this treaty, and thereby roused the vehement displeasure of

The Panama Canal was completed in 1914. Here, in June, 1913, work proceeds on Culebra Cut, deepest excavated portion of the Canal. Gold Hill is on the right, Contractor's Hill on the left.

President Roosevelt. At one time he actually contemplated forcible seizure of Panama. Later on he was foolish enough to boast: "We took Panama."

Colombia's refusal to ratify the treaty antagonized Panamanian elements with Colombia. They were afraid that the United States would choose the alternate Nicaraguan route. With strong American urging and support these elements revolted and proclaimed an independent Republic of Panama on November 3, 1903. The United States reacted swiftly. American warships, which President Roosevelt had ordered to Panama to "maintain free and uninterrupted transit across the Isthmus" before Panama seceded, prevented Colombian forces from landing to quell the revolution. Three days later the United States was the first power to recognize the independence of Panama.

In November 1903 the Hay-Bunau-Varilla Treaty (Bunau-Varilla was Panama's first minister to the United States) was negotiated between the United States and the new government of Panama. We guaranteed the independence of Panama and Panama granted us in perpetuity the use of a five-mile zone on either side of the future canal with full jurisdiction. We paid $10,000,000 for it and still pay $250,000 rent each year. Work started on the Canal in 1904 under the direction of Colonel George Goethals but had to be interrupted until typhoid and malaria were overcome. This was successfully accomplished in a historic battle against these fevers.

The Canal cost more than $400,000,000, but the tolls have repaid the original cost many times over. Far more important than the profit is the fact that the Panama Canal greatly strengthened the United States as a world power.

Russo-Japanese War

The Russo-Japanese War began formally on February 10, 1904, after the Japanese had attacked Port Arthur and bottled up the Russian fleet two days before. It put the Open-Door Policy for China in great jeopardy. Russia had advanced her aggressive policy in the Far East by completing the Trans-Siberian Railway and leasing Port Arthur. She not only maintained heavy troop concentrations in Manchuria, but penetrated into northern

Theodore Roosevelt's vision saw the benefits to world trade that the Canal would bring, although opposition pressures at home were great.

The sinking of the Russian armored cruiser, *Admiral Uschakow*, by the forces of Admiral Togo at the battle of Tsushima May 27–29, 1905, during the Russo-Japanese War.

Korea where Japan had established special interests.

President Roosevelt was disturbed by these events which directly affected American commercial interests. He realized that complete defeat for either Japan or Russia was undesirable, since this would destroy the existing balance of power in the Far East. He at once asked the two belligerents to respect the Open-Door Policy in regard to "neutrality" and "administrative entity" for China. Both hedged on accepting Roosevelt's proposal. Russia rejected the idea of neutralization for Manchuria which was one of Roosevelt's conditions.

In actual fighting Big Russia was getting the worst of it from Little Japan. The Japanese were victorious during the opening stages of

28

the war. Lack of preparedness and internal corruption hampered the Czar's military forces. As a sign of Japan's rising prestige, Japan's diplomatic representatives in the United States, England, France, Germany and Austria were elevated from ministers to ambassadors. After the historic naval battle of Tsushima Straits in which the Russian fleet of thirty-two vessels was annihilated by Admiral Togo's fleet, the Japanese Government asked President Roosevelt to take the initiative in bringing about peace. Russia, her back to the wall, agreed to allow President Roosevelt to act as a mediator.

Through this country's good offices, a peace conference was begun at Portsmouth, New Hampshire, on August 5, 1905. The final treaty was signed on September 5. This successful intervention in the cause of peace further enhanced United States prestige and in 1906 won for President Roosevelt the Nobel Peace Prize.

Theodore Roosevelt won the Nobel Peace Prize for his part in settling the Russo-Japanese War at the peace conference held in Portsmouth, New Hampshire, 1904. *Left to right:* Count Witte, Baron Rosen, Roosevelt, Baron Komura and Minister Takahira.

6.

Early Trust Regulation

The first big industrial combination to make its appearance in American business was the Standard Oil Trust, formed in 1879. It controlled 90 to 95 per cent of the oil refined in this country. In my father's paint and oil store in Merrill, Wisconsin, I had personal experience of the utterly ruthless way in which this monopoly was maintained and enforced. There were times when the Standard Oil Company actually gave away petroleum products to keep a rival company from doing business.

Other large combinations soon controlled other commodities, such as beef, whisky, sugar, tobacco, lead, and linseed oil. Selfish and harmful monopolies dominated many aspects of business. Several states passed anti-trust laws, but these laws could not regulate interstate commerce. The demand for action by Congress became nationwide.

The Sherman Antitrust Act was passed on July 2, 1890. It was the first of several federal measures designed to regulate trusts. In essence, the Sherman Act declared illegal "every contract, combination in the form of a trust or otherwise, or conspiracy in restraint of trade or commerce among the several states or with foreign nations."

Because the act was loosely drawn, it failed to solve the problem. The chief weakness was its obscure and ambiguous phrasing and the failure to define terms such as "trust," "combination," and "restraint." Of necessity it had to be supplemented.

President Theodore Roosevelt was the first chief executive to lead a strong fight against the trusts. He became known as a "trust

THE BETTMAN ARCHIVE

On Monopolies and Trusts. "In the hands of his philanthropic friends." 1897.

buster" although he tried to distinguish between "good" and "bad" trusts. He recommended legislation to abolish abuses which would not actually destroy combinations. He pledged enforcement of anti-trust laws and demanded a "square deal" for all. He said: "We do not wish to destroy corporations, but we wish to make them subserve the public good."

President Roosevelt didn't get the legislation he desired, but he ordered Attorney General Philander C. Knox to file suit against the Northern Securities Company, a large railroad holding company, demanding its dissolution. The Supreme Court ruled in the government's favor. This greatly strengthened the Rough Rider President's prestige with Congress and the country. During his administration forty-four anti-trust suits were started by the government. In the succeeding Taft administration there were more than twice that number. The most notable resulted in the dissolution of the Standard Oil Company of New Jersey and the American To-

29

"Who'd ever have thought we'd go fishing together"—
W. R. Rogers, 1906.

bacco Company. When the Supreme Court upheld the government's suit to dissolve the Standard Oil Company, it applied the so-called "rule of reason" to the Sherman Act. In the case of the American Tobacco Company, the Supreme Court ordered the reorganization of the "tobacco trust," rather than its dissolution.

The trust abuses brought the unusual phenomenon of muckraking which reached its height between 1904 and 1910. A group of prominent writers aroused public opinion with sensational disclosures of dishonesty, corruption, and other evils in business as well as in machine politics. Magazines of national repute and circulation, such as *Collier's, McClure's, American,* and *Cosmopolitan* filled their pages with exposures. Ida M. Tarbell's *History of the Standard Oil* began in *McClure's* in 1903. Lincoln Steffens wrote *The Shame of the Cities.* David Graham Phillips' *The Treason of the Senate* appeared in 1906 and Ray Stannard Baker's *The Railroads on Trial* appeared in *McClure's* in the same year.

The great American fortunes, the beef trust, and the life insurance companies all came under fire. I reported the insurance investigation for the Brooklyn *Daily Eagle* and well recall my admiration for the skill with which a young lawyer named Charles Evans Hughes cross-examined unhappy insurance executives. He soon became governor of New York State, and but for a handful of votes in the single state of California would have become president of the United States.

Many writers in those days also attacked the country's social evils, such as slums and prostitution. Some exposures were weakened because they overemphasized the sensational and lost their effectiveness as a public service.

This overemphasis on what was lurid and startling led President Roosevelt caustically to compare some of the magazine writers with the muckraker in *Pilgrim's Progress* who was so busy raking filth off the floor that he could only look downward. After the Supreme Court decisions in the Standard Oil and American Tobacco Company cases were handed down, muckraking subsided.

30

7.

Revolution in Mexico

Even today a frequently heard word in Mexico is *revolution,* but in recent years it has meant talk rather than action. Mexicans proudly declare that the chief ideals of their revolution predated the Russian Revolution by seven years. They point out, too, that the United States was a quarter century behind Mexico in launching its New Deal era of social change. The Mexican revolution of 1911 still continues to transform Mexico.

When this revolution started all the elements of political and social revolt had developed. Porfirio Diaz had controlled Mexico with absolute authority from the early eighties. Like most dictators, he can be credited with some worthy accomplishments. Order was established throughout a primitive country and Mexican prestige was raised. There was vast material progress in finance, public works, mining, industry, and railroads. A great deal of foreign capital, especially American money, had been invested in Mexico. But Diaz' government favored the upper class and the working classes were mercilessly exploited. Education was neglected. The situation was made for revolution.

On May 25, 1911, Diaz was overthrown by a movement headed by Francisco Madero. He became president and an era of revolution had begun. Madero had no real understanding of the issues. He lost control in 1913 when he was overthrown by Huerta, who was not recognized by the United States.

Although millions of dollars in American investments were at stake the United States had no firm Mexican policy. This was particularly true during the Taft administration, when the Mexican revolution began. In 1914, due to many overt acts against American interests, President Wilson had to ask Congress for permission to use force to protect American lives and property. On April 21 of that year the United States bombarded Veracruz, marines went ashore, and we occupied the city. This incident united Mexican public opinion behind General Huerta, and war between the United States and Mexico was narrowly averted. When Huerta was ousted from office by Venustiano Carranza, civil war broke out between Carranza and Francisco Villa. Along with eight other American nations, we recognized Carranza as the *de facto* president of Mexico in 1915.

In March 1916 Villa, with some 400 raiders, crossed the United States border to Columbus, New Mexico, and in broad daylight shot everyone in sight, exchanged shots with an army patrol, and then disappeared into the Chichuahua Hills. The American press and public demanded punishment. President Wil-

Pancho Villa—most famous of Mexican revolutionists. In 1916 he raided Columbus, New Mexico, and killed 20 Americans.

General Pershing and his troops pursued Villa into Mexico in retaliation.

son, after ineffectual diplomatic exchanges with Carranza's government, ordered a punitive expedition into Mexico under the command of General John J. Pershing. Pershing crossed the Rio Grande with 6,000 troops, largely cavalry, just a week after Villa's daring raid.

It was a difficult time for Wilson. Because of the war in Europe, he was more than eager to avoid war with Mexico. Also, it was a presidential election year, and Wilson's campaign was shaping up on the slogan, "He kept us out of war." General Pershing's expedition, due to a variety of causes, some of which were political, was a dismal failure. American troops were withdrawn from Mexico in February 1917. Though war was averted, trouble and unrest in Mexico went on for several more years. Carranza was killed in 1920 after a revolt led by three prominent generals. Álvaro Obregón became president and Villa surrendered to the insurgents. They gave him a handsome estate which he enjoyed until he was assassinated in 1923. Since that time revolutionary unrest in Mexico has gradually subsided.

The Mexican revolution was a classical example of social change on a large scale. After the violent phases ended it became a sort of institutionalized revolution with new achievements still in progress. In a way the Mexican revolution was the forerunner of the nationalist revolutions that followed the two world wars and that are still in progress in the remaining colonial areas of the Near East, the Far East, and Africa.

U.S. troops and supplies advance into Mexico in pursuit of Pancho Villa.

8.

Campaign of 1912—
Taft, Roosevelt, Wilson

The second presidential campaign in which I took an active part as a speaker for the Democratic candidate was in 1912. The first was when I worked for Bryan in 1896. When the Republican convention assembled in Chicago two years before World War I began, the continuing bitter feud between Theodore Roosevelt and President William Howard Taft reached its climax. That historic personal quarrel which caused the first major split in Republican ranks had a peculiar background. In 1908 Roosevelt picked Taft as his successor. He threw all his power and prestige behind Taft's nomination and election. Despite gossipmongers who spread rumors that Taft was ungrateful to Roosevelt, the friendship between the two men was unimpaired. Taft had written to Roosevelt, "You and my brother Charley made my nomination and election possible." Roosevelt went off on his African venture in 1909 feeling confident that Taft would follow the governmental policies he had launched.

But it soon became obvious that Taft was not a Roosevelt-type executive. Nor was there any glamour in his administration. Gone were the dramatic quarrels and continuous excitement of the Roosevelt days. It soon became evident that Taft's conservative policies and behavior had antagonized the progressive element in the Republican party. The first big rift between the president and the progressive wing was over the Payne-Aldrich tariff bill. Other differences soon developed. Everything

Taft did seemed to split the party more decisively.

When former President Roosevelt returned to this country from Africa and Europe (he received the Nobel Prize in 1906 and in his acceptance speech suggested a League of Nations) he tried hard for a time to maintain his confidence in President Taft. He even wrote: "There is at least a good chance that a reaction will come in his favor. Everyone believes him to be honest and most believe him to be doing the best he knows how. I have noticed very little real abuse of him, or indeed attack upon him."

Roosevelt's confidence was short-lived, especially after the interim election in 1910 in which the Republicans lost the House of Representatives and maintained but a slim majority in the Senate. Roosevelt realized that a progressive leadership was necessary to avoid defeat in 1912. He threw himself into the fray and campaigned vigorously in the congressional election. After the Republicans lost, the insurgents in the party started their campaign to block Taft's nomination in 1912. They felt convinced that he could not win a second term and they began a search for his successor. The National Progressive Republican League proposed Robert La Follette, but Roosevelt would not endorse him and the movement collapsed.

Roosevelt, who gave frequent interviews to New York reporters, myself among them, was then contributing editor of the *Outlook*. He charged in his magazine articles that Taft failed to continue the Roosevelt policies. He was not only increasingly critical of the Taft administration, but in 1911 his attitude toward Taft became openly hostile. Taft, who in political matters was sometimes naïve, was unable to understand Roosevelt's motives in his hostile articles and speeches. He said: "I don't know what he is driving at except to

33

make my way more difficult . . . it is painful to see a devoted friendship going to pieces like a rope of sand."

There was fault on both sides, but since Taft was under the domination of the Republican conservatives, he had abandoned practically all of Roosevelt's pet policies. Naturally, Roosevelt was furious. As the months went on and the 1912 convention drew nearer, Theodore Roosevelt decided that he himself had to become the candidate to rescue the party from defeat. A movement on his behalf was under way when a group of governors got up a petition calling on him to head the Progressive forces in their fight for the "New Nationalism." Roosevelt replied: "My hat is in the ring. I will accept the nomination for president if it is tendered to me, and I will adhere to this decision until the convention has expressed its preference."

When the boom for Teddy Roosevelt got under way, Taft took the offensive and the fight was on. It was open war. The two men who had been such close friends and associates now went at each other with ever-increasing invective. Said Taft, replying to Roosevelt's charges, "I deny all of them, but sometimes a man in a corner fights. I am going to fight." As the Roosevelt-Taft battle developed, the middle-of-the-roaders within the party, hoping to escape a defeat at the polls, suggested that both men withdraw in favor of a candidate acceptable to both. Neither would do so. Roosevelt boasted proudly, "I'll name the compromise candidate. He'll be me."

In the primaries in thirteen states Roosevelt won 278 delegates to 48 for Taft. However, the Taft forces, led by party bosses and the Republican machine, organized the convention in Chicago and seated the more than 200 Taft delegates Roosevelt had successfully opposed. This bitter fight only served to aggravate the party split. When Roosevelt realized

34

that the Taft forces had control of the convention, he said: "So far as I'm concerned, I am through. I went before the people and I won. Let us find out whether the Republican party is the party of the plain people . . . or the party of the bosses and the professional radicals acting in the interests of special privilege."

This was interpreted to mean that Roosevelt would not accept the convention's choice and would run on a separate ticket. When Taft was nominated two days later the opposition got together in a separate meeting and pledged support to Roosevelt. Teddy told his followers: "If you want me to make the fight, I will make it, even if only one state should support me." A short time later, when financial support was obtained for the new organization, the Progressive party came into being and in its convention, also in Chicago, nominated Roosevelt. He told reporters, "I feel strong as a bull moose."

So the bull moose became the symbol of the Progressives, and "Onward, Christian Soldiers" became their campaign song. I will

A Berryman cartoon depicting the campaign of 1912.

never forget the religious fervor and whole-hearted enthusiasm of those early Progressive party meetings. Although I had always been a Democrat, my allegiance wavered until Woodrow Wilson was nominated and I joined the Democratic College Men's Speakers League.

With the split in the Republican party there was little doubt that the Democrats would win. The campaign was chiefly a contest among the three personalities involved—the rational and liberal Wilson, the crusading Roosevelt, and the placid, party-ruled Taft. Wilson's policies, labeled the "New Freedom," were not much different from Roosevelt's New Nationalism. These notes of progressive liberalism were new on our political scene and made Taft's policies and viewpoint seem decidedly reactionary.

There was one element of excitement and drama during the campaign when Roosevelt was shot by an anti-third-termer as he was leaving a hotel in Milwaukee to make a speech. In his customary dramatic way Roosevelt said: "I will make this speech or die. It is one thing or the other." He delivered his speech with the bullet still in his body. Taft and Wilson both interrupted their campaigns until Roosevelt recovered, which was not long afterward, since the wound was not serious.

The election resulted as almost everyone had predicted—Woodrow Wilson carried forty states. Taft had only three and a half million votes, while Roosevelt had more than four million. After the election Roosevelt's comment was: "The fight is over. We are beaten. There is only one thing to do and that is to go back to the Republican party. You can't hold a party like the Progressive party together." In matters of politics T. R. usually showed the same shrewd good sense that distinguished another member of the Roosevelt family who also became president.

9.

World War I and Reactions in the United States

In 1914 it was the "Big Bertha" on which Germany relied to shatter the French and Belgian forts that barred the way to Paris. The forts were destroyed and overrun but the French capital was never reached. In 1944 Hitler counted on his secret weapons, the V-1's and V-2's, to win World War II. They did heavy damage but were not decisive.

"Big Bertha," the first long-range artillery weapon to be developed, could hurl shells at Paris from a distance of seventy-six miles. The shells destroyed precious monuments but had no military effect. So many years have passed that "Big Bertha," just like Verdun and Marne and the Argonne, is little more than a name to our younger generation. Yet to those of us who were covering World War I news, the memories of the crucial struggles in that conflict are still very real.

Like the Battle of the Bulge in 1944, the Battle of Verdun was launched in winter and, like the Ardennes offensive, was a desperate German effort which failed. Verdun was actually a campaign, rather than a battle, lasting from February until October 1916. General Pétain, whom Marshal Joffre had put in command, finally gained the victory which made him a sanctified French figure who fell from grace in World War II.

The Verdun campaign cost some 350,000 French casualties and more than half a million German. Soon after World War I, I visited the Verdun battlefield where bayonets were still sticking out of trenches covered by shell explosions and where the mortuaries

General Pershing, leader of the American Expeditionary Forces, landed at Boulogne, France, June 13, 1917.

were filled with bones and bodies gathered from the battlefield. In 1943, at the height of another war, I was again in France and made a broadcast from a secret transmission station in the depths of a Verdun fortress.

The turning point in World War I was the Second Battle of the Marne in the summer of 1918. By that time General Pershing had landed in France to announce "Lafayette, we are here." He led a great American expeditionary force of 3,000,000 troops. General Foch had been named commander in chief of the Allied armies at a time of crisis in April 1918, after the great offensive launched by the Germans in March.

Actually, Sir Douglas Haig, commander in chief of the British forces, General Pershing, our commander, and King Albert of Belgium retained extensive control of their separate armies. It was during the first 1918 German offensive that the Americans first played a substantial and dramatic role. This was in the

Battle of Château-Thierry in June. Just a few weeks later General Ludendorff, the German commander, threw his war-weary troops into an all out attack west and east of Rheims. The German troops crossed the Marne but made little progress against strong French and American forces.

Then General Foch began his successful counteroffensive in which nine American divisions took a leading and effective part. The Germans were forced back over the Marne to the Vesle River. This strategic counteroffensive was of particular importance in World War I, mainly because it thwarted General Ludendorff's plan for an attack in Flanders. It also enabled General Foch to seize the initiative and hold it through the months to come. After the Second Battle of the Marne, the Allied and American forces gradually began a sustained offensive, a series of local attacks that merged into a general movement. Victories at Amiens . . . the Somme . . . the St.-

36

World War I was fought in the trenches and the infantryman was the noblest of soldiers.

Mihiel salient . . . the Argonne . . . Ypres . . . eventually led up to November 11, 1918, when Germany surrendered and the Armistice was proclaimed.

It is interesting for such a German-American as myself to look back over the two world wars and reflect on the difference in American thinking and, American reaction to things German in the two wars. In World War I the American people were greatly influenced by three years of pro-Allied and anti-German propaganda such as the disproved atrocity stories about Belgian children. There were also many legitimate reasons for anti-German feeling such as the deliberate sinking of the *Lusitania,* the ruthless submarine warfare in general, and such individual acts as the unnecessary execution of the war nurse, Edith Cavell, as a spy. Not since the furor of the Spanish-American War, when the press played up the cruelty of the Spaniards in Cuba, had the American public been so aroused.

Germany surrendered to the Allied Forces in this famous railroad car at Compiègne, November 11, 1918.

Yet there was little sound justification for the hysterical attack on everything of German origin. Fritz Kreisler and other artists of Germanic origin had to cut short their public appearances. Wagner operas could not be given, and teaching the German language was verboten. Renowned artists and educators as well as patriotic German-American citizens were subjected to attack and humiliation. Everything German was taboo. Even hamburgers had to be renamed. There were, to be sure, a few German spies and agents in this country. But the American public, it seemed, was engaged in its own witch hunt. In 1915 the United States Secret Service obtained possession of documents signed by Ambassador Bernstorff and Captain Franz von Papen revealing in considerable detail sabotage activities in the United States. These were publicized and certain members of the foreign diplomatic corps were expelled.

The Black Tom munitions explosion of July 30, 1916, resulting in a loss of $22,000,000 and another war factory explosion at Kingsland, New Jersey, in January 1917, were believed due to German sabotage. It is an interesting sidelight that years later—in 1939—Germany was found guilty of those sabotage acts of World War I by a Mixed Claims Commission, but Germany never paid the $55,000,000 damage award. By then Hitler was in complete control of Germany.

There was a happy contrast in conditions when a more mature America faced World War II. Our hatred was first focused on Japan because of Pearl Harbor although Hitler deservedly had a bad press in this country from the day he achieved power in 1933. But our anger was directed against Hitler and the Nazis rather than against Germans as a whole. We had learned that German-Americans were almost unanimously loyal to the country of their adoption and there was no feeling against them. The German language, while less popular than French or Spanish, continued to be taught, and German music held its place in concert programs.

This helps to explain the speed with which good relations were resumed with West Germany after the war and the extent to which this country contributed to German recovery. Communist Russia deservedly became the villain while we promoted German rearmament and the reunion of communist-controlled East Germany with the West German Republic. If there should ever be a third world war it might well find Germans and Americans fighting on the same side.

The sinking of the *Lusitania*, May 7, 1915. A drawing.

10.

Woodrow Wilson

Set in a stone wall along the shore of lovely Lake Geneva at Geneva, Switzerland, is a plaque dedicated to Woodrow Wilson. The inscription under his name first reminds the passer-by that he was the founder of the League of Nations. Then, in much smaller letters, we are reminded that he was also president of the United States.

It is one of the ironies of history that Woodrow Wilson was great enough to inspire the world to accept his plans for a League of Nations but was not great enough to lead the United States into the League. Wilson was more prophet than politician, a man of vision who was greater as an educator than as a leader who could translate vision into action. He was always too impatient with the inevitable opposition to his ideals and aims. He took criticism too hard and while his moral leadership helped the Allies achieve victory in World War I, he was unable to translate victory into the terms of an enduring peace.

My first impression of Woodrow Wilson came to me as a Harvard undergraduate when I heard him deliver a brilliant commencement address. His book on the workings of Congress was my favorite textbook in a course on government. Both his speaking and writing were clear, forceful, and persuasive. A few years after graduation I was happy to join the Woodrow Wilson League of College Men and give street-corner talks in his behalf during the 1912 campaign.

Wilson's lot was far from easy after war broke out in Europe. As a true liberal and idealist, he sincerely strove to bring about common justice and common peace. He embarked on his administration as President determined to achieve the liberal reforms he had promised. He had a great gift for exposition. This was exemplified in his messages to Congress. He delivered these in person, a custom that had been dropped by presidents since 1797.

Even today his speeches and writings are shining examples of good exposition. When the European war broke out, he devoted himself to the cause of peace. He admonished the country to "be neutral in thought as well as in act." After the exchange with Germany of his expertly phrased diplomatic notes about submarine warfare, he still strove valiantly to

WIDE WORLD

Tablet in memory of Woodrow Wilson, Palace of the League of Nations, Geneva, Switzerland.

keep this country out of the war. He felt, and he may have been right, that as a neutral the United States could lead the world to a sound peace. Everyone remembers his "Too Proud to Fight" speech which had such an unhappy reaction. His continued negotiations with the German leaders merely evoked promises that were not kept. The Germans, who have always been poor diplomats, failed to realize that Wilson, despite his British blood, was a sincere idealist genuinely working for peace. The Kaiser's advisers completely misinterpreted Wilson's peace efforts.

After Wilson was re-elected in 1916 on the "He kept us out of war" slogan, he at once asked both Allies and Germans to state their peace terms. Both sides were evasive. Then, on January 22, 1917, Wilson made his famous "Peace Without Victory" speech. In this he advocated that the war be ended by a reasonable non-vindictive peace. But by this time public opinion both in this country and abroad was sure of Germany's ultimate defeat. Because of increasing American sympathy for the Allied cause, Wilson's speech was severely criticized in this country, even though he was merely trying to play the role of peacemaker. The Allied countries were bitter about Wilson's intervention which they called pro-German while the Kaiser's High Command was so foolish as to react by stepping up submarine warfare. This induced Wilson to ask the Senate for "armed neutrality"—the right to arm our merchant ships. The Senate, thanks to the stubborn opposition of a few "willful men," blocked the resolution. Germany's tactless proclamation of unlimited submarine warfare then forced Wilson's hand.

In his conduct of the war, once we were in it, Wilson allowed no political interference. "Force to the utmost" became his proclaimed purpose. He was in complete control, although he called on such Republicans as

Herbert Hoover, General George W. Goethals, Charles M. Schwab, and Frank Vanderlip to assume important posts.

Wilson's announcement of his "Fourteen Points" peace plan to Congress in January 1918 was an important factor in bringing about Germany's surrender. Here are the points:

1. Open covenants openly arrived at.
2. Freedom of the seas.
3. Removal of economic barriers.
4. Guarantees for reduced armaments.
5. Impartial adjustment of colonial claims with the interest of populations considered.
6. Evacuation of Russia and leaving her alone for the acid test of good will.
7. Belgium evacuated and restored.
8. French territory, including Alsace-Lorraine, to be freed and restored.
9. Italy's frontiers restored along lines of nationality.
10. Peoples of Austria-Hungary to be autonomous.
11. Rumania, Serbia, and Montenegro to be evacuated and restored.
12. Turkey to be sovereign and its Empire to become autonomous, with the Dardanelles open.
13. An independent Poland to have access to the sea.
14. League of Nations to be formed.

These fourteen points, which Wilson characterized as "the only possible program" from the United States standpoint, were publicized to the German troops along the front by loudspeakers and leaflets. The Wilson peace terms did much to undermine German and Austrian morale. In August 1918 Austria asked for a peace based on the Fourteen Points and through the efforts of Colonel House the

40

Allies accepted Wilson's program "in principle."

It is ironic to think that just when Wilson was on the road to success in his fight for "peace with honor" he was repudiated by the American public. In October 1918 he appealed (unwisely as we now know) for a Democratic Congress but the voters gave him a Republican Congress. Americans wanted a more vindictive peace, and were not keen on the League of Nations. Wilson won the League of Nations when he went to Paris to direct the peace negotiations, but had to sacrifice half of his Fourteen Points.

Although Wilson could and did compromise with foreign diplomats at Versailles, he would make no concession to American senators in Washington when they opposed Article Ten of the League of Nations. They finally turned down the treaty with which the

Woodrow Wilson and Thomas Marshall, the vice-presidential nominee, at the Democratic convention in Baltimore, 1912.

Wilson directed peace negotiations at the Paris Peace Conference in 1919 following World War I. *Left to right:* Orlando, Lloyd, Clemenceau, Wilson.

REFUSING TO GIVE THE LADY A SEAT.

Wilson's dream for the League of Nations was shattered by the United States Senate.

During his administration, Woodrow Wilson succeeded in transferring world leadership from Europe, where it had been since the collapse of the Grecian Empire, to the United States. But while we struck the final blows that won the war, we failed to win the peace. Lloyd George got what Britain wanted—the German fleet, the German merchant marine, German trade, and German colonies. Clemenceau got Alsace-Lorraine and revenge—the Old Tiger said after Versailles, *"C'est une belle journée."* Wilson got the League but without the American membership that might have prolonged its life.

After Versailles there were many interesting expressions of opinions about Wilson and the Treaty. Lloyd George said of Wilson, "He [Wilson] was incapable of taking criticism or advice. He was sure God, Wilson, and the people would triumph." Marshal Foch spoke about the peace—"This is not a peace—it is a twenty-year armistice." Will Rogers expressed it this way: "The Armistice terms read like a second mortgage, the peace reads like a foreclosure." And General Smuts said: "We have not achieved the peace for which the people were looking."

By advocating the League of Nations, Woodrow Wilson became, in a sense, the spiritual father of the United Nations. The Covenant of the League is the foundation of the Charter of the United Nations. There is one further world-wide heritage of a Wilson idea. When Woodrow Wilson preached self-determination of peoples he opened a Pandora's box. From Vietnam and Indonesia in the Orient to all of North Africa, the world's subject and semi-independent peoples insisted upon complete and immediate freedom. More than any other single leader since George Washington, Woodrow Wilson championed the right of every people to its own way of life. His name will live.

League Covenant was incorporated. Wilson was inflexible in regard to compromise if it meant going against his principles. Article Ten, he said, was the "heart of the Covenant." As things turned out, it was nothing of the kind. It must be remembered that the president appointed only those who agreed with him to high positions. Weakened by disappointment, he toured the country in 1920 to fight for his ideals. It was a losing fight. The Republicans won both Congress and the presidency and Wilson, his health greatly impaired, collapsed and never recovered. He became a martyr to a lost cause.

42

The first sitting of the League of Nations, 1920.

11.

League of Nations

Just eight years after Germany had surrendered in 1918, a German delegation stood at the door of the League of Nations assembly hall in Geneva, Switzerland, waiting to enter. It was one of the high spots of the League's short-lived twenty-six-year history when Germany was admitted to membership on September 8, 1926. I shall always remember the dramatic and solemn moment when the German delegation led by Dr. Gustav Stresemann, Germany's ablest postwar Foreign Minister and diplomat, formally marched into the assembly hall with typical German dignity. The applause was modest and polite, the atmosphere tense. Dr. Stresemann rose to make the first German speech ever heard by League delegates. He urged world-wide disarmament, reduction of economic barriers, and was optimistic about the hope for continued world peace.

Aristide Briand, France's Foreign Minister, in reply, delivered one of the finest examples of great oratory that it has been my good fortune to hear. Raising and lowering his organ-toned voice, thrusting his leonine head and heavy body forward or drawing himself up to his full height and throwing out his arms, he held the audience spellbound. Reaching his

43

"Can Eliza save the child?"

climax, he declared, "Peace in Europe will be maintained when France and Germany work together." Then, after his denunciation of all military trappings, he cried out passionately, *"En arrière les fusils, les canons, les mitrailleuses, en avant la democratie, la liberté, la paix!"*

These final words electrified the delegates. They rose to their feet as if on signal and greeted this dramatic close with a storm of applause. Dr. Camerlengh, the League's outstanding translator, performed the amazing feat of making the speech sound almost equally good in English, winning another hearty round of applause at the end of his translation.

My first direct contact with the League of Nations was in 1921 when I went to Geneva to cover the Assembly's September meeting for the Brooklyn *Daily Eagle*. The United States was never a League member but what struck me then and at later meetings was the extent of unofficial United States participation in various activities. An American benefactor provided the League with a magnificent library. Able Americans such as Manly Hudson occupied important League posts and unofficial organizations like the United States League of Nations Association publicized the worth of the League.

I myself worked for the League one summer, studying the operations of the League's powerful broadcasting station and making a report on how the radio programs might be improved. I was always impressed by the atmosphere of enthusiasm and hope that pervaded all League meetings. Men such as Foreign Minister Eduard Benes, of Czechoslovakia and Prime Minister De Valera of Ireland were always optimistic about what the League was doing for the smaller powers. Here was a forum where every country could be heard. Benes was a tennis fan, as I have always been, and I recall that he told me League problems reminded him very much of a tennis game. Sometimes the score was against you but since every point counted you could still win even though you were only one point away from defeat. The essential thing was to fight hard to the end.

The absence of the United States, Germany, and Russia from the initial deliberations of the League was a decided handicap and weakened its prestige and power. It was also handicapped because it was tied in with the vindictive Versailles Peace Treaty. The decade from 1920 to 1930 was nevertheless a period of worth-while growth and accomplishment. From then on difficulties developed and the League went into a gradual decline.

First there was the Japanese aggression in Manchuria which brought world-wide protests led by China. The League investigated

44

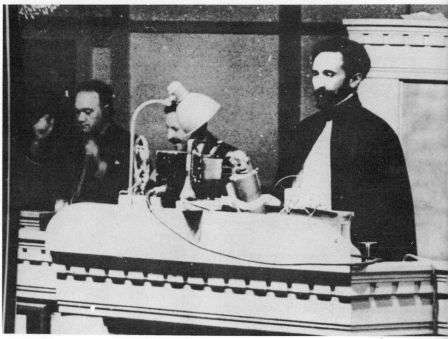

Haile Selassie makes his last appeal for justice to the League of Nations, June 30, 1936.

but did nothing except make an innocuous report. Then came Italy's aggression in Ethiopia. This led to League sanctions which France and England failed to enforce, thus striking a heavy blow at League prestige. Germany's aggression in the Rhineland and against Austria followed and again nothing was done.

I was in Geneva, when Haile Selassie, Emperor of Ethiopia, went before the world tribunal to plead his case against Italian aggression. Rarely have I listened to a more moving address. Fascist journalists from Italy created a disturbance as the Emperor began and had to be removed from the press gallery. Then the monarch said: "I am here today to claim the justice due to my people and the assistance promised eight months ago by fifty-two nations. They declared that an act of aggression had been committed in violation of international treaties. I decided to come myself to testify against the crimes perpetrated against my people. And to give Europe warning of the doom that awaits it if it bows before the *fait accompli*. The hour has struck for weak people to appeal to the League of Nations to give its judgment in all freedom. God and history will remember your decision. What answer am I to take back to my people?" Not the League but another war restored Ethiopia's independence.

The League had failed in its major purpose of preserving peace. It did serve greatly as a world forum and as a method of cooperation among lesser powers. In disputes between small powers, the League several times prevented war. The League also administered the Danzig area as well as the disputed Saar territory. In 1935 it conducted the plebiscite which returned the Saar to Germany. League

45

studies and reports, during the twenty-six years of its existence, made valuable contributions to social welfare, health, narcotics control, transportation, and a variety of other international activities.

Officially or unofficially, the United States participated in most aspects of the League's vain efforts to consolidate peace. Presidents Harding and Coolidge personally came to favor our entry into the League, but never took active measures to further our admission. President Hoover felt that public opinion would prevent war as effectively as the League. By 1931, despite our not belonging to the League, two hundred and twelve persons had been appointed to represent the United States at forty different League conferences. We also maintained five permanent offices at Geneva to look after United States interests. In 1931, when, for the first time, a great power violated the League Covenant and seized alien territory, the United States stood with the League against Japan. We even asked Britain to join with us in a special protest to Tokyo, but Sir John Simon, then British Foreign Minister, declined.

Despite this rebuff, we accepted representation in the League Commission which investigated Japan's acts and condemned them. If Britain and France, who always dominated the League, had decided on sanctions, the United States was ready to support them. From 1919 through 1939 there were few important instances where our non-membership meant non-cooperation.

That, I think, is the answer to those who believe United States absence was the only cause of the League's final failure. It failed because France and England, Russia, Japan, Italy, and Germany were more concerned about national advantage than about the larger obligations of the Covenant. The last three withdrew from the League when they began their aggression against weaker powers. Soviet Russia was ousted from the League for attacking Finland. Careful study of the League of Nations' failures should help its successor to do better. The United Nations has already gone a big step beyond the League by taking joint military action against aggression in Korea.

12.

Russian Revolution

Of all history-making events which I have followed for the past six decades, the most significant was the communist revolution in 1917. When Lenin and Trotsky seized power in Russia and overthrew the Czarist regime they launched a movement which will help shape mankind's destiny for a long time to come. My Harvard contemporary, John Reed, wrote a book about the Russian cataclysm called *Ten Days That Shook the World*. As I look back I realize how right I was in 1918 when I called this Bolshevik revolution the most important and probably the most enduring result of World War I. At that time I was war editor of the now-defunct Brooklyn *Daily Eagle,* supervising war coverage. Just as the triumph of communism in Russia was the dominant result of World War I, Russia's rise to world power was again the most important single result of World War II.

This communist revolution was the first really complete revolution the world has known. It was at once social, economic, politi-

Stalin movement can be so described. The Bolsheviks overthrew private property, the Greek National Church, the monarchy, and existing class distinctions. They substituted mass action for individualism—mass parades, mass decisions, mass everything; even tennis had to be communized. When I was in Leningrad nine years after the revolution I actually witnessed a tennis parade.

Of course the masses were well organized and dominated by a few men, but the early Bolsheviks were always careful to keep up the pretense of a people ruling itself through delegated power. The delegates always vote "yes" but they do assemble and they do vote.

As World War I ended I had a great desire to investigate and observe the communist experiment at firsthand. In 1926 I went to Russia by way of Finland. Few newspapermen were stationed in the Soviet Union and there were no tourists. I found the Russians friendly and curious about the outside world. The communist officials I interviewed were cooperative. As the United States was in the throes of Prohibition, I was interested in Russia's experience with the same problem. The Commissar of Health told me that Russia had abandoned Prohibition in 1921 because the commissars discovered that enforcement was impossible. The Russian peasant continued to make and drink his own vodka. So the-always-practical Bolsheviki leaders abandoned Prohibition and substituted temperance education. Excessive drinking continues.

In 1926 I visited industrial plants, cultural centers, libraries, and theaters. I became convinced then that for many years to come the Kremlin would be on the side of peace. Even

The Czar and his family.

Petrograd was the scene of the bloodiest revolt.

A barricaded street in Petrograd, 1917, during the revolution.

in 1926 Russia had all the land, resources, and people she required. Having suffered repeated invasion during the first five years of Soviet history, she remembered and feared outside aggression. She still fears it. Today, more than three decades later, I still believe that Russia has to be for peace. But in 1926 Russia was still the lone communist wolf confronting a hostile capitalist world which would be unified in the face of communist aggression.

By 1926 I was firmly launched on my career as a radio news commentator and sought for permission to broadcast over some of Russia's twenty-four radio stations. To my surprise it was granted on condition that I select a suitable subject. We were able to agree on "The Desirability of World Peace."

Selling receiving sets to the general public was restricted by the simple device of keeping prices out of reach. The few Russian customers were still buying parts for crystal sets. In the free world, especially in the United States, stations are supposed to transmit what the people want; in Russia, they transmit what the government thinks the people ought to want.

The Communists were using radio broadcasts most effectively as a propaganda medium, setting the pattern for government-controlled stations throughout the world. When I returned from this 1926 visit to the Soviet Union my first magazine article in *Century Magazine* was captioned "A Visit to Propaganda Land." What had chiefly impressed me was the shrewd way in which the Soviet Government utilized films, radio, posters, museums, stage, press, and platform to make people think what the government wanted them to think.

Radio was a marvelous new instrument, made to order for that particular Soviet purpose. Every dictatorship throughout the world has found a potent weapon in radio. The Communist International, with headquarters in Moscow, started foreign penetration by radio broadcasts in the early twenties. It erected the high-powered Comintern station over which I had the privilege of speaking on world peace—about the only topic on which a pro-capitalist bourgeois could be permitted to speak. It is my understanding that this was the first and last time a non-communist has ever extemporized over the Comintern station.

I spoke during the daily English hour in Moscow and later over the Crimean station during the German hour. All the high-powered Soviet stations used half-a-dozen different languages for their propaganda broadcasts. When I asked the manager of Russia's Radio Corporation what type of entertainment his listeners preferred, he answered glibly: "They like to hear the Red leaders speak." When I told him that Americans preferred popular music to most speeches, he said, "Well, I suppose the majority of our listeners also prefer music, but we don't give them too much of it."

Since there were so few home-owned sets in Russian villages, millions of villagers were supposed to participate in the Moscow ceremonies and government broadcasts by way of loud-speakers placed in clubs, reading rooms, and lecture halls. It was on the occasion of the Djershinsky funeral in 1926 that the chain-station network system was first used. This was the same year in which the National Broadcasting Company became the first American radio network. The Soviet leaders realized by this time that radio broadcasting provided them with a powerful instrument for fostering loyalty to the Communist party—and to put out communist propaganda.

Now, in the daily press, we often read "Moscow radio says" or "Tass radio announces."

In their use of radio, as in so much else, the

communist leaders were and are stark realists. Their chief illusion, obvious in 1926 as well as on my four later visits, was that world revolution was on the way and bound to come before long.

On my second visit to Russia, in 1929, I was with a United States Chamber of Commerce delegation representing American business and industry. Thus I had a comprehensive opportunity to observe the Soviet system after a three-year interval. It was possible to make comparisons with what I saw in 1926. I was impressed with the better clothing of the people and the greater amount of merchandise for sale in the shops. The Soviets had also come to have a high regard for American achievement. I recall our visit to a tractor plant which was to turn out 40,000 three-horsepower tractors per year, a plant designed by Henry Ford's architect.

It was on this trip that I had a revealing interview with the late Anatole Lunacharsky, first Soviet Commissar for Education. That famous and indeed notorious Bolshevik with the head of an intellectual, the eyes of a tired cynic, and the lips of one who loved the good things of life, expressed himself to me in this fashion: "The very existence of capitalist society constitutes a war against humanity. The bourgeoisie will never change, will never surrender their possessions of their own free will. They must be taken by force. Our task is to explain this to the people and organize them for the struggle. Then, when the proletariat is organized, we propose to present our ultimatum to the possessing classes."

Such was the completely outspoken and ruthless revolutionary doctrine held by the Communists in 1929. It has not changed. Perhaps the one thing I remember most vividly about that 1929 visit was the extent to which Stalin had already consolidated his power. Stalin worship was in full cry, and more often than not one saw his picture alone, rather than with Lenin, as was always the case in 1926.

Many people believe that the greatest internal triumph achieved by the Soviet Union is the conciliation of the varied nationalities within its borders. More than a quarter of the present population is composed of sixty different nationalities with widely contrasting languages and cultural differences, varying from the wild oriental nomadic tribes to such a highly civilized national group as the Ukrainians with a Western heritage.

According to the Soviet Constitution, these

Giants of the Revolution: Lenin and Stalin.

50

peoples are all represented in the Council of Nationalities and are allegedly granted local autonomy. They have never had any political liberty, but considerable cultural autonomy was permitted to develop during the twenties. In 1929 I visited the German Volga Republic, where 600,000 Germans still spoke a pure German. They even retained the provincial accents which their ancestors had brought from Bavaria and Silesia in the eighteenth century. Their principal occupation was farming and their agricultural productivity was far ahead of that in other sections of Russia.

This Volga German Republic was liquidated in 1941 (the Moscow Communists were afraid to put the loyalty of those Volga Germans to the test) and has never been re-created. Since the war, the Communists have inaugurated a much sterner policy with regard to national groups. They have returned to the old policy of the Czars when European Russia held in bondage all racial and national groups within the Czar's far-flung domain. Russian nationalism and Pan-Slavism have once more taken over.

Twenty years after the revolution and just after my fifth visit to Russia, I made this observation in a radio broadcast: "Russia has not achieved communism. She never will achieve it though her leaders tell us otherwise. She has, however, almost in spite of herself, come a long way on the road to a kind of semi-autocratic government with which her system of state socialism is not necessarily incompatible. Those who know something about the peace-minded temper of the Russian people do not find it surprising that this Socialist state prefers to remain at peace with the NATO powers while it continues to carry forward the process of infiltration, penetration, and more or less peaceful aggrandizement which has been so successful since 1944."

WOMAN'S HOLY WAR.
Grand Charge on the Enemy's Works.

Currier & Ives depict the holy war of Carrie Nation.

13.

The Prohibition Era

It was on January 16, 1920, that Prohibition became effective in this country but the Prohibition party and the Women's Christian Temperance Union had been making it a political and social issue for many decades. When the Drys finally achieved their victory just as our soldiers returned from France, it was evident at once that this long-delayed de-

51

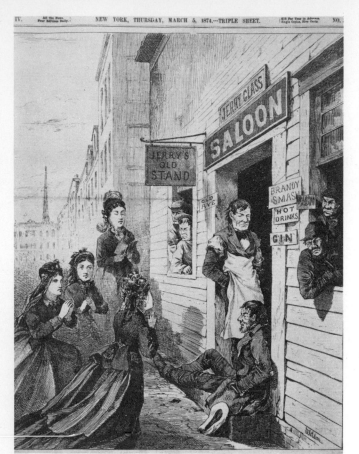

The temperance crusade—"who will win?"

term "intoxicating beverage," enforcement might have had a better chance. But Volstead and the other Prohibition leaders had become fanatics. The Act, which Congress finally passed over a presidential veto, defined an intoxicating beverage as one with "one half of one percentum or more of alcohol by volume," which barred all wines and led to the creation of a watery brew that was optimistically called "near beer."

I became acquainted with Andrew Volstead on a transatlantic voyage to Bremen, Germany. He was a tall, angular, hard-faced Minnesotan of Scandinavian ancestry who looked like the cartoonists' Prohibitionist. His normally mild manner disappeared when the conversation touched the liquor problem. My wife and I played deck tennis with his charming daughter and they accepted our invitation to join us at the famous Bremer Rathskeller for their first German dinner. I had wagered with my wife that I could persuade Volstead to taste wine and succeeded by ordering a glass of the Rathskeller's famous "Rosewein," which is supposed to be 200 years old, although it had probably been diluted several times. A thimbleful imparts a delicious flavor and fragrance to a glass of ordinary Rhine wine.

Volstead was intrigued with the rose color, the strong perfume, and the thought that this liquid was created long before we ceased being a British colony. He raised the glass and took a sip. The Rosewein is as sour as strong vinegar when taken straight, so it did not encourage him to become a wine-bibber. But I've always felt that I achieved some sort of triumph when I persuaded the author of the Volstead Act to taste wine. I still have the bill for that evening's entertainment. The glass of Rosewein cost one million marks. The entire bill for four persons totaled four and one half million marks. These were Germany's post-

cree was poorly timed. The returning soldiers felt that something had been put over while they were away. A famous cartoon showed the Statue of Liberty greeting the shipload of soldiers with a beer mug held upside down. The heroes came home to something they had not anticipated and did not want.

First advocated in 1917, the 18th Amendment, known as the Prohibition Amendment, was finally ratified in January 1919. With the passing of the National Prohibition Enforcement Act, commonly known as the Volstead Act, in October of that year, the Amendment was translated into law. If the Volstead Act had contained a reasonable definition of the

52

war inflation days and the actual cost was $1.60.

As one looks back on the Prohibition experiment, it is hard to understand how we ever got into it. We know now that Prohibition was never effective in the "wet" states, and it merely helped to promote in those states a fantastic decade of lawlessness. What we forget is that the 18th Amendment was primarily directed against the saloon and its evils and only secondarily against the manufacture and sale of liquor. As developed in the United States, the saloon had become a bad institution. There were virtually no restrictions on the sale of liquor in saloons in earlier days. Many of them sold liquor to minors and habitual drunkards.

I well remember that each spring the main streets of Merrill, my Wisconsin home town, were unsafe for women and children for several weeks because of the drunken lumberjacks who squandered their winter's earnings as they staggered from one saloon to the next. There was a saloon on every corner—one more disreputable than the next. When I thought that Prohibition would help us get rid of the saloon I was all for it. But I soon realized that the speakeasy was a poor substitute. The system of saloon licensing was haphazard and the activities of saloons were virtually unsupervised. The saloon was also the meeting place of criminals. Many saloons, instead of being the poor man's club, were places where he was clubbed. They were the headquarters for ward politicians and had a corrupting influence on municipal politics. The liquor trade and the negative aspects of law violation were closely related to the saloon. Thousands of saloons operated in a decent and law-abiding manner. But there were so many of the other kind as to give them all a bad name.

If it had not been for the saloon, Prohibition could never have passed. Most of those who voted for it were voting for the elimination of the saloon. Long before Prohibition the saloon had been recognized as an evil. Temperance propaganda was part of the American scene since colonial days. With the establishment of the Antisaloon League in the nineties, a concerted drive against the saloon was begun. Carrie Nation started her one-woman crusade with a hatchet to smash sa-

Aftermath of the Volstead Act.

Prohibition agents examine a confiscated still.

loons in Kansas. Although she was a fanatical temperance advocate, the national temperance movement never gave her much support. She died in 1911, nine years before her objective was realized.

By 1906 saloons were illegal in more than half the area of the United States. Anti-liquor propaganda in high schools began to show results and the dry advocates became a potent political force. The physiology books I studied in public school had chapters devoted to showing in word and picture the evil effects of alcohol on the human body. Prohibitionists became allied with powerful church groups such as the Methodists and their strength and tireless devotion to the cause surpassed that of the liquor interests.

Most people forget that by 1919, when the Drys forced Prohibition on the country as a war measure, two thirds of our people had outlawed liquor by local option. Ninety per cent of the United States had already voted itself dry. By fanatical insistence on forcing complete Prohibition on an unwilling minority the well-meaning teetotalers hurt the temperance movement almost beyond repair.

54

It was primarily the rural and country areas that voted for Prohibition. Few large cities ever voted themselves dry. Organized labor fought against Prohibition, but the majority of business interests supported it. Another factor that contributed to the passage of the Prohibition Amendment in wartime was the association of beer with the Germans during World War I. Most of the big breweries in the country were German-American owned— Schlitz, Pabst, Blatz, Anheuser-Busch, Rheingold, Piel are all German names. Because I was born in Milwaukee, I was once introduced to a home-town audience as "the seer that made Milwaukee famous." For years the brewers had fought against any restrictions on the sale of beer. Thus they became identified with the enemy forces and were easily labeled anti-American.

Prohibition meant much more than just a closing of distilleries, bars, saloons, and the padlocking of warehouses. It ushered in an era unforeseen by its well-meaning advocates. It brought a period of unprecedented lawlessness and corruption. Bootlegging, rumrunning, highjacking, and racketeering were the order of the day in every port and big city. Some 53,000 bootleggers were put in federal jails or on parole. In 1932 alone there were 80,000 Prohibition convictions.

From the Caribbean to the Bay of Fundy, the eastern seaboard swarmed with rumrunners. Ordinary citizens of all classes of society violated the law without shame. Speak-easies and blind pigs sprang up everywhere. "Joe sent me" was the password of the day. Speakeasies flourished even on the country's Park Avenues and Michigan Boulevards, as well as in New York's Bowery and Chicago's Madison Street. Raids were periodic, but not too frequent due to widespread police corruption.

Greed and Prohibition helped create a new monster on the American scene—the gangster.

Human life meant nothing to those terrorists —the public enemies vying for gang leadership. One principal beneficiary of the 18th Amendment was Al "Scarface" Capone who terrorized and dominated Chicago with his crime syndicate which controlled vice and gambling, making enormous profits. It was on February 14, 1929, when the infamous St. Valentine's Day Massacre took place. Five members of Capone's gang, three of them dressed as policemen, machine-gunned six members of the rival Bugs Moran gang and won undisputed control of the vice and liquor rackets of the entire Chicago area. A few months later thirty Chicago gangsters held a conference in Atlantic City. With gang leaders from other cities they mapped out a division of territories for operation, like so many world statesmen sitting down at a conference table. Capone headed an organization that took in more than $60,000,000 a year, but the Chicago police never touched him. When he went to jail years later it was due to federal prosecution for income-tax evasion.

Prohibition was one of the great political issues in the campaigns of the twenties. Even within the Republican and Democratic parties there were sharp differences of opinion that appeared at every political convention. In 1928 Al Smith, the Democratic candidate, was an avowed wet, yet the Democratic South was dry. In 1932 the rival candidates, Franklin D. Roosevelt and Herbert Hoover, both favored repeal. President Hoover was often misquoted in regard to his "noble experiment" phrase. While he was president, Herbert Hoover once told me that his oath of office compelled him to enforce a law which could not be enforced. He never called it a noble experiment. This is what he did say: "Prohibition is a great social and economic experiment—noble in motive and far-reaching in purpose." That he was opposed to the 18th Amendment is evident from this quotation from his memoirs: "Strong alcoholic drinks are moral, physical, and economic curses to the race. But in the present stage of human progress this vehicle of joy could not be generally suppressed by Federal Law."

Prohibition was destined for repeal, but the depression of the early thirties helped hasten it. It was on March 22, 1933, that President Roosevelt signed the Repeal Bill and the experiment was over. Because the saloons are still with us, the temperance forces are once more on the march. But this time they are more concerned with regulation than with prohibition. And they want the curbs to be applied by the separate states and not by the federal government.

"Scarface" Al Capone, leading gangster of the prohibition era.

At the Washington Disarmament Conference of 1921 Charles Evans Hughes, U.S. Secretary of State, convinced the major naval powers to reduce their naval strength and to maintain the Open-Door Policy in China.

14.

The Washington Disarmament Conference—1921

When President Harding took office in 1921 he had no blueprint for world peace. Nor did he have any definite idea on how to build a foreign policy after Wilson's historic failure to secure Senate approval for the League of Nations and the Treaty of Versailles to which it was tied. His campaign slogan was "normalcy," and that meant isolation.

Realizing that he had no knowledge of foreign affairs, Harding, who was never able to put the right man in the right job, wanted to make Senator Albert B. Fall his Secretary of State. The more astute leaders in the Republican party saw that such an appointment meant disaster. They overruled the president-elect and saw to it that Charles Evans Hughes was appointed to the top cabinet post. Hughes maintained close contact with the League of Nations by means of unofficial observers, and he did his best to develop an intelligent foreign policy toward Europe, where we had just fought and won World War I.

Senator William Borah who, with Senator

Henry Cabot Lodge, had led the successful Senate fight against United States membership in the League of Nations, advocated resumption of trade with Russia. Hughes was stubbornly opposed to having anything to do with the Bolsheviks, who were struggling for survival against attacks from within and without. He turned down the proposal of normal trade relations with the new Soviet state.

Borah also favored disarmament. In 1920 he had made a Senate proposal to conclude an agreement with Great Britain and Japan to limit naval construction. The Senate (including Harding, who was still a member) voted down the Borah proposal. Borah feared war with Japan, but he had no trust in European diplomacy and was suspicious of British imperialism. He was the ablest leader of the Senate isolationists.

Soon after the Harding administration took over, Secretary Hughes persuaded President Harding to give Senator Borah's proposals for naval disarmament a try. In this move he was unexpectedly aided by Lord Lee of Farcham, British First Lord of the Admiralty, who said that Great Britain would go along with an Anglo-American treaty to limit their navies to the same size.

The Anglo-Japanese Alliance was about to expire. With pressure from the Dominion prime ministers, Lloyd George was persuaded to drop this two-sided alliance and replace it with a broader union of powers to include Great Britain, Japan, China, and the United States, thus covering the whole Pacific area. Secretary Hughes wanted more than merely an agreement about Pacific issues and problems. He proposed that the United States call a nine-power conference in Washington to include Great Britain, France, Italy, Portugal, Belgium, Holland, China, and Japan. Naval disarmament was to get top priority with the Pacific and Far Eastern problems second.

Hughes was playing for high stakes, but he knew what he wanted and how to go about getting it.

Once he had assumed the initiative, Secretary of State Hughes maintained his leadership when the delegates of the powers met in Washington on November 12, 1921. President Harding opened the conference with an appeal for world peace. Then Secretary Hughes electrified the gathering by announcing that the United States which had launched the world's greatest warship building program, stood ready to halt most of its naval building. We were even prepared to scrap those capital ships already under construction provided the other countries with interests in the Pacific would also limit their building programs.

Here was a bold pronouncement, something new in world diplomacy. It is recorded that William Jennings Bryan, who was in the visitors' gallery for the conference, yelled with joy when Hughes made his spectacular announcement. The conference adjourned over the weekend to consider the United States proposal. Hughes, by his words in the historic opening session, sunk more warship tonnage than had ever been destroyed in any of the world's historic sea encounters. It was a big moment the following Monday when Lord Balfour accepted the proposal "in principle" for His Britannic Majesty's Government. For the first time the United States had achieved naval parity with Great Britain. We offered to scrap 845,000 tons, Great Britain was asked to scrap 583,000 tons, and Japan 480,000 tons.

I covered this historic meeting for the Brooklyn *Daily Eagle* and learned two things. The first was the skill of the British in dealing with the press at a conference of this kind. Their first purpose was to help and not to hinder the international army of newsmen who were covering the conference. They tried to answer all questions whether or not British interests were involved. They provided reams of background information without being asked. Without giving away secrets they helped us to avoid being wrong. Their press conferences were held more regularly than those of any other group so that they were often the first to give out important news. Their chief press officer was an experienced diplomat as well as an expert on public relations. As a natural result the British point of view was more fully and fairly presented to the world at large than that of any other powers, including the United States. At many later international meetings, including a recent one at Geneva, I have had occasion to admire British skill in presenting what has sometimes, from our point of view at least, been a bad case. An exception is the Cyprus issue, which, from the point of view of British public relations, has been badly handled.

The second thing I learned at this Washington meeting was President Harding's ignorance of foreign affairs. The Chief Executive was foolish enough to carry on ad-lib press conferences during these difficult nego-

tiations. He sought to answer offhand questions on conference matters that he should have referred to Secretary Hughes. I remember one embarrassing occasion when it turned out that he had a complete misconception about which Pacific islands were included or excluded in a treaty with Japan. The State Department was obliged to issue an immediate correction.

After three months of negotiation the Washington conference agreed on nine separate treaties, three of which were vital. First was the agreement to fix the tonnage of capital warships at the ratio of 5-5-3, that is 5 for the U.S., 5 for the British, and 3 for Japan, since they were the largest naval powers. Italy and France each had a much smaller ratio. The Anglo-Japanese Alliance was ended. A ten-year treaty was signed by the United States, Great Britain, Japan, and France to respect each other's rights in the Pacific. All the participants at Washington signed a treaty that endorsed the open-door policy for China, the principle of which had been set forth years before by the United States. In addition,

In compliance with the naval disarmament treaty the U.S. destroyed over 800,000 tons of its naval strength, more ships than had ever before been sunk in battle.

Japan, which had overextended herself in China, agreed to restore Kiachow and the Shantung Peninsula to China.

Secretary of State Hughes deserved the credit he received for his successful conduct of these negotiations. Especially in view of the negative role played by President Harding, Hughes showed convincingly that at least the United States had the power and the diplomatic skill to put into effect broad-gauged foreign policies which a previous Republican administration had vainly sought to promote after the war with Spain. The United States played the dominant role in the 1921–1922 conference. Aside from assuming the lead in the reduction of armaments—it was the first such voluntary agreement in world history—the treaties Hughes concluded had another significance. They marked our temporary success in upholding the territorial integrity of China. The United States had taken another big forward step in world affairs, even though the strong antiforeign feeling which followed the end of World War I continued to keep us out of the League of Nations.

15.

The Rise of Mussolini

The Fascist march on Rome on October 27, 1922, put Benito Mussolini squarely on the map of Europe. It put Fascism into power and set off a train of events that led Italy straight into a minor war which she won and a major war which she lost. Italy had not yet recovered from the effects of World War I when the internal disorders, the postwar disillusionment, and economic and political troubles enabled Mussolini to consolidate dictatorial power and impose strict controls on Italy's political and economic life.

When I visited Italy in 1921 there was already some talk about Mussolini. He was an active socialist editor in Milan. His Fascisti were sometimes the leaders in suppressing left-wing uprisings. Fascism itself was beginning to show its revolutionary nature. The Party, which featured black shirts and the Roman Consul's fasces was gaining more and more control of cities. The Fascist congress at Naples in 1922 was attended by almost 100,000 members. At this meeting Mussolini demanded the resignation of the wobbly government headed by Luigi Facta. Premier Facta refused to resign and asked the King of Italy to proclaim martial law to restrain Mussolini's followers. The King refused, Facta then resigned, and the march on Rome followed.

Mussolini did not head it, as is generally supposed, but four days after the Fascisti seized Rome, the King called Mussolini from Milan to form a cabinet. Like Hitler, Mussolini was called to power by constitutional procedure. Once firmly in the driver's seat, he took one step after another to secure total power. It was not until seven years later, in 1929, that Italy had been changed from a constitutional monarchy into a Fascist state.

My first meeting with Mussolini was in 1931 when he invited a group of newsmen to the Palazzo Venezia in Rome to show us the plans he had developed for remodeling the Eternal City. Mussolini showed tremendous enthusiasm about his plans as he walked to and fro in front of a whole series of maps and plans explaining what he intended to accomplish. He accompanied his talk with vigorous gestures, indicating with pointed fingers and waving arm where whole sections of the city were to be torn down to make way for his Via Imperio.

Il Duce was always easy to talk to. Interviews were easier to get with Mussolini than with Hitler. There was an atmosphere of peace and well-being in Italy throughout the early years of Fascist rule. Actually, if we pass over the usual restrictions imposed by a dictatorship, Mussolini had done a good deal for the impoverished country and the easygoing Italian people. His disastrous career of foreign aggression began only later.

It was a real chore to interview Hitler, whose unresponsive personality always fell on me like a dead weight. Mussolini, on the other hand, was keen, alert, and responsive. He had a sense of humor and loved to exchange sallies with a questioner. You knew he was acting a part, but you sensed that he enjoyed his own performance. While he made major mistakes that cost him his life and ruined his country, he was too intelligent and too much of a realist to deceive himself for long. To Mussolini, the interview was a game like a fencing match in which he was past master. He would ask as many questions as he answered. His thrusts and parries had a rapierlike quality. While he loved the good things of life and showed no moral restraint in reaching for them, he did not neglect his work because he loved pleasure.

When I saw him in 1935, just before he defied the League of Nations and invaded Ethiopia, his mood was serious. He was surrounded by guards (there had been several attempts on his life) and there were checks and double checks as I was moved from room to room in the Palazzo Venezia for my interview. Mussolini had met Hitler for the first time the year before in Venice. I am convinced from what I know of the two men that the stories of their mutual dislike are true.

In talking to me about the history of his relations with Ethiopia, Mussolini outlined his long-standing endeavors to get a square deal for Italy in Africa from France and England. He felt that Italy was in a better position than France or England to cooperate with the Ethiopian Government to the mutual advantage of both countries. Italy had well-developed colonial territories adjoining Ethiopia. The British and French repeatedly blocked an agreement between Italy and Ethiopia which Haile Selassie was willing to accept. Instead, France and England suggested Italy occupy a dry, uncultivated, and unpopulated area in North Africa. Mussolini's reply was: "Do they think I am a collector of deserts?"

Mussolini assured me that several times he was on the point of signing a mutually satisfactory agreement in the Ethiopian capital when French and British diplomats in Addis Ababa intervened and blocked agreement. He reminded me that the secret World War I Treaty of 1915 promised Italy compensation in Africa if she should enter the war on the Allied side. Doubling his fists and with a heavy scowl, he said: "Everyone agrees that this promise was not kept. Now I'm going to rely on Fascist power and not on French and British promises."

I had just been following the League of Nations debates on Ethiopia at Geneva. So I reminded Mussolini that if he invaded Ethiopia the League would impose sanctions.

At this his penetrating eyes blazed belligerently. He rose from his seat and with an accent of contempt replied: "The League! The League! What did the League do when Japan invaded Manchuria?"

This Mussolini interview suggests the historic importance of the United Nations military intervention in Korea. For the first time in history a world organization devoted to peace actually went to war against those who broke the peace. Mussolini dared defy the

Mussolini in the famous march on Rome.

Il Duce!

League of Nations because it had failed to intervene against Japan. Tomorrow's would-be aggressor may shrink from action because the United Nations has shown that it can and will intervene.

Mussolini began his invasion of Haile Selassie's ancient empire in October of 1935. Within seven months the Italian Government formally proclaimed the annexation of all Ethiopia and the King of Italy was given the title of Emperor of Ethiopia.

The League of Nations did vote sanctions against Italy as the aggressor nation. England and France refused to execute the sanctions by the simple process of closing the Suez Canal but attempted a compromise settlement before the Italian forces finally occupied Addis Ababa. On July 4, 1936, the League of Nations voted to discontinue sanctions, which was an admission of failure. It marked an unhappy milestone in the history of collective action against aggression.

In October and November of 1935 about 60,000 Italian soldiers were shipped through the Suez Canal. The Italians had a total army of 320,000 troops compared to Haile Selassie's 35,000 lightly armored troops. The best of the Ethiopian forces were the untrained tribesmen armed with spears and old rifles. Italy's 400 bombers killed thousands. The world still remembers that Vittorio Mussolini, the Duce's son, said that bombing Ethiopian cavalry was "wonderful sport and exceptionally good fun."

Well-trained and well-supplied Italian troops soon completed their unhindered conquest of Ethiopia.

16.

The Rise of Adolf Hitler

The original cover of *Mein Kampf* as published in Germany.

"He is an outstanding demagogic orator who lacks the power of decisive action. His total lack of humor, his tense speech, his self-centered egotism, and a certain sense of melancholy make one feel that here is a man destined by fate to fill a tragic hour of history. Hitler is a fanatical popular leader who could lead the German people into a new Valley of Despair. He suggests failure rather than success."

That was my partially correct analysis of Hitler as written right after my first interview with him in 1932, a few months before he achieved power. Ever since the days of the early twenties, when I visited Nazi headquarters in Munich, saw the might of Hitler's private army, and realized the impact of *Mein Kampf* which Hitler wrote in jail after his Beer Hall Putsch failed, I was eager to talk to this Austrian demagogue.

Hitler had an intense aversion to interviews —mine was the last he gave to any foreign correspondent before becoming chancellor. It was also the last in which he discussed a great variety of topics with complete freedom. My piano-playing Harvard classmate, Ernst Hanfstaengl, better known as Putzi, who was Hitler's liaison officer for the foreign press, arranged the interview for me and Louis Lochner, the veteran Berlin correspondent of the Associated Press.

Ever since Dorothy Thompson had written her uncomplimentary *I Saw Hitler,* the Nazi leader had been chary about receiving American reporters. For a year he refused all requests. He consented only after his 1932 meeting with President Hindenburg did not get him the post of Reich Chancellor. His party had just suffered an election loss of thirty-four members in the Reichstag and he was eager to restore his faltering prestige at home and abroad. When statesmen and politicians spend time on interviews they expect to get something in return. It may be nothing more than publicity or even entertainment. After being interviewed by one famous American woman reporter, who must be nameless, Hitler complained to Hanfstaengl that if he had to see women correspondents the least he could ask was that they be good-looking.

Hitler's personal car and chauffeur drove us

63

Von Hindenburg made Hitler Chancellor of Germany, January 30, 1933.

from Munich to Berchtesgaden where we lunched at the little hotel two hundred yards from Hitler's Swiss chalet on the Obersalzberg, while Hanfstaengl went over to announce our arrival. This was before the construction of the Eagle's Nest on top of the mountain. Later, as we stepped out on the open porch at the front of Hitler's chalet, my first impression of the man was unfavorable.

He came out of the front door just as we arrived. Hanfstaengl whispered to him who we were and he greeted us without a smile or a word of welcome in an atmosphere of latent hostility. He was dressed in solemn black, including his necktie. He abjured colors in his personal dress except as provided by the Nazi uniform. His slick black hair parted in the middle and his clipped black mustache added

no dignity. I had made up my mind not to listen to a Hitler tirade as an interview and resolved to interrupt him if he launched into one. We sat down and without giving Hitler or Lochner a chance to open the conversation, I plumped my first question, which was about his anti-Semitism. It evoked the typical Hitler tirade which I interrupted with other questions. Hitler had little capacity for logical, consecutive thought or analysis. But his mind was quick and keen. Among other topics, the forty-five-minute interview touched upon the Von Papen cabinet, which had excluded the Nazis, Franco-German relations, and the political situation in Germany.

Hitler obviously disliked being questioned about politics and the Nazi party. He was eager to close the interview and did so when he saw Captain Ernst Roehm approaching the house. With a show of impatience, Hitler permitted Hanfstaengl to use Lochner's AP camera to take a snapshot of us standing on the porch of his house. It may be typical that the man was not even on friendly terms with his huge shepherd dog who bounded on the porch during the interview, apparently seeking a recognizing pat from his master. Hitler shouted gruffly, "Platz," and the dog, his tail down, slunk under the table. A minute later, as Hitler began another oration, the dog sneaked away.

As a human being Hitler was so unimpressive that most of us who talked with him before he came into full power refused to believe that the German people would ever be stupid enough to tolerate him as a leader. We underestimated him because he was an introvert, an ascetic, and narrow-minded. We failed to allow for the man's fanatical drive, his mag-

netic power, and his single-minded devotion to his ideas.

Decent human beings could hardly anticipate the utterly unscrupulous methods the Nazis were ready to use. The phony Reichstag fire was just one example. Although he had been made Chancellor by Hindenburg on January 30, 1933, Hitler still lacked a Reichstag majority. He needed an excuse to oust the communist members so that the Nazis could gain control. His propaganda chief, Goebbels, said, "We must do something striking."

They did. The carefully prepared fire broke out on February 27 and provided an excuse to drive eighty-one communist members from the Reichstag. Their absence enabled him to win dictatorial power. The Nazis accused the Communists of starting the fire. At the slow, trumped-up trial, the communist defendants, who got the better of Goering when they were on the stand, were acquitted, but a poor half-

H. V. Kaltenborn gained his first interview with Hitler in 1932. *Left to right:* Carl von Wiegand of the Hearst papers, H. V. K., Adolf Hitler, Louis Lochner of the Associated Press.

The Reichstag Fire of February, 1933, which Hitler used to cement his dictatorial powers.

A sea of Nazis parade before Adolf Hitler at the Nuremberg Stadium.

witted Dutchman, Marinus Van der Lubbe, was convicted and beheaded for the crime the Nazis themselves committed.

Hitler's fanaticism, which ultimately resulted in the mass murders of thousands of innocent Jews and Poles, got off to its start with the Blood Purge within his own party in the summer of 1934. On the pretext that there was a plot against his life, Hitler ordered the execution of about 1,000 Nazi leaders, including Ernst Roehm, head of the Storm Troopers, and General Kurt von Schleicher who preceded Hitler as Chancellor. This Blood Purge gave Hitler complete control of the Reichswehr and made him supreme in his power as dictator.

My first unfavorable impression of Hitler, which was substantiated by my later contacts, left me with an intense dislike of the man. He was narrow, bigoted, humorless. His information—and he had a lot of it—was lopsided. His most consistent trait was the utter sincerity with which he believed his own lies. He was selfless in his indifference to most things of the flesh. He cared nothing for tobacco, meat, alcohol, or exercise. Even his taste for women was erratic and intermittent.

But the man had a remarkable instinctive intelligence for leadership. He was a sort of Pied Piper who could appeal to every negative quality in the German mind and heart. He knew how to capitalize German defeat, German economic prostration, Germany's apparently hopeless situation in the world. He promised everything when nothing seemed possible. He combined propaganda with personality. In him the little man, the forgotten man saw his dreams come true. And with that complete German myopia which is unable to see the non-German aspect of any issue, the politically illiterate Germans tolerated the screwball leadership of the man whose real name was Schicklgruber.

17.

Lindbergh Flight and Early Days of Aviation

The most thrilling peacetime event that stands out in the sixty years of my newspaper experience was the lone-eagle flight of Charles A. Lindbergh across the Atlantic in May 1927. Nothing in the history of aviation did more to stimulate flying than Lindbergh's masterly accomplishment. The element of drama which dominated this successful adventure had universal appeal. Never will I forget the general excitement in the Brooklyn *Daily Eagle* newsroom when my eyes glimpsed the flash on the ticker, "Lindbergh lands" and I was able to cry out: "He made it!" If this had meant victory in a war in which Lindbergh was our lone champion we could not have been happier.

His was a solo flight; he flew nonstop from New York to Paris. Seldom, if ever, had anyone been thrust so suddenly from relative obscurity into world-wide fame. People talked of nothing else. Press and radio played up the Lindbergh story as an epochal tale of personal accomplishment. The former flying cadet and airmail pilot became a world hero overnight.

His achievement also won him the Orteig prize of $25,000 for the first nonstop New York to Paris flight. Lindbergh's was no fluke accomplishment. His planning was complete and perfect. The flier himself supervised every step in the building of the plane, planning the flight, and equipping his monoplane, the *Spirit of St. Louis.* He knew every detail of his plane so well that it was a part of him. He was quite logical in speaking of himself and his plane as We. His second book, the *Spirit of St. Louis,* shows the infinite skill, patience,

Charles Lindbergh at the time of his transatlantic flight of 1927.

and persistence with which this flight was planned and executed. It gives the reader a sense of personal participation in a great adventure.

Lindbergh's historic flight of thirty-three and a half hours was not the first transatlantic flight. Actually it was the second nonstop crossing, but it was the first solo flight and by far the longest. In 1919 two English fliers from World War I, Captain John Alcock and Lieutenant Arthur W. Brown, flew nonstop from St. John's, Newfoundland, to Clifden, Ireland, a distance of 1,900 miles in slightly more than sixteen hours. The month before this first transatlantic flight was accomplished the NC-4, one of four Curtiss flying boats under the command of Lieutenant Commander Albert C. Read reached England from Trepassy

Lindbergh and the most famous plane in the world.

68

The Wright brothers made the first powered flight in 1903 at Kitty Hawk.

Bay, Newfoundland, after several stops enroute.

Although commercial long-distance aviation was well on its way toward becoming a reality, Lindbergh's flight in 1927 provided a stimulus which lasted for years. Aviation was less than a quarter century old when he lifted his plane from the soggy Long Island ground. Powered flight had long been the dream of mankind but only became a reality with the first flight by the Wright brothers, Orville and Wilbur, on the sand dunes of Kitty Hawk, North Carolina. This was on December 17, 1903. Two of their flights that day, one of 120 feet and the other of 852 feet and lasting a minute, marked the birth of the modern air age.

This was the beginning of an era which has remade our concept of the world we live in, developed the airplane as a weapon of war, as

Louis Blériot depicted making his famous flight across the English Channel in 1909.

a means of transportation and a highly important factor in our domestic economy. In 1904 the brothers Wright made the first maneuvers with an airplane and in 1905 Orville Wright kept his plane up for more than a half-hour. In 1909 the Frenchman Louis Blériot flew his monoplane across the English Channel from Calais to Dover in thirty-seven minutes. That same year I had my first flight sitting on the wing of a rickety monoplane next to the daredevil pilot, clutching the wing struts as he hedge-hopped across fields in the outskirts of Brooklyn. We never got more than ten feet off the ground since our joint weight was too much for the engine. The pilot was killed in a crash a few weeks later.

By 1919 the Russian Sikorsky had developed a twin-motored plane which helped lay the foundations for the multiengined planes as we know them in commercial and military use today. But in that year a World War United States Army pilot gave me my first stunt flight in a plane that was much like the biplane in which I had made my first flight except that there was a saddle seat for one passenger behind the pilot. He put me through such 1919 stunts as the Immelmann turn (a fighting maneuver introduced by a famous German Army pilot), the falling leaf, which was a steep side-slip maneuver to lose altitude, and the loop-the-loop, during which a novice lost all sense of direction while getting a sore neck. My chief recollection of that flight is the weird whining of the straining strut wires. My most recent experience of how uncomfortable a plane ride can get was during the Korean War when a pilot teacher carried me on a jet-plane reconnaisance mission over North Korea. When we were shot at over the North Korean capital he took what he called evasive action, a series of high-speed up-and-down maneuvers that almost left me unconscious.

Recalling some of aviation's firsts, it was in 1918 that the Post Office Department inaugurated the first regular airmail service. Army planes began a daily round trip between Washington and New York. The first transcontinental airmail route was established between New York and San Francisco in 1920. It was Brigadier General William Mitchell—more affectionately known as Billy Mitchell—who, more than anyone, is largely responsible for the early progress of military aviation in the United States. This distinguished soldier had studied aviation for many years and was the first American flying officer to cross the lines in World War I. He laid the basis for the tactical Air Service in Europe and later commanded the Air Service of the First Army Corps, the First Army Air Service, and the Air Service of the Group of Armies. After the war, General Mitchell was in charge of training and organizing the Air Service for the United States Army. Plainly outspoken but having great vision as to the future of the airplane in time of war, he wrote about it in his book, *Our Air Force*. It was most unfortunate that because of his views and criticism of national defense policies he got into the mess he did with the higher-ups in the Army and was subsequently court-martialed and suspended. Now the story of that whole affair has been made into a successful moving picture.

The Lindbergh flight initiated a whole chain of remarkable accomplishments in aviation. Just a few weeks after Lindbergh landed in Paris, Charles A. Levine, piloted by Clarence D. Chamberlain, became the first transatlantic passenger in a flight from Roosevelt Field to Germany. In 1930 two Frenchmen, Captain Dieudonne Coste and Maurice Bellonte, made the first nonstop Paris to New York flight, and in 1932 Hugh Herndon and Clyde Pangborn made the first nonstop Pacific flight from Japan to the state of Washington. That same year Amelia Earhart, who was

In 1918 the Post Office inaugurated the first regular air-mail service.

lost in 1937 on a round-the-world flight, became the first woman to fly the Atlantic alone. Like Lindbergh, she got a traditional ticker-tape parade upon her return to New York. In 1933 Wiley Post made the first solo round-the-world flight in his *Winnie Mae*, doing 15,596 miles in less than eight days.

The record round-the-world flight of Howard Hughes in July 1938 was significant on three counts. It was a striking demonstration of the progress of civil aviation in the ten years after the Lindbergh flight. It carried home in dramatic fashion the smallness of the world. It showed that for military purposes forts and frontiers had lost their traditional meaning. The government had nothing to do with it, except to wish it well. It was the individual enterprise of the civilian sportsman-aviator who accomplished the flight with four companions in less than four days, flying by way of Europe and Siberia. At that time I commented that we have every right to be proud that American aviators, American engineers, and American machines combined to make possible a flight around the world in less than four days. Courage, ingenuity, skill, endurance, and scientific precision all played their part in this high achievement. Those same comments would still apply to what is being done today in the spectacular development of aviation.

My own early experiences in aviation include a passenger flight in Germany in 1924, a transatlantic passenger flight in 1939, military plane crossings in 1940 and 1941, a trans-Pacific survey trip in United States Navy planes in 1942, a round-the-world flight in 1947, and a Korean combat mission in a jet plane in 1951. My very first airplane ride was the one I made with a stunt pilot in 1909. This is a paragraph from the account I wrote for the Brooklyn *Daily Eagle:* "The pilot sits on a saddle seat centered between two wings and ahead of the engine. There is no seat for a passenger but I am told to sit on the front edge of the left wing alongside of the pilot. He shows me where to hang on to the struts and wires to keep from falling off. The engine starts with a terrific racket and the plane bumps along the grass. Soon we leave the

71

ground for a few seconds, only to drop back with a terrific thud. We bob up again after moving forward for a hundred feet. The wires twang angrily each time we hit the ground. In less than two minutes we were at the end of the field and the flight was over."

Here is a much more eloquent description of flying from the emotional angle. In his book, *Spirit of St. Louis*, Lindbergh writes: "What freedom lies in flying! What godlike power it gives to man. I'm independent of the seaman's coast line, of the landsman's roads. I'm like a magician concocting magic formulae. The symbols I pluck from paper applied to the end of a compass will take me to any acre on earth where I choose to go."

Although I must have flown half a million miles I still experience an emotional lift each time I leave the ground.

18.

Kellogg-Briand Pact—1928

As a result of talks with Professor James T. Shotwell, of Columbia University, in March 1927, the French Foreign Minister Aristide Briand startled the world with a novel proposal. He suggested a pact among nations for the "outlawry of war." A short time later Nicholas Murray Butler, president of Columbia, revived this proposal to outlaw war in a letter to the New York *Times*. On June 11, Secretary of State Frank B. Kellogg, whom President Coolidge had appointed to succeed Charles Evans Hughes, formally acknowledged Briand's proposal. Briand submitted a draft and the United States and France exchanged pledges never to go to war against each other.

As a result of talks with Idaho's Senator Borah, Secretary Kellogg—he was called "Nervous Nellie" because of his fussiness and lack of confidence—was urged to extend the agreement to all other nations. On January 11, 1928, a draft treaty was published and brought to the attention of other powers. It was proposed that all signatory powers should renounce war as an instrument of national policy. This Kellogg-Briand Pact to outlaw war—it was also called the Paris Pact—was signed in Paris in August 1928. Eventually more than sixty nations signed it.

I was in Paris to report the formal signing ceremonies. While I appreciated the purpose of such a pact, I could not share the enthusiasm of those who honestly believed that by signing an agreement to renounce armed conflict war would be forever outlawed. At best, the Kellogg-Briand Pact was a political gesture which had a certain moral value. By signing this pact the major and minor powers went on record as recognizing the horror and futility of war. At that time the world was putting a great deal of confidence in newly signed pacts and agreements.

The best one could hope from the Paris Pact was that the signatory powers were at least expressing an honest intention to keep the peace. I well remember the feeling of doubt that assailed me as the representatives of the major powers went through with the signing ceremony in the handsome Salle des Horloges of the French Foreign Office, scene of many historic meetings. Germany was happy to sign because she had been disarmed. We were happy to renounce war because we were in the high tide of postwar prosperity. But as Japan's representative stepped to the table I recalled my talks with Japan's military leaders the previous year and wondered how much more Japanese penetration China would accept without fighting back. Soviet Russia was still too busy with internal problems to think of war. While Mussolini's Italians wanted no more war, they were soon to be thrown into it by an imperialist-minded dictator.

The 1928 agreement had no force behind it. There were no military or economic sanctions. The Pact rested on the moral force of world opinion. Although the United States was not a member of the League of Nations, the League implemented the Kellogg-Briand Pact by a general act providing for conciliation and arbitration in the event there was aggression by any nation. That was the period when we pretended to be aloof from the League while we actually participated in most of its important political and economic endeavors. Geneva was always full of official and unofficial United States observers who carried a good deal of weight.

The Kellogg-Briand Pact evidenced further participation by the United States in world affairs. Briand told me that he felt the Pact showed the re-entry of the United States on the larger world stage. He was right. We were becoming conscious of the larger role we were destined to play and the Kellogg-Briand Pact was a step—albeit a minor one—toward world leadership.

Secretary of State Kellogg was less conscious of his country's imminent role as the greatest single power than he was of the role he himself had played in signing this pact of peace. He was a small man and a modest man, a relatively minor Midwestern politician whom fate had thrust, for a brief moment, into the center of the world stage. He confided to me that nothing had pleased him more during his stay in France than the gift he received from the

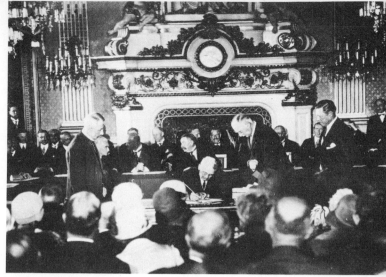

BROWN BROTHERS

Secretary of State Frank Kellogg signed the pact for the United States.

mayor of Le Havre, France, as he first landed on French soil. It was a gold pen with which to sign the Paris Pact. On it was inscribed this clever variation of a well-known Latin epigram: *"Sivis pacem para pacem."* I wonder where that pen is now that all the great powers are once more acting on the original version: *"Sivis pacem para bellum"*?

The Kellogg-Briand Pact to outlaw war was signed in Paris, 1928.

BROWN BROTHERS

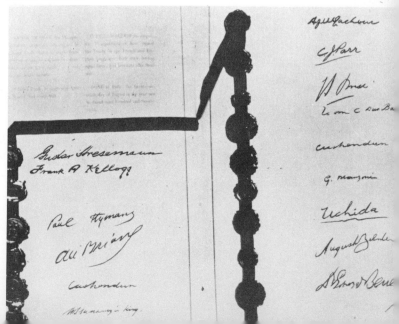

Governor Al Smith and his famous cigar.

19.

Al Smith and the 1928 Campaign

At the Democratic party convention in Houston, Texas, in June 1928, Governor Alfred E. Smith of New York was nominated for president on the first ballot. The bands broke into "The Sidewalks of New York," the Smith theme song. The Happy Warrior was the apt nickname Franklin D. Roosevelt gave to Smith when he placed the governor's name in nomination. Smith won easily in Houston. Four years before, at the sixteen-day Democratic convention in New York, in 1924, the best he could do was to prevent William G. McAdoo from winning. The two arch rivals were deadlocked until the 103d ballot, when the tired delegates nominated John W. Davis, who was defeated by Calvin Coolidge.

Al Smith's campaign theme song was opportune. He actually was from New York's East Side, a fact of which he was always proud. He had little formal education and once told a reporter, "The only book I ever read was *Life and Battles of John L. Sullivan*. Yet Smith hated prize fights. He enjoyed his political battles and always fought clean. Because he was vigorously and picturesquely outspoken, Smith always provided good copy. We who reported him in the press and later on the air loved him both as a man and as an unfailing source of good copy.

He started his political career as a party worker in the Downtown Tammany Club. Tom Foley, the East Side boss, soon picked him as a candidate for the State Assembly. That meant certain election. Henry Campbell, who sponsored Smith, bought him a cutaway coat and a full-dress suit to start him on his Albany career.

Smith served eight terms in the State Legislature and Charles Murphy, Tammany chief, picked him as assembly leader. The late Sen-

Al Smith received this enormous brown derby, his campaign symbol, from New York boy scouts during his campaign for the presidency.

ator Robert Wagner, father of New York's mayor, and Al Smith were Tammany's team of bright young men in the state capital.

In 1918 Smith became governor of New York, a post to which he was elected four times. Only Governor Clinton also served four terms. Smith had many devoted and loyal followers, such as Belle Moskowitz, the unselfish social worker. Her knowledge and experience supplemented his, and he knew when to take her advice. Smith was a Tammany man but throughout his governorship and his public life there was never a suggestion of corruption. He maintained a strict code of personal integrity in both his public and private life. In his first campaign for governor he stated in a speech: "I know what is right. If I ever do anything that is wrong it will be deliberate and you can hold me to account for it." When he was inaugurated at Albany the first time, many thousands of New Yorkers went up for the ceremonies.

Many times Al Smith and I were fellow speakers at the annual Guggenheimer-sponsored Washington's Birthday celebration. It was held at the Brace Memorial Newsboys' Home on the lower East Side not far from where Al Smith was born. He himself had been a newsboy and he loved talking to this juvenile audience even after he became governor. While the number of newsboys became smaller as the years passed newsstands and home delivery displaced the juvenile hawkers—the audience was made up of East Side teen-agers, most of whom were earning their own living or, like the youthful Al Smith, even helping to support their families. They admired Smith and he certainly knew how to get their attention and hold it throughout his speech. I always felt lucky when I was called on to speak before Al Smith arrived because when he finished the boys wanted the food for which most of them had come and no more oratory. By watching Al Smith talk to those boys I learned a great deal about how to win and hold a difficult audience.

Smith was by nature and experience an excellent executive. He had a genius for drama-

75

tizing political issues. When asked to what he attributed his success, he replied: "Just being around." Smith never lost touch with the common man. He could make the public understand and support liberal legislation by what Raymond Moley called "sidewalk statesmanship." He often showed courage, as when he risked his political future by denouncing William Randolph Hearst who wanted to be governor of New York.

When Robert Moses first met Al Smith, his shocked comment was: "He looks the picture of a Tammany politician with his brown derby on one side of his head and a big cigar in the corner of his mouth." Though poles apart in background and education, these two men became great friends and collaborators. It was Al Smith who started Bob Moses on his magnificent career of public service.

To win the presidential nomination in 1928 Al Smith had to overcome powerful enemies. He was an avowed wet and advocated amending the Volstead Act. He was a Catholic and expressed his religious creed in a notable magazine article. In the Democratic ranks there was strong opposition to him on both points. But when McAdoo, his powerful 1924 opponent, would not be a contender for the 1928 nomination, the field was wide open for Smith despite internal party opposition. United States Senator Robinson, a dry, was nominated as vice-president, which led a commentator to remark that the Democratic donkey left Houston with a wet head wagging a dry tail. The prominent industrialist, John J. Raskob, boomed Smith and became the campaign chairman. Many rich Republicans joined the bandwagon because of Smith's stand on Prohibition, the farm bill, and the tariff, which were the main issues. They also helped swell the Democratic campaign fund which reached record heights.

Smith fought a vigorous campaign, stumping around the country tirelessly. He maintained a constant heavy oratorical barrage against the Republicans. He repeatedly challenged his opponent, Herbert Hoover, on the issues. But Hoover's campaign was so subdued that he didn't once mention Smith's name during the contest. The brown derby, the genial smile, the big cigar and the campaign song, "The Sidewalks of New York," won Smith many friends all over the country except in the Democratic South. His mispronunciation of radio as "raddio" caused raised

Al Smith and the Democratic national chairman, John Raskob, favored repeal of Prohibition.

eyebrows and became a byword. Mispronounced or not, Al Smith used the radio on every possible occasion. His East Side accent and his folksy ways probably hurt more than they helped. Radio sales rose to unprecedented heights during the campaign period. Expressions such as "Let's look at the record," and "No matter how thin you slice it, it's still baloney" became Smith trade-marks and caused his audiences to shout with delight. He was in every sense the Happy Warrior as he fought for election.

During the 1928 campaign Smith made a personal plea to Franklin D. Roosevelt to run for governor of New York. He felt it would help him win. Ironically, Roosevelt won the governorship, but Smith lost the state to Hoover by more than 100,000 votes. Smith's protégé was to become his nemesis. Smith carried only eight of the forty-eight states. Partly because he was a Catholic but mainly because of his stand on Prohibition and the Ku Klux Klan he even lost six traditionally Democratic southern states.

Smith's defeat in 1928 hurt him very deeply and alienated him from politics. For the first time in his life the Happy Warrior became bitter. Later he even broke with Franklin Roosevelt, mainly because he couldn't go along with Roosevelt's New Deal philosophy. He felt that Roosevelt had become too class conscious. At the Jefferson Day dinner in Washington in 1932 Smith said, "I will take off my coat and fight to the end against any candidate who sets class against class." The gap between Smith and Roosevelt widened as the New Deal was translated into legislation. Smith said in 1936, when Roosevelt was nominated for a second term, "I think I'll take a walk." Along with other conservative Democrats Smith did take a walk and supported the Republicans against the man he had persuaded to become governor of New York.

"Bringing home the Bacon" by Berryman.

Smith's alienation from his own party and its great leader was a sad thing for him personally and for millions of Americans who regretted Smith's departure from public life. He became president of the corporation that owned the Empire State Building but was never completely at home as a business executive. He continued to serve many good causes but ceased being a public leader except as a memory. He died on October 4, 1944, at the age of seventy. A $5,000,000 Al Smith memorial building at St. Vincent's Hospital in New York City was provided by public subscription.

77

WORST STOCK CRASH STEMMED BY BANKS; 12,894,650-SHARE DAY SWAMPS MARKET; LEADERS CONFER, FIND CONDITIONS SOUND

FINANCIERS EASE TENSION

Five Wall Street Bankers Hold Two Meetings at Morgan Office.

CALL BREAK 'TECHNICAL'

Lamont Lays It to 'Air Holes' —Says Low Prices Do Not Depict Situation Fairly.

FINDS MARGINS BEING MET

'Susceptible of

Wall Street Optimistic After Stormy Day; Clerical Work May Force Holiday Tomorrow

Confidence in the soundness of the stock market structure, notwithstanding the upheaval of the last few days, was voiced last night by bankers and other financial leaders. Sentiment as expressed by the heads of some of the largest banking institutions and by industrial executives as well was distinctly cheerful and the feeling was general that the worst had been seen. Wall Street ended the day in an optimistic frame of mind.

The opinion of brokers was unanimous that the selling had got out of hand not because of any inherent weakness in the market but because the public had become alarmed over the steady liquidation of the last few weeks. Over their private wires these brokers counseled their customers against further thoughtless selling at sacrifice prices.

Charles E. Mitchell, chairman of the National City Bank, declared that fundamentals remained unimpaired after the declines of the last few days. "I am still of the opinion," he added, "that this reaction has badly overrun itself."

Lewis L. Pierson, chairman of the board of the Irving Trust Company, issued last night the following statement:

"Severe disturbances in the stock market are nothing new in American experience. The pendulum always swings widely and it would seem as though the long-expected break should bring about an equilibrium.

"The position of the Federal Reserve Bank is unusually strong ... of member banks are moderate.
... ... earnings in many industries,

LOSSES RECOVERED IN PART

Upward Trend Starts With 200,000-Share Order for Steel.

TICKERS LAG FOUR HOURS

Thousands of Accounts Wiped Out, With Traders in Dark as to Events on Exchange.

SALES ON CURB 6,337,415

Prices on Markets in Other Cities Also Slump and Rally —Wheat Values Hard Hit.

The most disastrous decline in the ... and broadest stock market ... financial dis...

20.

The Stock Market Crash of 1929

The crash heard around the world! In effect that was what the Stock Market crash of October and November 1929 turned out to be. It was no mere domestic affair in which large segments of American society lost the money with which they did their gambling on 10 per cent margins. The golden bubble of unprecedented securities speculation burst with a repercussion that set in motion a world-wide depression. The crash helped change the course of history.

It brought the worst panic known to Wall Street. In one day 16,000,000 shares of stock were dumped on the New York Exchange. Within three days stock averages dropped 68 points. By November 13, when the disastrous speculative orgy of the twenties had definitely ended in disaster, the market value of listed stocks had dropped by $30,000,000,000. This was almost as much money as the country had spent fighting World War I.

A few people had predicted the crash. Roger Babson announced for months that the market was headed for a major break. But the speculators preferred to believe those financial and economic leaders who felt there was nothing fundamentally wrong with the market or the business and credit structure. The country was enjoying prosperity, commodity prices were high, and business—with normal fluctuations—was still good in the months before the crash. But stock prices rose out of all proportion to general conditions and speculation on 10 per cent margins continued unchecked.

Herbert Hoover, who had been president only a few months before the collapse, attempted to curb stock-market gambling through the Federal Reserve. He wrote a memorandum to a Board member in which he said: "Unless our financial policies are guided with courage and wisdom this speculation . . . can only land us on the shores of depression." But the market boom which had started in the Coolidge-Mellon era continued to soar onward and upward. President Hoover issued repeated warnings to the press, to bankers, and to President Whitney of the Stock Exchange, but to no avail.

Then, suddenly, public confidence cracked. The big selling wave started to knock down the high prices and to wipe out paper fortunes. The experts characterized this stock-market crash as a local matter that wouldn't affect anyone except speculators who were playing the market. Few of them foresaw the international reaction that was to come. Big financiers continued to buy stock; big business exuded unjustified confidence. President Hoover was put under pressure to issue an optimistic statement. He hedged: "The fundamental business of the country, that is the production and distribution of commodities, is on a sound basis." But he refused to say anything about stocks.

The "speculative flurry," as Andrew Mellon called the hectic market activities that ended with the crash, may have been over, but the prosperity slogan of "two chickens in every pot" and "two cars in every garage" soon gave way to breadlines and street-corner apple sellers. Business and industry ground to an almost complete halt and the deep, dark days of depression, with all their human misery, set in. It took the stock-market crash to destroy the prosperity that followed World War I. The golden twenties were a memory.

We lost much more than our prosperity. The crash pointed up how New York had become the world's financial center. Foreign countries promptly lost their confidence in the United States and its economy. They felt that a market crash of such proportions proved that the underlying American economy must be unsound. Economic nationalism and isolation became the order of the day here and abroad. Our depression soon led to depressions elsewhere.

The apple seller became a depression symbol.

UNEMPLOYED
BUY
APPLES
5 EACH

People feared the worst and panic led to bank runs. The scene before New York's Broadway Central bank was repeated across the nation some months after the Wall Street crash.

In Germany in 1929 there were riots and demonstrations due to unemployment. This strengthened both the Communist and Nazi parties. Depression set in, and the Germans could no longer count on continued United States help. For four years before the market crash, loans from the United States had afforded the Germans some semblance of good times. The crash ended prosperity and helped bring Hitler. Foreign Minister Gustav Stresemann died just about the time stock prices were beginning to decline in New York. His death along with our stock-market collapse marked the beginning of the end of the Weimar Republic and paved the way for the rise of the dictator who was soon to lead the world into another war.

As an aftermath of our stock-market crash the Bank of England was forced off the gold standard in September 1931. Two years later we, too, gave up the gold standard. The abandonment of sound money marked the end of an economic era and altered the course of history. By cooperating and maintaining the gold standard, the major powers provided a steadying element for national government finance and promoted international economic stability. Once the gold standard was abandoned, the powers embarked on all sorts of restrictive policies. Economic nationalism replaced cooperation.

The London Economic Conference in 1933, which was called for stabilization, might have done much to salvage our declining prestige abroad and to restore sound currencies. The Conference was deliberately wrecked by the man who called it. President Roosevelt, under bad advice, succumbed to the current fever of economic nationalism. He refused to accept a sound-currency program which was still supported by the remaining gold-bloc nations—France, Belgium, The Netherlands, Italy, and Switzerland. He repudiated his own Secretary of State Cordell Hull and insisted on limiting United States participation in the conference to tariff treaties. In a radio message he rebuked the delegates for taking up the currency problem first. I was in London, covering the Conference for the American radio audience and well remember the reluctance with which the American delegation carried out a policy which its members did not approve.

The Conference broke up without any accomplishment. This was a severe blow at international economic cooperation. It signalized the American drift toward isolation and economic nationalism. Thus the crash that was heard around the world in October 1929 echoed for many years thereafter. But it did lead to the creation of the Federal Security Commission and a system of controls on stock speculation that has been effective ever since.

21.

Admiral Byrd Flies Over Both Poles—1929

It was less than three decades ago that Rear Admiral Richard E. Byrd flew over the South Pole and a little more than thirty years ago that he made his epoch-making flight over the North Pole. Our greatest living explorer—one of the great explorers of all time—has devoted most of his adult life to polar exploration.

It was on May 9, 1926, that Admiral Byrd—he was Commander then—and Floyd Bennett, his pilot, flew from King Bay, West Spitsbergen, to reach the North Pole. They used a Fokker monoplane, the *Josephine Ford*, and

Making final preparations for the eventful flight to the South Pole on the big Ford monoplane *Floyd Bennett* which carried Admiral Byrd, Bert Balchen,

Harold June and Captain Ashley McKinley on the 1,600-mile trip, November, 1929.

East Base, where 26 men of the Byrd Antarctic expedition spent an Antarctic winter.

covered the 750 miles and back in fifteen hours. They accomplished what the Norwegian explorer Roald Amundsen and his American companion, Lincoln Ellsworth, had failed to do one year earlier in two flying boats. For his successful flight over the North Pole, Byrd was given the Congressional Medal of Honor.

Admiral Byrd's first Antarctic explorations began in 1928. He headed a large scientifically equipped expedition, which included three airplanes. In January 1929 he established and built his base at Little America on the Ross Barrier in Antarctica. From here the members of the expedition flew to make important discoveries. On November 28 and 29, 1929, Byrd, piloted by Bert Balchen in the plane they named after Floyd Bennett, flew to the South Pole and back from the Little America base.

The second Byrd Antarctica expedition, lasting from 1933 until February 6, 1935, was equipped with four planes, four tractors, and an autogyro, as well as the most up-to-date scientific weather equipment. Notable discoveries were made on these expeditions, chief of which were the huge Edsel Ford Range and the territory which Byrd named the "Marie Byrd Land" and claimed for the United States.

One major accomplishment of Admiral Byrd's second Antarctic venture was the demonstration that there is no strait between the Ross and Weddell seas and that Antarctica is an entire continent. Byrd himself remained alone from March 22 until October 12, 1934, at an advanced base 123 miles south of his main base. There he conducted the first extended study of meteorological conditions in this region.

In 1939 Admiral Byrd was made commander of the United States Antarctica Service. After World War II, in 1946 and 1947, he headed the United States Navy Expedition which explored almost 2,000,000 square miles, carried out a geological survey and gathered important weather data. During World War II Byrd served on the staffs of Admirals King and Nimitz.

82

Rear Admiral Byrd made Antarctica exploration big business. He wrote three books about his ventures and adventures, all of them best sellers. He became one of the country's most popular lecturers at $1,500 per lecture. But he kept none of the proceeds for himself. He donated them to the causes he himself has served with such devotion. He is still exploring the Antarctic. Early in 1956 he returned home once more after establishing another expedition in the far South.

At a Paris conference in mid-1955 the United States and the Soviet Union reached friendly agreement on the establishment by both countries of more bases in Antarctica. This Paris meeting brought together the organizers of the International Geophysical Year. This is an eighteen-month period from July 1957 to December 1958 which will be marked by many explorations, experiments, and expositions.

As explained by Professor Vladinus Balousov at the Paris meeting, the Soviet Union plans an expedition across 1,600 miles of unexplored Antarctica territory. The Russians will establish three new bases, one of which would be near the South Pole. The United States is planning to create and maintain six bases, one of which will also be in the general area of the South Pole.

It must be remembered that Antarctica is a continent of between five and six million square miles, so that even a dozen bases scattered over this vast area are hardly likely to interfere with one another.

The Soviet Union borders on the Arctic for thousands of miles which gives her a natural interest in both the North Pole and South Pole areas. Thanks largely to Admiral Byrd, the United States is well in the lead in Antarctic exploration, which is an important part of that comprehensive study of the earth with which forty nations will mark the Geophysical Year.

President Roosevelt presents the Distinguished Service Medal to Admiral Byrd in 1940 for his most recent Antarctic expedition, as Secretary of the Navy Knox looks on. The Admiral received his original D.S.M. for his transatlantic flight in 1927.

HARRIS & EWING

22.

The Scottsboro Case

NEW YORK TIMES, NOVEMBER 8, 1932

York Times.

1932, by The New York Times Company.

X, ESDAY, NOVEMBER 8, 1932.

NEW TRIAL ORDERED BY SUPREME COURT IN SCOTTSBORO CASE

Ruling Finds Seven Negroes Condemned in Alabama Were Denied Right of Counsel.

TWO OF 9 JUSTICES DISSENT

Police Wield Clubs Freely on Radicals Attempting to Picket Court Chamber.

MANY HURT, 14 ARRESTED

Alabama Judge Expects New Trial In March—Holds Move for Change of Venue Likely.

Text of Supreme Court decision in Scottsboro case is on Page 12.

Special to THE NEW YORK TIMES.

WASHINGTON, Nov. 7.—New trials were ordered by the Supreme Court today for seven Negroes condemned to death at Scottsboro, Ala., on charges of attacking two white girls. Seven members of the court joined in the opinion handed down by Justice Sutherland, asserting that the Negroes had been denied the right of counsel. Justices Butler and McReynolds, the other two members of the bench, dissented, saying that the youths had not been deprived of any of their constitutional rights in the Alabama court.

An hour before the decision was announced, Capitol and metropolitan policemen and a corps of detectives vigorously wielding clubs, had driven 100 Communists and other radical demonstrators off the plaza at the front of the Capitol. Tear gas

HOOVER AND RO[O] WITH NATION LEADERS OF

Polls Open in This State F[or] Chief Candidates in Neu[...]

The polls in New York Sta[te...] o'clock in the morning and clos[...] adjoining State of Connecticut [...] but in New Jersey they will re[...]

Following are the candid[ates] President and Vice President,

area:

NEW[...]

For Governor—Herbert [...] van, Republican; Louis Wald[...] Preservation party; Aaron [...] Communist.

For Senator—Robert F. [...] Republican; Charles Solomo[...] ervation party; Jeremiah D. [...] stone, Communist.

NE[...]

For Mayor—John P. [...] publican; Morris Hillquit, [...] William L. Patterson, Com[...]

For Governor—Wilbu[r...] Republican; Jasper McLe[...] Labor; Albert Levitt, Ind[...] munist.

For Senator—Augus[...] Republican; Devere Alle[...] Milton C. Conover, Inde[...] munist.

For Senator—W. W[...] Democrat; Herman F. [...] Labor; Esther H. Elf[...] munist.

ROOSEVELT [...] VOTES FOR 'NE[...]

Victoria Price and Ruby Bates were not the fine flower of southern womanhood, but they were southern white girls. They wanted a ride on a freight train, so they took one on March 25, 1931, from Chattanooga, Tennessee, to Paint Rock, Alabama. By that ride the girl tramps set off a chain of events that led to the celebrated and far-famed Scottsboro case. Even today, when questions of southern justice for Negroes arise, the Scottsboro case comes to mind.

Fellow hitchhiking juvenile delinquents on the same freight train with the two white girls included seven white boys and twelve Negroes. As a result of a fight between the whites and the Negroes, nine of the Negro boys were arrested when the train reached Paint Rock. They were charged by the authorities with raping the two girls. That is how the *cause célèbre* which so aroused the country got under way.

The first trial at Scottsboro, in Jackson County, Alabama, began on April 6, 1931. Three days later eight of the defendants were convicted and sentenced to death—the ninth Negro boy was only fourteen and was not convicted. That was the first round in what was soon proved to be a mockery of justice, since the case was trumped up and no convincing evidence was produced.

Feeling ran high at Scottsboro. Mobs surrounded the courthouse during the trial and there were open threats of lynching. The defendants had to be guarded by the military.

From the beginning the trial proceeded in an atmosphere of tense, hostile, and excited public sentiment. A Jackson County newspaper, in reply to criticism about an all-white jury, said, "A Negro juror in Jackson County would be a curiosity and some curiosities are embalmed."

After the United States Supreme Court had set aside the decision of the first trial on the

84

ground that the prisoners did not have the assistance of counsel, a new trial was ordered. Because of the prejudice in Jackson County, the second trial was held in Decatur, Morgan County. Again the jury verdict was conviction and death. However, that trial was declared a mistrial when Circuit Judge James E. Horton, of Athens, declared there was a lack of evidence. He stated, "The testimony of the prosecutrix [Victoria Price] in this case is not only uncorroborated, but it also bears on its face the indications of improbability. It is contradicted by other evidence and in addition thereto the evidence greatly preponderates in favor of the defendant. It is therefore ordered that . . . the verdict of the jury in this cause and the judgment of the Court sentencing this defendant to death be set aside and a new trial ordered."

The dramatic third trial, with Heywood Patterson the chief defendant, again ended in conviction and the death sentence. The fatal circle again closed in the Scottsboro case, as far as the Alabama courts were concerned. But not in the court of public opinion.

Throughout the trials the cause of the young Negroes was championed by liberal organizations. As usual, the Communists exploited it. Negro societies were much concerned with it. Samuel Leibowitz, the defending lawyer, now a judge in New York City, who had taken over the case, was actually defending the 14th Amendment. This enraged the Alabamans and their neighbors. Some of the more rabid retaliated by terrorizing and shooting Negroes on outlying plantations.

Public sentiment against the miscarriage of justice ran rampant the country over. Virtually every newspaper carried strong editorials about the Scottsboro decisions. Even southern newspapers voiced strong opposition to the verdicts and the trials. The Richmond *News Leader* said, "The men are being sentenced

The eyes of the world were turned to the state of Alabama in 1931. State troopers maintain order while the second trial of the Scottsboro boys begins.

The Scottsboro boys face their second trial. The decision, as in the first case, was reversed and they had a third trial ahead.

to death primarily because they are black. The second trial confirmed all the suspicions aroused by the first." Another Richmond paper said, "The apparent lack of fairness in trying these helpless Negroes is deplored by the vast majority of Southerners," and a Raleigh paper stated: "All southern justice will be discredited by the shocking verdict in Decatur." North and south, east and west, the editorial opinion was the same.

Along with dozens of other radio commentators, I expressed my criticism of the Scottsboro verdicts on the air by comparing the unfair procedures of Alabama in dealing with Negroes with those that Hitler was then using in Germany against the Jews. This caused an Alabama newspaper to flay me as a flibbertigibbet. My remarks determined the attorney general of Alabama, Thomas E. Knight, to have me put off the air, because he felt "the state of Alabama has been scurrilously slandered."

He formally asked the Federal Radio Commission to take action against me for my allusion to Alabama's concept of justice, declaring that he knew the Negro defendants accused of assaulting two white girls "had a scrupulously fair trial."

In defense of what I said I pointed to the record and explained: "It is difficult for a defender to obtain justice when the entire atmosphere is charged with prejudice against him. That was certainly true in Alabama in the case of the so-called Scottsboro defendants, as it is true in the case of any Negro in the South charged with attacking a white woman. It is something the judicial authorities cannot overcome, although they may try. The very fact that the Supreme Court of the United States had to reverse the first Scottsboro trial because it was unfair, that the second trial was upset by the very Alabama judge who presided, and that a careful reading of the record of the third trial shows numerous grounds for reversal seem to justify my statement. As for disciplining, the Radio Commission will tell the gentleman from Alabama that it has no censorship authority over programs or expression of opinion."

Nothing ever came of the attorney general's attempt to have me banned from the air, but in response to a request from the Federal Radio Commission, a vice-president of the Columbia Broadcasting System sent me a gentle rebuke for commenting on a case which had not had its final judicial review. Since a thousand other editors had voiced similar comments at the same time I did not worry.

The final upshot of the Scottsboro case was this. The state of Alabama dropped all charges against four of the defendants. Four others were sentenced to prison, one for assaulting a sheriff. One was sentenced to death, but in 1938 the sentence was commuted to life imprisonment. Thus public and judicial indignation at a sentence of death against eight Negroes innocent of the crime with which they were charged finally saved their lives and prevented a serious miscarriage of justice in the state of Alabama.

23.

The Bonus March in 1932

The most significant dramatic moments in the careers of our two greatest living generals, Douglas MacArthur and Dwight D. Eisenhower, came with the surrender of Japan and Germany in 1945. But who now remembers that tensely dramatic event in their careers when they led a force of federal troops in Washington, D.C., against a group of fellow Americans?

It was on July 28, 1932, that President Herbert Hoover ordered General MacArthur, as Chief of Staff, to expel those remnants of the "Bonus Expeditionary Force" which remained in the national capital as a result of the ill-conceived Bonus March at the height of the depression. With General MacArthur and acting under his orders were Colonel Dwight D. Eisenhower and Major George Patton. The connection of these three outstanding military leaders with this rather unhappy event is not a circumstance they ever liked to recall, even though each one was only performing his duty with soldierly obedience.

The Bonus March idea originated with a group of more or less impoverished ex-servicemen who descended on the Capitol with the

Bonus Marchers at the Capitol, 1932.

intention of remaining there until Congress gave them some kind of a handout.

Because of general unemployment, the veterans demanded immediate cash payment of the deferred bonus. They refused to wait until the adjustable compensation certificates were due. When President Hoover pointed out the danger of such an immediate drain on the badly strained United States Treasury, the American Legion rightly refused to endorse the Bonus March. In this refusal it expressed the sentiment of most ex-soldiers. That didn't deter those veterans who insisted on getting some cash from the government right away.

Communists were quick to infiltrate and take command of some Bonus March units. The original ex-servicemen marchers were also joined by several thousand ne'er-do-wells, including bums, hoodlums, and ex-convicts. By the time it reached Washington the Bonus Army was little more than a motley rabble-rousing mob. It established itself in shacks and makeshift hovels on Anacostia Flats at the edge of Washington and also took possession of unused government buildings near the Capitol. Charles Michelson, publicity chief of the Democratic National Committee, dubbed this miserable and unsanitary encampment "Hooverville."

When Congress rejected the veterans' demand for immediate payment of the bonus, most of the marchers, including a good part of the more respectable elements, went back home at government expense. Some two thousand, including the Communists and the homeless tramps, stayed on at the camp. Secretary of the Treasury Mills, who feared for President Hoover's life, instructed General Pelham Glanford, head of Washington police, to clear the Bonus Marchers from all government property. But the half-hearted efforts of the Washington police were ineffectual. The

88

The U.S. Army made a spectacular drive against the marchers and forced them from their shacks in sight of the Capitol. The marchers in leaving burned their shantytown, but despite sensational newspaper headlines there was not a single casualty.

police were stoned, and in this first effort at eviction two veterans and two policemen were killed.

It was then that President Hoover reluctantly decided that he had to call on General MacArthur and the Army to restore order and drive the marchers out of Washington. The infantry threw tear-gas bombs while cavalrymen and tanks carefully pushed back the motley crowd of campers. The hovels on Anacostia Flats were burned and the marchers were scattered without a single casualty. General MacArthur said a short while later, "It was an ugly mob that mistook consideration for weakness. To let the situation go would have made it worse. It was the insurrectionists themselves who fired their billets. Bonus Marchers were preying on the population and everyone was relieved when they were gone. It was the first riot I've ever seen in which there was no bloodshed."

Two soldiers, who were to earn great fame, lead the U.S. troops as they moved out the Bonus marchers. *Left to right:* MacArthur and Eisenhower.

Looking back at the Bonus March we can all agree that it was an unhappy incident in our domestic history. It proved a damaging blow to President Hoover's political status. Yet the Hoover administration did more for the veterans than any that preceded. From 376,000 disabled, sick, and destitute veterans or their widows and orphans on federal pay rolls at the start of President Hoover's administration, the number had increased to 853,-000 at the end.

As a result of my radio comments on the Bonus Army, I received a record volume of letters, many of them vituperative, some threatening me with violence. Along with most of our government leaders and thinking people I opposed immediate cash payment of the bonus. The United States has done more for its war veterans in the way of special pensions and rewards than any other country in the world. Our liberality toward the veteran dates back to the Revolutionary War. Today, the government is spending nearly four and a half billion dollars a year to aid the 20,000,-000 veterans who, with their families, constitute 40 per cent of our people. As a veteran myself, I have always felt ashamed that my comrades should demand special consideration because they were privileged to serve their country in uniform.

Let us always be generous to the disabled veteran and take care of the families of those who died, but let us refuse to be exploited by those men who, because they did their duty in time of war, without hurt or sacrifice, seek special favors which they do not deserve.

24.

The New Deal Begins

On May 27, 1935, the United States Supreme Court in a unanimous decision declared the NRA unconstitutional. The Blue Eagle, well-known symbol of the Act, was dead. The New Deal's most enthusiastic experiment in social legislation was declared illegal and invalidated on three grounds, with Chief Justice Charles Evans Hughes writing the decision: 1. Excessive delegation of legislative power to the Executive; 2. Lack of constitutional authority for such legislation; 3. Regulation of business wholly intrastate in character.

President Franklin D. Roosevelt called that Supreme Court ruling the most important decision since the Dred Scott case of 1857. Since then another Supreme Court ruling on a thorny social problem, segregation in public schools, has also, and more correctly, been compared with the Dred Scott case.

It was to help relieve the major depression of the early thirties that the National Indus-

90

F.P.G.

Franklin Delano Roosevelt received the Democratic nomination for President in 1932. Although the depression was the major issue, Prohibition was not forgotten.

MARCUS, NEW YORK TIMES

trial Recovery Act was passed on June 16, 1933. The Act was received enthusiastically by a large number of Americans. It promised employment, prosperity, and other benefits. In New York it brought forth a peacetime demonstration rarely, if ever, equaled. Two hundred and fifty thousand people "paraded for prosperity." For ten hours they marched, expressing in this parade their hope for better times, their confidence in the multiple actions of the Roosevelt administration. Millions lined the sidewalks to cheer the marchers. Business declared a half holiday. Mr. and Mrs. New Yorker and their children were on hand to demonstrate support for President Roose-velt and for General Hugh S. Johnson who had just been appointed to administer the National Recovery Act. Not since the days when Fifth Avenue echoed to the tread of a victorious army returned from France after World War I had New York seen such a tumultuous outburst of approval. The march of baker and banker, show girl and stenographer, longshoreman and merchant moved on and on. It was a city afoot, marching, they hoped, on the road to recovery.

The National Industrial Recovery Act, which created the National Recovery Administration (NRA), was to defeat the depression by establishing trade associations; suspending

91

Passage of the NRA was received enthusiastically by most Americans. New York saw its greatest peacetime demonstration when 250,000 people "paraded for prosperity."

antitrust laws; drawing up codes of fair competition; guaranteeing collective bargaining and requiring employers to accept prescribed wage provisions.

While the NRA was initially successful, affecting about 500 fields of business and about 22,000,000 employees, code violations became increasingly frequent. Cutthroat competition, unfair price fixing, and other evils developed. The National Recovery Review Board reported that the NRA was encouraging monopoly and operating to the detriment of the small businessman. Finally, it was the Schechter Poultry Corporation case, known as the "Sick Chicken Case," that resulted in the invalidation of NRA by the Supreme Court. The NRA, like the AAA, which was also ruled illegal, would have collapsed because of its own internal defects had the courts not decreed instantaneous death.

THE INGENIOUS QUARTERBACK!

The Agriculture Adjustment Act of May 12, 1933, which established the Agriculture Adjustment Administration (the AAA) for the benefit of the farmer was an equally important piece of legislation in the initial phase of the New Deal. Ever since it was set aside by the Supreme Court the farm problem has become a political football. Wherever and whenever a federal subsidy has once been established, whether as a protective tariff for the businessman or a handout for the farmer, it usually spells loss of control for the party that removes it.

Although President Roosevelt had called a special session of the 73d Congress to deal with the banking crisis, he decided to keep Congress in session to deal with unemployment and farm relief. This session, which, among other items, enacted such legislation for relief and recovery as the CCC (Civilian Conservation Corps), the FERA (Federal Emergency Relief Act), TVA (Tennessee Valley Authority), PWA (Public Works Administration as part of NRA) lasted from March 9 to June 16, 1933. This period was later dubbed "The Hundred Days." (Named after Napoleon's Elba to Waterloo period, March 20 to June 28, 1815, in which he sought to regain power.)

The AAA was intended to restore the purchasing power of the farmers, to eliminate surplus crops of the basic farm commodities by curtailing production and establishing parity prices. A feature of the Act was the subsidy principle whereby farmers would receive direct payments for reducing acreage and crops. The Act was passed on May 12, 1933. The AAA was invalidated in 1936 on the ground that the processing tax and the production control features were unconstitutional. It launched us on a continuing political controversy over farm relief and farm legislation. So far federal intervention in the farm problem has satisfied neither the farmer nor the taxpayer. Even today, more than twenty years later, it is far easier to agree that certain things should not be done than to agree on just how the federal government should help solve the farmer's problems.

These two major setbacks to early New Deal legislation, as well as other conservative Supreme Court decisions, were a severe check on the President's leadership. They led directly to his unhappy attempt in 1937 to reorganize the federal judiciary, by "packing" the Supreme Court (he wanted to increase the membership from nine to fifteen) and instituting other reforms.

My chief memory of the early days of the New Deal is the hopeful enthusiasm that dominated Washington. I spent a whole day wandering through various offices at the White House, busier than I have ever been before or since, talking with everyone from the President down and watching the comings and goings of the endless parade of businessmen, bankers, farmers, and politicians who counted on the new administration to pull them out of the difficulties created by the complete collapse of the country's economy.

The spirit of hope which the new President had launched with the ringing declarations of his inaugural address—"We have nothing to fear but fear itself"—had infected everyone. Even the morose Louis Howe, then the President's most intimate adviser, assured me everything was going marvelously. When I asked what particular job he had around the presidential office he replied with a simile worth recording: "I'm the man who goes around with the oil can. Whenever I hear about a squeak in the machinery I locate it and pour on a little oil." Many wise visitors to the White House sought out Louis Howe before they asked to see the President himself. If he decided to help you, your chance of get-

President Roosevelt's press conferences during the early days of the New Deal were known for their cheerfulness and enthusiasm.

ting what you wanted was very much improved. On less important matters "Missy" Le Hand, the President's private secretary, could be of great help. She once showed me what the public never heard about or saw during F.D.R.'s lifetime—the large collection of weird and wonderful canes sent to him by admirers who had noted his need of a cane during the few steps he ever took in public.

"Missy"—like every Washington reporter—loved the weekly press conferences. "Sometimes," she confided to me, "I'd make up my mind to stick to my work, but when those familiar gales of laughter began to reach me, I'd drop everything and run in to share the fun."

And they were fun! President Roosevelt was a completely happy man during the first months of his first term when everything was going his way and the entire country was backing almost everything he did. I have been in Washington under every president since McKinley but cannot recall such a completely happy and harmonious period in the nation's capital. Here was a time that truly deserved to be called a political honeymoon.

The fireside chats from the White House became a national institution.

25.

Huey Long and His Share-the-Wealth Movement

"Every Man a King!" Not so long ago everyone was talking about this Huey Long slogan. Yet it is a quarter century ago that "Kingfish" Huey Long coined this appealing phrase to advance his Share-the-Wealth movement. Dissatisfaction with the social, fiscal, and other aspects of the Roosevelt administration led to the emergence of several organized anti-administration groups along about 1934. There were the Liberty Leaguers, the Old Age Revolving Pension advocates, better known as partisans of the Townsend Plan. But of all the recovery panaceas that arose to plague the New Deal which most Americans found radical enough, certainly the wildest was inspired by Huey Long. He simply demanded that the federal government make "Every Man a King" by guaranteeing a minimum annual income of $5,000 to every family.

And remember, that would be $10,000 in present-day money.

Huey Long was an ardent supporter of Roosevelt at the Chicago convention in 1932, but it wasn't long after Roosevelt's inauguration that he broke with the President and his New Dealers. I remember talking with Long at the inauguration. Even that early he voiced his suspicion of Roosevelt's sincerity. "He says 'yes' to me all right," Huey declared, "but then the next man comes along and he says 'yes' to him, too. In the end it's 'no' for both of us."

He accused the New Deal of being the dupe of Wall Street and said to Postmaster Farley anent Roosevelt, "What the hell is the use in my coming down to see this fellow? I can't win any decision over him."

The first real excitement of the 1932 Democratic convention was the seating of Huey Long's delegation from Louisiana. It was the first national appearance of the "Kingfish" who had established a personal dictatorship in his home state on the basis of a one-man political machine. It was also my first opportunity to meet this unique American phenomenon. The man was distasteful to me personally, but

The "Kingfish"—1935.

Louisiana's Lower House in session, April, 1929, hearing evidence in connection with the impeachment of Governor Huey Long.

I was full of admiration for his demagogic abilities.

Although his activities in Louisiana—then a somewhat backward state—provided important public improvements, such as schools, roads, and hospitals, his methods were corrupt and violent. He was an unscrupulous dictator and used ruthless methods to gain his objectives. He not only made a mockery out of the democratic form of government, but by flaunting some laws he reduced the respect for all laws. I was saddened when I observed the

The funeral of Huey Long in Baton Rouge, La., September 13, 1935 took place before the state capitol, itself a monument to Long, and was attended by 150,000 fond Louisianans.

deferential way in which he was approached by important leaders of the Democratic convention.

At Chicago I came to respect the Kingfish's skill as a clever manipulator, as a politician, and as a speaker. In personal habits he was coarse, vulgar, and crude. He was no orator in the usual sense, but his speeches were simple, direct, and spiced with pertinent biblical allusions.

Huey Long used the same oratorical technique and dictatorial manner during his senatorial days and whenever he made speeches in behalf of his Share-the-Wealth movement. Not only in Louisiana, but throughout the South, he won millions of followers with his slogan. In March 1934 he boasted, "Two hundred and fifty thousand earnest men and women are now dedicated to an unrelenting fight to divide up the wealth of this land of plenty so that children will not starve and their parents beg for crusts." By this time no children were starving and no parents were begging for crusts, but many thousands were willing to follow Huey Long while he promised them something for nothing.

Huey Long had aspirations to become president. He even wrote a book about it in 1935, called *My First Hundred Days in the White House,* which he hoped would win him the 1936 nomination and election. Before the book was published, the Kingfish was shot down in cold blood by the son of a political opponent. The bullet struck him down as he was walking through the state capitol at Baton Rouge on September 8, 1935. He died two days later.

The significant thing about Huey Long was the tremendous support and following he obtained for his wild-cat Share-the-Wealth idea. He convinced his followers that the liberal was not the champion of the forgotten man. It was evident that Roosevelt's appeal to Americans that they put their faith once more in the forgotten man at the bottom of the economic pyramid had less appeal than the crudely socialistic policy of the Louisiana dictator. This was a rather frightening revelation to those who insisted: "It can't happen here." It was happening in Louisiana and was spreading when Huey Long was killed. There was much speculation on what might have happened had he lived.

After Huey Long's death, the Rev. Gerald L. K. Smith succeeded to Long's leadership in the Share-the-Wealth clubs and later became allied with the Townsend movement. Both of these groups then formed a coalition with the notorious Rev. Charles Coughlin for social reform. The Smith-Townsend-Coughlin coalition gained considerable strength and much publicity. In 1936 it emerged as a third-party movement. But it lacked the powerful leadership which the able Kingfish might well have provided.

In this young country of ours, which is tolerant of everybody and everything, there will always be a lunatic fringe ready to accept a movement or a leader with a generous promise. Whether it be as modest as "ham and eggs" for breakfast or as far-reaching as the millennium here or heaven hereafter, it will not lack followers whenever there is an able leader to expound the cause.

In good times the Huey Longs of tomorrow will not get far, but such a leader must be taken more seriously if the shadow of a serious depression should once again lead lazy or deluded thousands to demand that the government solve all their problems. The trend of the day is to expect the state to solve problems for the individual. Self-reliance is less popular. Workers, farmers, oldsters, the sick, the crippled, and the lazy are all demanding that the state intervene more and more to help them "share the wealth."

Alfred M. Landon provided H. V. Kaltenborn with a radio "first." It was the first time a presidential candidate was privately interviewed over the air ways.

26.

Governor Landon and the 1936 Election

"For three long years the New Deal administration has dishonored American tradition and flagrantly betrayed the pledges upon which the Democratic party sought and received public support." That was the opening sentence with which the Republican party platform of 1936 launched into the presidential election. Governor Alfred M. Landon, of Kansas, was the Republican candidate. Senator Vandenberg of Michigan could have had the nomination, but he wasn't interested. "I don't want it and I wouldn't take it," he told me in an off-the-record interview. "Think of the mess I'd inherit as Roosevelt's successor."

The Republican platform which Vandenberg helped shape enumerated all the sins and grievances of which, in the eyes of the G.O.P., the New Deal was guilty.

The 1936 Republican convention was one of the dullest of the many which I have attended. Roosevelt's re-election was expected. There was little Republican enthusiasm, and a feeling of defeatism dominated the delegates. They realized that it would be difficult, if not impossible, to win the presidency away from Roosevelt and the New Deal. One of several uninspired theme songs was:

Landon, oh Landon,
Will lead to victory
With the dear old Constitution
And it's good enough for me.

Governor Landon, who got the nomination on the first ballot, was presented at the convention and in the ensuing campaign as a plain country boy with a good heart and an honest purpose. He was budget-minded, affable, and sound; he was to save the country from the evils of the New Deal. "Life, Liberty,

Already they were asking in 1936
—"Has the President aged?"

HARRIS & EWING

and Landon" was the slogan devised by the Republicans to capture votes. The sunflower, the state flower of Kansas, became the emblem for the campaign buttons. If you wanted to, you could even buy one at Tiffany's—a nineteen-petal gold sunflower set with yellow diamonds for $815.

It was unfortunate for the Republican cause that Governor Landon had such a colorless personality. He presented such a marked contrast to the suave, smiling Roosevelt, that highly competent experienced campaigner who could not only speak effectively, but knew how to turn on the charm as he posed for the press photographers. There probably was no available Republican candidate who could have beaten Roosevelt that year. If Huey Long had not been shot, he might have had some effect on the outcome. As it was, Landon carried only two states.

From the start, it was apparent that Governor Landon was not at his best in platform speechmaking. He was much more convincing in an informal radio interview. On the air,

several months before Landon was nominated, I opened my CBS broadcast with these words: "This evening it is my pleasure and privilege to interview Governor Landon, of Kansas, who is generally considered to be the outstanding possibility for the Republican nomination for president. While many of you may have heard the governor over the air in his previous speeches, there are many sidelights of a man's personality and his point of view which cannot be revealed in a formal speech. And now I will address my first question to Governor Landon."

The governor was much more at ease, much more effective and dynamic in this interview than in any of his previous speeches. I went over the questions with him beforehand. They covered the general issues of the coming election, his proposed campaign tactics as well as his views on foreign policy, New Deal ideas, Social Security, and the depression. In the actual interview I used only those questions for which he had effective answers. On the air his replies sounded honest and forthright.

99

BROWN BROTHERS

two months ago. . . . If you will look into the facts of the situation, you will find that on four different occasions since March 1933 this country has started on a definite movement toward recovery. And on each of these four occasions it was set back again by some new reckless experiment or disturbing move by the present administration. How can we feel any confidence that this won't keep on happening? . . . What the young people of America really need, and earnestly desire, is not relief but opportunity."

So far as I know this was the first time a presidential candidate had ever been interviewed so that the whole country could listen in. The Hearst newspapers which were supporting Landon printed the full text of the interview. Not long afterward I was approached by an emissary of the Republican National Committee with a proposition. Would I do a similar radio interview with Governor Landon on a regular night each week during the campaign? The offer of a handsome weekly stipend was included with the proposal, but I did not accept. I could not jeopardize my position as an independent radio commentator by linking myself with any party candidate.

This Landon technique came back to my mind recently as I listened to an incredibly dull radio report by Secretary of State Dulles. I remembered how interesting the secretary had been the night of the televised Cabinet meeting at which he made a similar report by the question-and-answer method. For unless a man has a real gift for speaking or a most fascinating message he just cannot hold a radio or television audience with a straight half-hour speech. I sometimes wonder why the interview method is not used on the air more frequently. It would make half the campaign speeches infinitely more effective with the listeners.

They revealed integrity and common sense. I kept the interview informal and was delighted to be able to tell the audience that the governor was just lighting his pipe before answering a question I had just asked. This showed me that he was completely at his ease. On the Democratic party and the depression he had this to say, "To be specific, let's take the administration's record in dealing with the depression. Some people say we reached the bottom of this depression in the summer of 1932. The present administration says we reached the bottom in the spring of 1933, when it came into power. Now, if, according to the administration's own statement, it came into power at the bottom of the depression, there is only one direction we could move from that point and that direction would be upward. That was three years and

100

27.

The Spanish Civil War

When Generalissimo Francisco Franco and his rebel forces landed in Spain from North Africa on July 19, 1936, he not only started the bloodiest civil war in modern history, but actually set a dress rehearsal for World War II. Many leading statesmen in Great Britain and France realized then, in view of the Rome-Berlin ties, that the Spanish revolt could easily spark a world war.

The opening weeks of the Spanish Civil War consisted of local struggles with the Loyalist Republicans quelling rebellion in some places, while in other cities Franco supporters seized control and set up military governments. There were bloody reprisals by both sides which embittered this civil war from its beginning. These resulted in the execution of thousands of innocent civilians.

Everything functioned as planned, except for the capture of Madrid by Franco. There, as well as in Barcelona and other important centers, the rebel forces lacked leadership and were overpowered by a spontaneous rising of industrial workers. A week after the Civil War started the Republican government still held two thirds of Spain's territory and dominated three quarters of the population. If it had not been for early outside help from Mussolini's Italy and Hitler's Germany the Franco forces would probably have been defeated within two months after the revolt began.

But almost at once the Spanish Civil War became the battleground of rival European ideologies. France proposed that all powers refrain from sending any war matériel to either side. A nonintervention committee, made up of fifteen countries including France,

Great Britain, Germany, Italy, and Russia, was established to execute this policy of non-interference. France and Great Britain were generally sympathetic with the Loyalists but adhered to the agreement of complete non-intervention. Hitler and Mussolini joined the nonintervention committee although they had no intention of remaining aloof from the conflict. They openly stated that they would help Franco win and from the beginning backed him to the hilt. I saw German planes on the airfield at Burgos, a Franco headquarters, in the opening month of the Civil War. Italian and German "volunteers" joined the rebels as soon as they could reach Spain.

"They Shall Not Pass." The world-famous slogan of the Spanish Loyalists.

Franco soldiers, well clothed and well fed, await word to advance during the siege of Madrid.

Communist volunteers and Russian planes did not reach Spain until much later. Franco soon had scores of German and Italian planes, thousands of troops and many German technicians. Four months after the Civil War began, Hitler and Mussolini recognized the Franco regime as the de facto government of Spain. Stalin supported the Loyalists because they were anti-church and included many Communists. The Russians worked hard to transform the Loyalist cause into a communist cause while advocating "moderation" in Spain's domestic difficulty. That line, however, didn't prevent them from sending military equipment and technicians to help the Loyalists.

From the first clash the ruthless nature of the Spanish Civil War was apparent. There was little difference between the two sides in regard to the commission of atrocities or the shedding of innocent blood. During the three-year duration of the Civil War at least 30,000 people were executed or assassinated; 15,000 civilians were killed in air raids that served no military purpose and more than 700,000 were lost in battle. The general estimate is that the

102

Civil War cost Spain 1,000,000 lives out of a total population of 24,000,000.

It was in the early weeks of the Civil War, before intervention had become a major factor, that I went to Spain from Paris. I was on the front repeatedly with both the Insurgent and the Loyalist armies. I visited prison camps, talked with soldiers of both sides, and interviewed prominent Spaniards. Not once did I hear an impartial analysis of the issues. There was only bitterness, hatred, and prejudice. Everywhere one felt the curse of war with its enmity and brutality. There was the gripping tragedy of an unnecessary conflict.

The Spaniards took a diabolic joy in their cruelty to one another but I could not help but admire their complete indifference to death and danger. In my desire not to seem a coward I took many foolish and unnecessary chances on my visits to the battlefronts. The Spaniards were both brave and fatalistic. Miguel de Unamuno, the venerable Spanish philosopher, explained it to me in this way. He said: "We Spaniards are a sick people. The Spaniard's spirit of desperation represents something of the fundamental tragedy of

In contrast, the majority of Loyalist forces were ill-trained recruits.

The tragedy of civil war is mirrored on the faces of these refugees fleeing into France from Barcelona before Franco's victorious entry into the city.

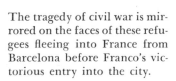

H. V. Kaltenborn interviewed a Franco officer outside Madrid.

man." He thought the Spaniard's lust for blood was due to his mixed blood to which both Moor and Saracen have made important contributions.

It wasn't easy to get into Spain and be accredited by both sides in the conflict. The Franco authorities passed me readily enough because among my papers was a lecture circular with a photograph of myself interviewing Hitler. Hitler was actively supporting the Franco cause.

However, this same picture almost prevented me from obtaining a pass for the front lines of the Loyalists because of their anti-Hitler feeling. Then I recalled that my lecture circular also had a similar picture of myself taken during an interview with a Soviet commissar. This placated the Loyalist commander and got me a pass. Thus I became one of the few correspondents accredited to the military forces of both sides in Spain's Civil War and I could go from one side to the other by crossing and recrossing the French frontier near St. Jean de Luz.

With headquarters established in Hendaye, on the French side of the Spanish border, I could reach both Franco headquarters, first in Burgos and then in Salamanca, as well as government forces defending the northern coast

of Spain in the Irun and St. Sebastian area. At Hendaye, on the Franco-Spanish border, it was possible to arrange for lines and transmission facilities for broadcasting. So, after visits to the embattled armies, I could speak to America from Hendaye, France, without censorship.

The highlight of my broadcasting experience during the Spanish Civil War came in the final weeks of my visits to the fronts while the battle of Irun was at its height. For reasons of personal ambition easily understood by working newspaper and radio newsmen, I was eager to make the first actual battlefield broadcast in radio history. After all sorts of difficulties I managed to get myself installed with a daredevil French engineer in a small haystack located at an excellent vantage point between the Franco and Republican lines. My French technician was eager to help me score the beat of which I dreamed. When, after a variety of misadventures, including a long wait because an intervening French operator had gone out for an apéritif, I finally got through to New York and told them I could describe the battle for Irun while it was in progress with actual audible sounds of rifle and artillery fire, word came back to stand by because there were commercial programs on the air which could not be interrupted. There was nothing to do but stand by, hearing the bullets whistle while I sought to remain inconspicuous by hiding in my haystack. Twice, while waiting, the transmission lines were cut by stray rifle bullets, but the intrepid Frenchman crawled out and made repairs. My haystack was right in the line of fire, but most of the bullets were high.

When the go-ahead signal finally came through from New York, darkness had fallen and artillery shots were less frequent. But the rifles and machine guns were still going strong so we got through to New York and I described the battle for the CBS network audience while the rival armies provided the sound effects.

The saddest thing about the Spanish Civil War from my point of view was the fact that the United States refused to let the legitimate government of Spain buy arms while the Franco forces were well supplied by Italy and Germany.

The United States maintained a strict policy of neutrality and our traditional isolation. President Roosevelt's New Deal took precedence over foreign affairs. He expressed the general opinion by saying: "We shun commitments which might entangle us in foreign wars." Yet, when the end of the Spanish Civil War came with the surrender of Madrid at the end of March 1939, the United States immediately recognized the new regime of Generalissimo Franco. But later, when the Communists demanded it, we made the mistake of following Red Poland's leadership and endorsed the United Nations resolution to withdraw all ambassadors from Franco Spain. For years we remained at odds with the Franco government until the Russian danger persuaded us to make an agreement with him for the construction of American military bases on Spanish soil.

28.

Sit-Down Strikes—1936

When they tie a can to a union man,
    Sit-down! Sit-down!
When they give him the sack, they'll take him back,
    Sit-down! Sit-down!

When the speed-up comes, just twiddle your thumbs,
    Sit-down! Sit-down!
When the boss won't talk, don't take a walk,
    Sit-down! Sit-down!

That was the song the strikers sang when an epidemic of sit-down strikes hit the country in 1937 and spread like a malignant contagion across the industrial scene. They had started in France the year before when a popular front government under Léon Blum took over power. Actually France witnessed them centuries earlier when the humble builders of the great cathedrals used the sit-down technique. This new kind of stay-in strike actually started in this country the last day of December 1936, when a few hundred workers seized a number of General Motors plants at Flint, Michigan, took possession, and staged a spectacular sit-down strike that lasted forty-four days. The company couldn't oust them, the strikers defied the courts, and Governor Frank Murphy refused to use troops to drive them from General Motors property.

Because the automobile workers were successful in this sit-down strike, forcing General Motors management to capitulate and sign a contract, it wasn't long before the same technique spread to rubber, steel, textile, oil, and

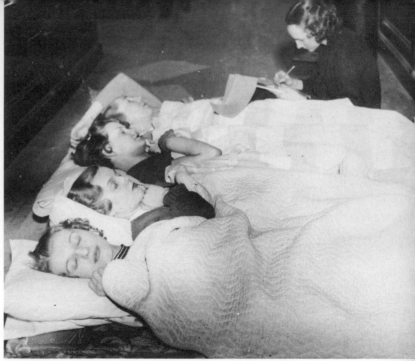

The sit-down strike was an effective nonviolent weapon. One hundred and fifty girls staged a sit-down strike in a Woolworth store in Detroit.

WIDE WORLD

shipbuilding industries, involving half a million workers. Even hospital and power-plant employees used sit-downs to threaten stoppage of essential services. Woolworth's five-and-ten-cent-store girls and telephone workers, too, staged sit-downs to win their aims. It wasn't until 1939 that the Supreme Court outlawed sit-down strikes, declaring them illegal. After that they were discredited by organized labor.

Sit-downing had its points. Here are four:

1. It enabled an aggressive minority to tie up a plant.
2. It placed the burden of violence on the employer and public authorities—"possession is nine points of the law."
3. It gave strike leaders complete control of the strikers.
4. It prevented operation of a plant by nonstrikers.

As America's first major sit-down strike, the Flint episode had enduring importance. It marked the first tentative recognition by a big

corporation of the United Automobile Workers, a new type of industrial union. It also marked the first time that an organized minority of strikers (counting all General Motors employees in Flint) successfully defied both courts and police in a company union town.

The United Auto Workers was among the first of the CIO unions to become all-powerful. The Wagner Act had been passed by Congress in 1935, creating the pro-labor National Labor Relations Board. It put labor in a strong position for organizing and bargaining. A few months later the CIO was formed under the leadership of John L. Lewis, head of the United Mine Workers, Sidney Hillman of the Amalgamated Clothing Workers, and David Dubinsky of the International Ladies Garment Workers.

The motor and steel industries were the first major targets of the CIO. "Ford next" was the cry of the United Automobile Workers after General Motors came to terms with

106

One of the most bloody labor riots of the thirties occurred during a strike at Republic Steel in 1937. Ten workers were killed.

WIDE WORLD

the strikers. Henry Ford didn't yield to the CIO pressure until a long and bitter losing battle finally made him come to terms. As for the steel industry, Myron C. Taylor, chairman of the board of United States Steel Corporation, conferred with John L. Lewis and agreed to recognize and bargain with the CIO steelworkers' union.

Tough Tom Girdler, chairman of Republic Steel, flatly refused to follow suit, saying, "I won't have a contract verbal or written with an irresponsible, racketeering, violent body like the CIO . . . Until they pass a law making me do it, I'm not going to do it." He didn't, but Republic Steel's strike resulted in the shocking "Memorial Day Massacre" of 1937 when ten CIO pickets were shot and killed by the police at the South Chicago plant of Republic Steel.

It was easy to have pat opinions about sit-down strikes at a distance. But those who dealt with them at firsthand, employers, workers, families, and public authorities, were compelled to translate them into human terms. During the first sit-downs I went to Flint to observe this development at firsthand in order that I might comment on it fairly and intelligently. Flint was tense. Out of a population of 165,000 some 42,000 were General Motors employees. This meant that the strike directly concerned everyone in town. No one in Flint was neutral. You cheered the strikers or you hated them.

No city busses were running because the drivers were on strike against the transportation company. The streets of the city were full of automobiles carrying signs, "Courtesy car."

The use of sound trucks was a new propaganda device introduced by the auto workers, with strike leaders barking their orders to the strikers. When the Michigan National Guard finally took over the Flint area, the first thing they did was to ban the sound trucks. The Flint police had the toughest job, for they got

107

no support from the National Guard whose commander had orders "not to take sides."

Flint was full of outsiders. Union leaders and union members from other cities, men who looked like detectives, members of strong-arm squads, strike breakers, idle men of all sorts wandered through the streets. As always in any kind of labor war, the women had to bear the brunt, but strikers' wives were with their men. Wearing red berets and arm bands, they paraded, cooked and delivered food, and reported for every kind of strike duty.

When the strikers inside Fisher Body Plant No. 1 finally allowed me to climb in by a guarded window and join them, sit-down striking seemed something of a lark. The strikers were all young, with a high average of intelligence. Their organization was excellent. Sentinels and pickets relieved each other in three-hour shifts. They were summoned to duty over a loud-speaker system. Every guard had a homemade policeman's club, manufactured on Fisher lathes. Some were wound with decorative leather strips. Ping-pong was a favorite game. It alternated as a pastime with classes in public speaking and parliamentary law.

The strikers were patriotic Americans who felt they were in the right. They exuded a kind of missionary zeal and were determined to see matters through to the end. After talking with leaders I advised against the use of force to put them out even though I knew they were wrong in seizing private property. Fortunately a settlement was reached without bloodshed.

One significant result of the labor troubles of 1937 was the parting of the ways between John L. Lewis and President Roosevelt. New Deal legislation had put organized labor in the strongest position it had ever occupied. Lewis's United Mine Workers had contrib-

uted a half million dollars to the Democratic campaign fund in 1936 and Lewis felt the President owed them his support. When the sit-down strike wave swept through industry and the administration proved unsympathetic to the new technique, Lewis felt that he was betrayed by the President he helped to reelect. When President Roosevelt made his epic "A plague on both their houses" statement the break between the two men became complete.

29.

Japanese Aggression in China and the Panay Sinking—1937

As they swarmed across the Marco Polo Bridge in July 1937, and captured Peiping as the second step in their conquest of China— the conquest of Manchuria was the first—Japanese soldiers carried forward the policy of military aggression that reached its climax at Pearl Harbor four and a half years later. At the same time, an undeclared war among major powers was going on in Spain as a part of that country's civil war. The Japanese, by their deliberate invasion of China, spread World War II to the Orient and launched a chain of events that still carries seeds of future wars.

"We act. Tokyo explains." This was the cynical comment of a Japanese army commander I interviewed in Manchuria a few years before Japan went all out in China. His remark epitomizes Japan's aggressive policy of expansion and conquest upon which Tokyo

The League of Nations again proved in-effectual in keeping peace.

Japanese Marines advance in the attack on Shanghai in 1937.

The U.S.S. *Panay* was sunk by Japanese bombers on the Yangtze River in 1937—an ill omen of things to come.

embarked when she brazenly invaded Manchuria in 1931. There she set up a puppet government under the guise of independence and named the province Manchukuo. In Japan, political policy and military policy often went separate ways. The aggressive and wanton action of the army compelled explanations by the Japanese Foreign Office. In most countries the government formulates the policy which is to be executed by the army. Not so in pre–Pearl Harbor Japan. That difference explains the importance of the series of Japanese "incidents" which foreshadowed war, whether the war was declared or undeclared.

Japan was dominated by army leaders who embarked on imperialist aggression. It should be remembered that the League of Nations never took action against Japan in response to China's protests against the occupation of Manchuria in 1931. It did go so far as to appoint the Lytton Commission. This group made a careful investigation, then a report unfavorable to Japan. The only result was that Japan gave notice and quit the League in 1933.

In her deliberate and unprovoked invasion of China, Japan violated two treaties she had signed with the United States and other leading powers. One, the Treaty of Paris, better known as the Kellogg-Briand antiwar pact of 1928, was signed by practically all countries. In its text each signatory renounced war as an instrument of foreign policy.

Japan also violated the Nine-Power Treaty of 1922 which guaranteed the inviolability of Chinese territory. Thus, the "China incident" of 1937 found the leading powers of the West lined up in organized effort against the aggressive power of Japan. But because nothing was done, all aggressor nations were encouraged. It was obvious that Japan had no more regard than Hitler or Mussolini for treaties, agreements, or covenants.

In the first three months of Japan's undeclared China war that followed the fall of Peiping, more than 100,000 Chinese and Japanese were killed. The senseless air raids on Canton and the rape of Nanking followed. The carnage in China surpassed that of the civil war in Spain. Japanese soldiers knew no bounds during those early days of the war in China. By 1939 the Japanese controlled 90 per cent of China's railroads and occupied most major cities. The way had been prepared for

110

the Japanese puppet government that was set up in China in 1940.

Even the United States was not without a China "incident" which cost American lives. On December 12, 1937, the United States Navy's gunboat *Panay*, on legitimate duty escorting ships on the Yangtze River near Nanking, was attacked and sunk without cause by Japanese bombers. This wanton act immediately created acute tension between the United States and Japan. President Roosevelt sent sharp notes. Ultimately we accepted the Japanese explanation of the bombing.

There are those who believe we should have used the *Panay* incident to take world leadership in resisting Japan's conquest of China. Even if other powers had provided only passive aid we could have defeated Japan then much more easily than we did after losing some of our best naval units at Pearl Harbor. As it was, the Japanese government continued its high-handed policy of utter disregard of foreign rights and property in China. The Japanese evaded or ignored the stream of protests from the United States, Great Britain, and France. The dangerous European situation, which Hitler and Mussolini created during the years Japan was waging her war of aggression in China, helped her to pursue her reckless aims without too much risk of Western intervention.

Yet it remains true that at any time between 1931 and 1939 Great Britain and the United States acting together could have checked the ever more powerful Japanese war machine with comparative ease. Instead, we continued to arm our future enemy with steel scrap and oil as we lost one opportunity after another to organize the world against Japanese aggression. Our one thought was to remain at peace while the Japanese imperial forces bought some 80 per cent of their imported arms, oil, iron, fuel, and motors from British and American companies. Between 1937 and 1940 the United States alone shipped $700,000,000 worth of scrap metal to Japan. Even in the summer of 1941 we were still shipping about 1,000,000 barrels of oil a month to Japan. American editors and commentators protested continuously, but the fear of war made us go on doing the things that promoted war. In going over my own broadcasts and radio mail of this period, I find that I emphasized the danger of our policy at least a hundred times, and the popular response indicated that the American people were ready to support strong action.

It wasn't until September of 1940, when Japan set up a puppet government in China and moved into Indo-China, that the United States policy of "moral protests" over Japan's aggression began to stiffen. But it didn't harden sufficiently to influence Japan's militarists. Sumner Welles, at the time, thought an "equitable settlement with Japan was possible." But by then the Tokyo-Berlin-Rome Axis had been formed and was in operation. Japan was also working out a neutrality agreement with Russia.

Japan's aggression had donned the velvet glove of the "co-prosperity sphere" which was to be the New Order for greater East Asia, with Thailand and Indo-China as part of it. The Chinese war which started in 1937 was still in deadlock. We were just beginning to make Japan feel that sooner or later she would have to fight the United States if she was ever to complete the conquest of China. But our concern was to stand up for a righteous policy without becoming involved in war. Instead of taking the initiative, we were being pushed by events and our reaction was slow and reluctant. Japan was anticipating events and soon got ready to strike her devastating blow against a poorly guarded American naval base at Pearl Harbor.

111

30.

Edward VIII Abdicates

In November 1936 I accompanied President Roosevelt on his triumphal visit to the countries along the east coast of South America. The Columbia network had sent along a broadcasting team headed by Paul White, the network's news director. For several weeks our broadcasts were featured. Then, just as we began reporting the climactic episodes of the unexpectedly enthusiastic Argentinian welcome, New York's interest in what we were doing disappeared. Our broadcasts were cut down or canceled. There was nothing in the Buenos Aires newspapers to provide an explanation until the Edward VIII love story finally broke the second week in December. On December 10 all broadcast reports on President Roosevelt's doings were arbitrarily canceled. "Schedule nothing till advised," New York ordered. Down in Buenos Aires we wondered whether the world was coming to an end. The explanation came the next day.

On the evening of December 11, 1936, there came hurtling across the ocean what Lowell Thomas called "the greatest broadcast of all time." It was Edward VIII, now the Duke of Windsor, delivering his brief abdication message to the world. "At long last I am able to say a few words of my own," he began. Then he continued, "I have found it impossible to carry the heavy burden of responsibility and to discharge my duties as king, as I wish to do, without the help and support of the woman I love."

In the United States people went on one of the greatest sentimental binges in our history. All the world watched eagerly as King Edward VIII, who had become widely popular as the Prince of Wales, stepped down from the world's last remaining mighty throne. "The woman I love" became one of the most famous phrases of the time. Here was a great human-interest highlight. A British king was giving up his throne to marry an American woman who was a commoner and who had been twice divorced. Here were three more or less good reasons why she could never expect to become Britain's queen. It would have taken a much stronger character than Edward VIII to wage a successful battle to make Mrs. Simpson Queen of England.

The drama of Edward's abdication had all the essentials to arouse public romantic interest—romance, religion, politics, and a throne. It rocked and shocked the British Empire. While all the world thrilled to this unfolding romantic drama—it broke first in the American press—the British heaved a sigh of relief when the climax was reached with Edward's abdication.

The bitter political and religious battle over the King's decision brought forth its champions, pro and con, and left a trail of bitter disillusion, sardonic satisfaction, and millions of words in print. Every Englishman and almost every American felt a sense of personal participation in the great debate that was climaxed by the unnecessary abdication. The King's own mother, Queen Mary, sought in vain to recall him to his duty.

Winston Churchill stood virtually alone in the House of Commons fighting for Edward's lost cause for a morganatic marriage. It was also Winston Churchill who rewrote Edward's broadcast and provided its simple eloquence.

Prime Minister Baldwin did his duty according to his own lights. He advocated abdication. He had promised to consult with the Cabinet and with the Dominion prime ministers about a possible marriage between the

King Edward VIII pleaded for "peace and understanding throughout the world" in a famous radio address shortly before his abdication.

King and Mrs. Simpson. Before he did so the Bishop of Bradford made his famous public utterance "hoping that the King was aware of his dependence on God's grace . . . some of us wish he gave more positive signs of his awareness."

Thereafter there was little chance of a morganatic marriage. The Archbishop of Canterbury summed up the story in these bitter words: "From God he received a high and sacred trust. Yet, by his own will he has abdicated—he has surrendered the trust. With characteristic frankness he has told us his motive. It was a craving for private happiness. Strange and sad it must be that for such a motive, however strongly it pressed upon his heart, he should have disappointed hopes so high, and abandoned a trust so great."

The momentous broadcast of December 11, 1936, ended with Edward, Duke of Windsor, saying, "And now we all have a new King. I wish him and you, his people, happiness and prosperity with all my heart. God bless you all. God save the King."

That invocation for divine assistance seems

The instrument of abdication.

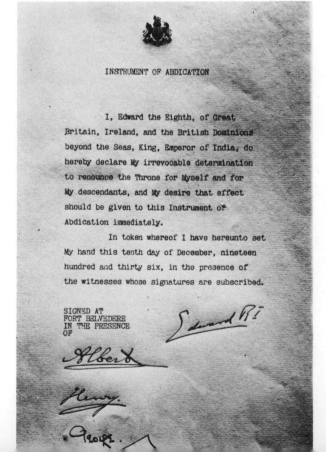

to have been heeded when Edward's brother, the Duke of York, took over the throne. King George VI and Queen Elizabeth, now the much-beloved Queen Mother, restored the monarchy to its rightful high place of dignity and veneration in the hearts of the people of the British Commonwealth of Nations and in the eyes of the entire world.

Edward VIII's abdication was the first voluntary abdication in English history. It focused attention on points of weakness as well as on points of strength and solidarity in the British Empire. Its scars have been healed, but its repercussions are still felt. Its principal characters are still in the public eye. In his revealing book, *A King's Story*,[1] the Duke of Windsor sheds considerable light on his life as Prince of Wales. In it there is the en-

[1] G. P. Putnam's Sons, publishers, New York City.

The Duke and Duchess of Windsor photographed in France after their wedding June 3, 1937. Mr. Herman Rogers (*left*) gave the bride away; Major E. D. Metcalfe (*right*) supported the Duke as best man.

tire background of the abdication. In his book he states that "Man is seldom master of his own fate. . . . I hoped time would solve my problem." And again, "Mine is the story of the life of a man brought up in a special way, as a Prince trained in the manners and maxims of the nineteenth century for a life that had all but disappeared by the end of his youth."

More recently the Duchess has told her side of the story in a book of memoirs that, like *A King's Story,* took its place on the bestseller list.

I liked his book better than hers because it is closer to straight autobiography and less of an *apologia pro sua vita.*

Having met both the Duke and the Duchess on various occasions I have developed increasing respect for the dignified manner in which they face and meet the challenge of an ever-curious world. Theirs is no easy task. An ex-king and emperor who is fundamentally shy is kept in the midst of a social whirl by a woman who enjoys society much more than her husband.

His heart is with the garden in their little country house outside of Paris. The Duchess likes people great or small. She takes trouble to put people at their ease and plays the role of a duchess as though she were born for the part. Yet somehow, despite the simple friendliness they both strive for and succeed in showing, one cannot help remembering that this man was born to the purple and turned his back upon it. He did this to be with a woman who is not and was not beautiful and who, for all her charm and dignity, does not even suggest the historic type of the eternal feminine that turns men's heads. They are just a nice, middle-aged couple. Romanticists that we are, there just seems to be something missing which leaves us feeling a bit sorry for them and for ourselves.

The fiery destruction of the proud airship *Hindenburg* dramatically
ended the promising experiment with lighter-than-air craft.

31.

The Hindenburg Disaster
Ends Dirigible Travel

The most dramatic tragedy of 1937, and the worst in the early history of air travel, was the explosion and burning of the German dirigible *Hindenburg* at Lakehurst, New Jersey. The giant ship, which had carried on a successful transatlantic service for about a year, arrived from Europe on May 6. Without any warning, while approaching the mooring mast, the huge gas bag exploded and burst into flames with a loss of thirty-six lives.

This disaster dramatically marked the end of air travel in lighter-than-air passenger ships. At best, travel in airships was short-lived. Count Ferdinand von Zeppelin began his work with rigid airships in 1898. His first one was 420 feet long and was propelled by two motors. In 1900 he made his first flight, attaining a speed of eighteen miles per hour. He covered only three and one quarter miles before the steering gear failed.

Commercial flights in Germany only started in 1910. The first time I ever saw a dirigible in the air was in Munich that year as it flew over the city. I was on my honeymoon and shared my wife's excitement as we saw the graceful cigar-shaped balloon speeding across the skies. Enthusiasm was universal as Germans visualized a new era of air travel that would carry passengers over deserts or oceans. Heavier-than-air passenger planes had not yet gone into regular service.

Then came World War I. The Germans built eighty-eight zeppelins, and some were used to bomb England. They were not effec-

115

The loss of the *Shenandoah* was the first of a sequence of disasters, which included the loss of the *Akron* and *Macon,* that ended America's efforts to use dirigibles as a military craft.

tive because they were too slow and were easy prey for antiaircraft guns and planes. But it was these zeppelins that made the first air raids in history and set an unhappy example for the wars to come. The Germans used them more successfully to scout for the German Navy. For example, they helped the German fleet keep track of the British naval units during the Battle of Jutland. Great Britain and the United States used the nonrigid type of airship successfully in both world wars to hunt submarines.

After the 1914–18 war the British dirigible, R-34, successfully crossed the Atlantic in July 1919. This marked the first lighter-than-air transatlantic flight. It crossed from the Firth of Forth, Scotland, to Mineola, Long Island, in 108 hours. On the return eastward flight, it took only 75 hours.

The *Graf Zeppelin,* under the command of

Dr. Hugo Eckener, circumnavigated the globe, the first airship ever to do so. Later this dirigible went into regular passenger service between Europe and South America.

My own experience with dirigibles began in the early twenties. I had been invited to Wilhelmshaven on Lake Constance to participate in trial flights of a dirigible the Zeppelin Works had completed for the United States as a part of war reparations. Several times the trials were postponed because the wind was too strong or wasn't blowing from the right direction. The dirigible couldn't be taken out of the huge hangar when a cross wind might press the light aluminum frame against the doorframe. After noting these difficulties and observing the crew carry out the delicate and difficult launching and landing operations, I made up my mind that the airplane would soon make the slow, clumsy dirigible obsolete for transport purposes. But in the face of the enthusiastic advocacy of the dirigible by Dr. Hugo Eckener and his partisans in this country, it required more than a decade and the *Hindenburg* disaster before the lighter-than-air advocates gave up the battle.

The tragedy of the *Hindenburg* in the spring of 1937 emphasized the continued ill fortune the United States experienced with this type of aircraft. On September 3, 1925, the United States dirigible *Shenandoah* broke apart at Caldwell, Ohio, causing the loss of fourteen lives. Shortly after midnight, April 4, 1933, the *Akron,* heading into a squall off the New Jersey coast, crashed, killing seventy-three men including Rear Admiral Moffet, chief of the Bureau of Aeronautics, who was a guest on board. The German tanker *Phoebus* rescued four men but stood by helplessly while many drowned in the heavy seas.

The Navy never found a reason for this crash and the public never knew why the *Akron* was sent out in the face of a squall.

Our last major tragedy was the United States *Macon* in 1935, after which this rigid type of airship was all but abandoned for naval use. The airplane has now taken over entirely from the rigid airships, but the nonrigid blimps are still used by the Navy to locate submarines and for advertising purposes. The helicopter has also made hovering, slow forward speed, and vertical landings possible for heavier-than-air machines.

32.

Hitler Takes Austria— Czechoslovakia Is Next

By February 1938 Hitler had long had Germany under absolute control. The purge of the Reichswehr had given him command of the German Army and he was in a position to put his timetable of conquest into operation. First on the list was his native Austria. He had reluctantly decided against marching into Austria in 1934 after the Nazis had murdered Chancellor Dollfuss in an abortive attempt to seize Vienna. At that time his army was not ready and he had no alliance with Mussolini. As I traveled from Italy at the height of this 1934 crisis, I passed numerous Italian units camped in the Brenner Pass area which had been mobilized just in case. Hitler wisely decided the time had not yet come to make Austria capitulate to his wishes. That was one time he listened to his generals.

On February 12, 1938, the Austrian chancellor, Dr. Kurt von Schuschnigg, paid a reluctant visit to Hitler at his Berchtesgaden retreat. Hitler had summoned him to force him to accept a pro-Nazi solution of the Austrian-German problem. Hitler received Von Schuschnigg with the utmost rudeness, refusing to greet him properly or even to address him by his correct name and title. Hitler began their conversation with an abusive harangue. "How have you dared for all these years to suppress and torture my people, my German people in Austria? God has made me Fuehrer and ruler of every man and woman of German blood in every country on earth. You shall bow to my will as all the rest of the world shall bow, or I will break you. I demand obedience from you and shall enforce it, if necessary with my armies. You will accept and sign before you leave this house the terms I have prepared or I will at once give the order to march into Austria."

The Austrian Chancellor was hardly prepared for such demands. Under the severe pressure which Hitler and the Nazis applied for several hours, Von Schuschnigg gave way and accepted Hitler's humiliating terms. These included amnesty to all Austrian Nazis who had been imprisoned for the Dollfuss murder and other acts; opening the "Fatherland Front" to Nazis, and taking certain Nazis into the Austrian cabinet. Four days later Dr. Arthur Seyss-Inquart, an avowed Nazi, was made Minister of the Interior with police control. Hitler promised independence of Austria but warned that he would keep German troops on the border to see that Von Schuschnigg carried out the terms of the agreement.

Very soon serious disorders were deliberately started by the Austrian Nazis. They began in various key cities, creating what was in essence an internal revolution. The Austrian Government could not cope with it without offense to Nazi Germany. The Nazis, on their part, violated the Berchtesgaden agreements

Vienna mourned the death of Chancellor Dollfuss, murdered by the Nazis.

Dr. Arthur Seyss-Inquart, pro-Nazi Interior Minister and later Chancellor, paved the way for Hitler's conquest of Austria. Here he is tumultuously welcomed by Linz Nazis.

A corporal in the German army returns to Vienna as conqueror—1938.

relative to "internal affairs" and seized power in the provinces.

To counteract this situation and make a last bid for national sovereignty, Schuschnigg announced on March 9 that a plebiscite would be held in all Austria the following Sunday. This was to prove to the world that the great majority of Austrians preferred independence. The announcement drove the Nazis to take measures which created a state of chaos

118

in much of Austria. The day before the plebiscite was to have taken place, Hitler sent an ultimatum to the Austrian Chancellor to postpone the voting or he would invade. He also demanded Von Schuschnigg's resignation.

Austria's President Miklas refused at first to accept the Chancellor's resignation, but with German troops massed at the border and ready to strike, he, too, asquiesced to Hitler's demands. Not a single real gesture of support came from the leading European powers to whom the Austrians had appealed for help. In their timid eagerness to avoid war, the European powers helped to make a later war inevitable.

Seyss-Inquart, the Nazi leader, succeeded Schuschnigg as Austrian Chancellor. At the same time the German Army began the invasion of Austria and the new Chancellor proclaimed Austria's union with Germany. On March 14, Hitler made his triumphant entry into Vienna and took formal possession of Austria as part of the Third Reich.

Hitler wanted to avenge himself on Vienna because of the humiliations he had suffered there in the early days of his career. His opportunity to gain that revenge was now at hand. He used it ruthlessly against all opponents of the Nazis. The Jews, in particular, suffered brutal assault and humiliation. Hundreds committed suicide, those who could escaped from the country, thousands were thrown into the concentration camps that Hitler had waiting for them. Anti-Semitism became the order of the day in Vienna as in Berlin.

The absorption of Austria into the German Reich was executed with such speed and energy that no international complications even arose. Four years before, Mussolini had still been able to stop Hitler with a military demonstration at the Brenner Pass. Now Mussolini was Hitler's captive. The Rome–Berlin axis had been formed and was functioning smoothly. Mussolini was deeply involved in the Spanish Civil War and could only accept the new situation created by Hitler's new aggression against Italy's peaceful neighbor. France and England were both committed to Austrian independence, but Hitler only sneered at their feeble protests. Their weak-kneed attitude made him the more certain that he would have his way again when the time came to deal with Czechoslovakia and Poland.

The Munich agreement showed that Hitler was right in his calculations at least on Czechoslovakia. Only Soviet Russia was ready to fight to prevent Hitler's seizure of this powerful little French ally. France and Britain admitted that they were too weak to try. But a year later, when the ever-hungry Fuehrer

Thousands of Viennese fled the new regime. Particularly the Jews suffered. Here a long queue forms before the Polish Embassy to obtain visas to Poland.

struck at Poland, they had to try because they finally realized that they were next in line once Poland was conquered. But by that time Hitler was too strong to be defeated by what remained of free Europe. Help had to come from beyond the seas. What might have been accomplished in 1938 by sending French, British, and Russian help to Austria and Czechoslovakia could not be done for Poland because it was already too late. Nor should it be forgotten that one reason the ruthless realistic Stalin signed a pact with his Nazi enemy in 1939 was that French and British leaders had already demonstrated their weakness while Hitler had demonstrated his strength.

33.

Munich—1938—First International Crisis Covered Step by Step on Radio

Will war be averted or is World War II about to begin? The whole world was asking that question in September 1938, when Hitler suddenly demanded that Czechoslovakia cede the Sudetenland to Germany. The climax came at Munich in late September when Hitler, Mussolini, Neville Chamberlain, and Édouard Daladier sat down to confer and ended by accepting Hitler's terms.

Some eighteen years have passed since the stormy three weeks that came to be known as the Munich Crisis which, because of the sellout of Czechoslovakia to Hitler, made the Bavarian city and the word *appeasement* synonymous. It also made Chamberlain's furled umbrella the symbol of the fateful surrender to aggression that was decided at Munich.

The historic story of the Munich Crisis began on September 12 when Hitler, in his Nuremberg speech before the Nazi Congress, demanded self-determination for Sudetenland Germans. It ended on September 29, when the four big powers at the final parley agreed to the dismemberment of little Czechoslovakia. When it was all over, the world, which was still more interested in peace at any price than in peace with justice, breathed a sigh of relief. Neville Chamberlain flew back to London to make his pathetically boastful "peace in our time" announcement to the anxious British people as he waved the scrap-of-paper promise Hitler had signed.

Premier Daladier, who, because of his feelings of guilt and shame at the parley's outcome, expected to be greeted by an angry French mob, returned to Paris to receive a hero's welcome. It was the German and Italian dictators who defeated the democratic leaders at the Munich meeting. Yet Europe was so willing to accept a shameful temporary peace that there was rejoicing in every European capital except Prague and perhaps Moscow, where appraisal of the results of Munich was more realistic.

The world knew that Prague would accept the Munich Agreement because it had no other choice. But the free peoples of Europe failed to realize, as late as 1938, that a dictator's appetite grows only by what he feeds on. At Munich four European leaders tried to set up a new balance of power without either American or Russian participation. The United States, which had been so largely responsible for the creation of the Czech Republic, was elated that peace had been maintained even though it was at the expense of that republic. The realistic Stalin called the Agreement "mollycoddling an aggressor."

120

Chamberlain, Hitler and Mussolini at Munich in September, 1938.

In September 1938 war came closer to the American people than it ever had come since the Armistice of 1918. Throughout the Munich Crisis the free peoples of the world, through radio and the press, got an exact accounting of every important move. Here was open diplomacy at its worst because every leader spoke for publication. Those controlled by public opinion were compelled to speak for peace at any price. Those who spoke as dictators voiced demands and threatened war if they were not granted. Radio, the new medium of communication, carried challenge and answer, the pleas for peace, and the threats of war to millions of homes in Europe and America which heard such a public debate for the first time.

The medium worked both ways in the free countries, and through it, the people carried

"Peace in our time." Mr. Chamberlain's furled umbrella was soon to become the symbol of appeasement.

Mrs. Neville Chamberlain, the wife of the Prime Minister, was acclaimed almost as wildly as her husband by London crowds after Chamberlain's return from Munich.

Hitler's triumphal entrance into Czechoslovakia's Sudetenland—1938.

UNDERWOOD & UNDERWOOD

back to their leaders their response to every move. Their continued response was a demand for peace. They got peace. But it was the kind of peace that paved the way to war. Radio, which transmitted instantly every important speech, message, action to and from every European and American center, acquired an importance it had never had before.

The events of those trying days are intimately familiar to me. During the twenty days and nights of the Munich Crisis I happened to be the only experienced American news analyst working for a radio network who was thoroughly familiar with the background of the crisis, the personalities involved, and the foreign languages which they employed. During the twenty days of the crisis I made 102 broadcasts lasting from two minutes to two hours each. Here was an international crisis in which radio participated every step of the way. It was the first complete play-by-play coverage of history in the making.

122

After the Austrian Anschluss, the late Paul White, able news director of the Columbia Broadcasting System, realized what lay ahead and immediately prepared to cover the next "crisis" more completely than the last. We expected that Czechoslovakia would be next on Hitler's list, but we couldn't know just when he would strike. At the time the CBS news department was not only fortunate in its news director but also in the fact that Edward R. Murrow was European manager. Between them they lined up a staff of expert journalists and commentators in every capital of Europe, ready to broadcast to America on the shortest notice. This staff included, in addition to Ed Murrow in London, such people as William L. Shirer in Berlin and Maurice Hindus in Prague. Thus it was possible for radio listeners to hear "America calling Prague . . . London . . . Paris . . . Berlin or Prague, Rome, and the other capitals calling America. At that time we were still permitted to carry on telephone conversations during which New York and up to five European capitals exchanged questions and answers while all America listened in. The telephone company condoned this violation of the rules only while the crisis lasted.

The two-way setup enabled Americans to hear personally from every leading figure in the Crisis—Chamberlain, Hitler, Mussolini, Daladier, Anthony Eden, Jan Masaryk, Benes, and Hodza. The focal point of CBS's coverage during the September crisis was New York, and the heart and center of the entire organization was Studio Nine where I stuck by the microphone night and day from the time of Hitler's speech at Nuremberg until the day after the Munich Agreement had been signed by Germany, Italy, France, and Great Britain.

It was my task to ad lib my comment on the news as it came over the wires. All talks were extemporaneous since I analyzed each news bulletin as soon as it was read and each speech as soon as it was completed. The studio engineers, producers, and announcers milled about as I talked and fresh news dispatches were constantly being carried in from the adjoining ticker room and placed before me. Despite the Crisis, the network continued to observe split-second timing even of the special programs. Sponsored programs were continued but were subject to interruption.

The intimate grasp of a complex situation which those broadcasts helped give our listeners also enabled them to realize our country's increasingly important role in world affairs. When hour after hour CBS brought the major voices and events of Europe into our very homes, the blind, ostrichlike isolationist view of foreign affairs was no longer tenable. The way was opened for more intelligent planning of means to protect ourselves against the chaos which seemed about to descend on Europe. That the Munich Crisis did take the

turn for peace may be due in some measure to radio. Certainly broadcasting rendered an important service to the world by providing instant information on events which were occurring far away but which could affect the destinies of all mankind.

As it turned out, Munich was just a beginning. Hitler got what he wanted and agreed to stay appeased. I didn't believe him. In my final Crisis broadcast I recalled the words of a British Prime Minister: "Today they ring the bells; tomorrow they will wring their hands."

In retrospect it is interesting to recall a passage from Hitler's book *Mein Kampf,* where he says: "Every nation that once submits to a foreign demand has lost part of its power to resist. Each time it makes a concession it is less able and less willing to resist the next demand. That is why the shrewd victor will always ask for what he wants by degrees. Once a nation has begun to give rather than fight back, it will keep on giving and giving, provided that the victor nation does not ask for too much."

When he insisted a year later on the occupation of Poland, Hitler asked too much.

H. V. Kaltenborn, an exhausted newscaster, made 102 broadcasts during twenty days and nights of the Munich Crisis.

NBC

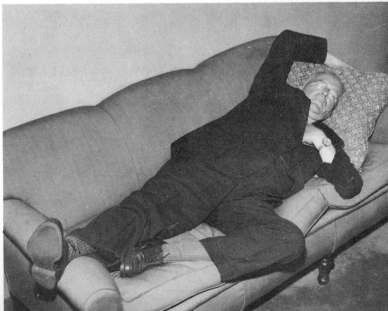

German Panzer tanks introduced the blitzkrieg to modern warfare as the Wehrmacht overran Poland.

34. War in Europe—1939

Poland fell soon after German infantrymen closed in on Warsaw.

On September 1, 1939, Hitler's air force roared over the Polish frontier in all its might. The first aerial blitzkrieg was under way. Poland crumpled like a house of straw under the impact of bombs and Hitler's mobile army. Warsaw surrendered on September 27. In less than a month a nation of 31,000,000 people with an army of a million and a half was conquered. Hitler, because he was well prepared for modern war, had scored the first important success of World War II.

For weeks the Fuehrer had brought pressure on Poland to surrender the Corridor which separated East Prussia from the rest of Germany. As a pretext for the "war crisis" he used a minor Danzig-Polish controversy over the customs duty on herring and margarine. Actually, what gave Hitler the green light for the start of his blitzkrieg was the infamous Hitler-Stalin pact of August 24, 1939.

The seven articles of this pact guaranteed that for ten years neither Russia nor Germany would make war on the other or join any alliance directed against the other. The pact was negotiated between two outstanding double-crossers, Ribbentrop and Molotov, on behalf of two aggression-minded dictators, Hitler and Stalin. The agreement, Hitler foolishly believed, cleared the way for German aggression against Poland without bringing on the dreaded two-front war. Hitler exultingly said: "Now I have the world in my pocket."

When the shocking news of this Hitler-Stalin pact burst on the world, I was in Paris, reporting on France's unpreparedness for war. Frenchmen were reluctant to believe that the Hitler-Stalin pact opened the way for Hitler to make war. France and Britain were backing Poland. When I asked France's Foreign Minister, Georges Bonnet, whether he felt that war was imminent, he replied, "No one can predict—the situation rests with one man." Our then American Ambassador, William C. Bullitt, told me, "There can be no question of selling out Poland either by the British or the French. France has said if Britain fights, France will fight, too."

In 1939 France was totally unprepared for war. Yet she had great confidence in her military preparations, in her huge army, and especially in the fortified Maginot Line. To me, it was obvious that the French national psychology was dominated by defeatism. Britain, too, was almost totally unprepared though

politically committed to Poland. Lord Halifax remarked to me, "We must act if Hitler invades Poland. We are pledged to intervene and we must keep our pledge. In any case our prestige and our Balkan interests demand action. The conquest of Poland would only be a first step."

Britain failed in her chief war aim, the defense of Poland. She could give that country no military help. As Winston Churchill wrote about the guarantee to Poland in *The Gathering Storm,* the first volume of his war memoirs, "God helping, we could do no other."

The communist press had a hard time explaining the alliance of Hitler and Stalin, who had hated each other so much for so many years. The New York communist *Daily Worker* gulped hard for twenty-four hours before shifting to a new line to explain the Hitler-Stalin alliance. The German people quietly accepted a Russo-German pact as preventing the kind of two-front war which had

WONDER HOW LONG THE HONEYMOON WILL LAST?

125

Not for long. Germany smashed into Russia in 1941. As did General Kutuzov before Napoleon, the Russians followed a scorched-earth policy and Hitler's forces had to employ every available means, such as horses and wagons for supplies, in their attempt to conquer the vastness of Russia.

As Hitler's forces invaded Russia early in the war, several million Soviet troops were made prisoner before their defenses tightened.

brought about their defeat in 1918. They were reminded of Bismarck's following up the Triple Alliance with a reinsurance treaty with Czarist Russia. Ribbentrop had wanted to put in the pact preamble some high-sounding phrases about the traditional Russo-German friendship. To which Stalin made this classic reply, "Leave it out. I can't sell that bunk to the Russian people after the Nazi Government has poured pails of manure over us for six years." Stalin at least was an earthy realist.

It was not long after France and England had declared war on Germany, and Poland had fallen, that the two thieves began to fall out over the division of their loot. The pretended "friendship" was visibly cooling off.

The pretense of a real alliance and the exchange of German industrial products for Russian raw materials continued, but each power greatly distrusted the other. The Comintern accused Germany of waging a war for world domination. Stalin was beginning to dislike his end of the deal.

By a boundary agreement between Stalin and Hitler, Germany took over half of Poland, paving the way for the Nazis to move in on Scandinavia and the Balkans. Russia took over the other half of Poland and cast her eyes on the Baltic states and Finland. As 1939 neared its fateful end, Russia announced that she had been "attacked" by little Finland. Molotov told the world that Finnish troops

Paying the piper. Hitler performed this joyous dance at Compiègne in 1940 after dictating armistice terms to conquered France.

were menacing Leningrad. A nation of 100,-000,000 threatened by Finland's 4,000,000! So Russia struck. For four months after Russia invaded Finland, the Finns, greatly outnumbered, fought back with skill and courage. Russia was expelled from the League of Nations for her wanton aggression, but that didn't keep Finland from losing the war. Final capitulation came in March 1940. This was another instance where the major League members failed to provide help when a big power attacked a weaker nation.

It is ironic to think back to the events of 1939 that resulted from the Hitler-Stalin Pact and then recall the exchange of Christmas greetings between the two aggressors. Hitler sent his "best wishes" to the peoples of what he called "the friendly Soviet Union." Not to be outdone, Stalin replied, "The friendship of the peoples of Germany and the Soviet Union, cemented by blood, has every reason to be lasting and firm."

A year and a half later Hitler launched his people into the two-front war he had always promised to avoid, thereby sealing his own fate and making certain he would lose the war. Stalin saw the unhappy Russians surrender by the millions because they abominated his government and foolishly hoped for something better under Hitler.

Better diplomacy by France and Britain should have been able to forestall so unnatural an alliance as that between a communist and a Nazi dictatorship. I said that when the Pact was signed, and am now more certain than ever that it is true. I added that by their Pact Nazi Germany sold out her last remaining moral and political assets to Comrade Stalin and also assured her own defeat in the war. Many Germans must have come to the same conclusion. The crushing influence of dictatorship is shown by the fact that not one German voice dared proclaim this truth.

35.

Three World Fairs—
New York, Chicago, St. Louis

The two architectural highlights of the New York World's Fair, which opened on April 10, 1939, were the dramatic Trylon and the huge Perisphere. Dominating the skyline for miles, they were the theme structures of the gigantic exhibition which was designed to reflect the world's tomorrow. The parachute drop was the most dramatic amusement feature. I had already encountered this in the Soviet Union many years earlier where it was used by the Kremlin to help recruit parachute units. Not many of the millions of visitors who saw or rode the parachute drop in New York dreamed that this fair would turn out to be a united world's last fling at gaiety and relaxation before the military parachutes started dropping over Europe. Less than five months after the fair opened, World War II had begun.

Everyone has vivid memories of the fair, which covered two square miles on what was a former city dump at Flushing Meadows. There were the vast and impressive displays of art, industry, and science; the Billy Rose Aquacade with Eleanor Holm as the star; the girlie shows of the Midway where the nudist girls wore ten-gallon hats, short boots, and a fringed belt; the marvelous French and other continental restaurants; the spectacular fountains and lights, the funny little trains, and the busses in which you traveled around the fair grounds while the horns tooted: "East Side, West Side, all around the town." Years later I encountered those same busses at an Air Force base in Texas where they tooted a different tune.

The St. Louis Exposition in 1904 was the first major "fair" held in the United States since the Chicago Exposition of 1892.

Chicago's Century of Progress gets ready for its opening day—1933.

The most magnificent of all—the New York World's Fair in 1939. 62 nations were represented.

Much comment was created by the impressive Soviet building. It featured huge photographs of the Soviet hierarchy some of whom had already been purged when the fair reopened for its second year. People recall, too, the fine Italian building. This featured Mussolini's dictum—"Obbedecire; Credere; Combattere." Thus the Duce propagandized to the free world the Fascist creed, that man was to obey, to believe, and to fight on order without thinking for himself.

Altogether, sixty-two nations participated in the World's Fair and there were more than 600 commercial and noncommercial exhibits. It cost $150,000,000 to build and attracted 45,000,000 visitors. All that remains now at Flushing Meadows are a few buildings used by the City of New York. Robert Moses almost succeeded in getting the United Nations to establish its headquarters in this area. They did use the New York City Building for several Assembly sessions.

My own personal contribution to the fair was the use of my voice to narrate the story of the City of Tomorrow, as exemplified in picture, panorama, song and word on the inside of the huge Perisphere. Since this was the theme story of the fair, nearly every visitor tramped up the long ramp and paid admission to the moving sidewalk that carried visitors around the huge Cyclorama showing how the ideal city of the future would be organized to provide every resident "with sunlight and good air." It was a happy prospect which my voice proclaimed. Joyous workers, healthy children, everything organized so that the benefits of country life were all provided for city dwellers.

Well, it hasn't happened yet, but at least I lived long enough to note that more and more city dwellers are moving away from the too thickly populated areas. Those that cannot move away are gradually getting a chance to live in modern apartments built in reclaimed slum areas. The story told inside the Perisphere may have given a little push in the right direction. And as Harvard's William James used to tell us: "If each one of us gives even a little push in the right direction we will make this into the melioristic universe in which I believe."

In contrast to the New York World's Fair was the Century of Progress World's Fair which opened in Chicago on May 27, 1933, and played to a mere 22,000,000 people. The Chicago Fair had been financed by a private bond underwriting, floated by Rufus Dawes, brother of Charles Dawes. The Century of Progress exhibits were better planned than the buildings which housed them. There was no over-all design and the fair suffered in consequence. The exhibits ranged all the way from the greatest art collection ever assembled in America to Sally Rand and her fan dance. Actually, she was the publicity hit of the fair and attracted the most enthusiastic crowds. Her old Earl Carroll routine act was new to the Midwest, but Sally Rand became notorious when the police raided her show and a tolerant judge released her.

Coming as it did in the very early days of the New Deal, the Century of Progress got off to a bad start financially. Then came a turn for the better with higher farm prices. This enabled thousands of nearby farmers to attend the fair. By the late summer of 1933 the fair had taken in about $35,000,000 and helped take Chicago out of its insolvency.

Before the New York World's Fair and the Century of Progress in Chicago another important fair in this country had been the St. Louis Exposition of 1904. This was held to commemorate the centennial of the Louisiana Purchase. The St. Louis show cost only $31,-000,000. It was a well-planned, highly impressive sight with the fifteen large exhibit build-

A highlight of Chicago's Fair—Sally Rand.

ings arranged in the shape of a fan. The theme of the exposition was the presentation of a summary of the world's knowledge. Of particular interest were the Congress of Arts and Science Building, the exhibition showing the advance in agriculture, the Government Building, and the anthropological exhibits from the Philippines.

In contrast to Sally Rand and the girlie shows of the midways at the Chicago and New York fairs, the main attraction of the St. Louis Exposition were the primitive natives from distant areas. Visitors were treated to the sight of pygmies, Eskimos, and aborigines all housed as they were at home.

I became so interested in the Igorots of the Island of Luzon that I paid them a special visit when I went to the Philippines in 1927. This savage tribe, which occupied a considerable area in the mountainous part of northern Luzon, stirred my imagination and made me want to visit the Philippines. As a

130

Spanish-American War volunteer I had been offered a chance to enlist for service in the Philippines instead of being mustered out in April 1899. I was sorely tempted by this opportunity to see something of Asia. But when I observed the primitive Igorots in St. Louis I was happy to have escaped my chance to suppress whatever longing for liberty they may have cherished. Our war against Aguinaldo and the Filipinos on the Island of Luzon is not a creditable chapter in our military history. Perhaps that is why it has been pretty well forgotten.

36.

Wendell Willkie and the 1940 Campaign

"Of course I will not run for a third term." Those were President Franklin D. Roosevelt's words in the summer of 1939 as reported by James A. Farley. But in 1940, when the war had begun and Hitler had overrun Poland, Denmark, Norway, Holland, Belgium, and France, Roosevelt changed his mind. Thus the Democratic National Convention, meeting in Chicago, shattered tradition by designating as its candidate the man who became the country's first third-term president. When his name was put in nomination the demonstration lasted almost an hour, establishing another evil precedent for the time-wasting nonstop ballyhoo that has characterized so many of our political conventions.

Wendell Willkie, the 1940 Republican nominee for President, greets jammed galleries at Madison Square Garden with a characteristic wave.

The Republicans also upset political precedent in 1940. By nominating Wendell L. Willkie they chose a candidate who was an absolute newcomer to the political scene. Here was a man who had never held public office nor even sought it. A Wall Street lawyer and public-utilities executive, Willkie was a political neophyte. He had even been a Democrat and helped elect Roosevelt in 1932. Yet a Republican convention kept shouting "We want Willkie" until it got Willkie. I remember the earsplitting vigor of those shouts because it was my task to describe the scene for a large audience of radio listeners while the shouting was going on.

The Republican convention in Philadelphia was one of the most curious and in many ways one of the most dramatic of the many I have reported. Contending for the nomination were such seasoned political figures as Thomas E. Dewey, Senator Robert Taft, and Senator Arthur H. Vandenberg, with Dewey the favorite. Newspaper publisher Frank Gannett was also nursing the vain hope that he might be tapped.

Although he was a newcomer in the political field, Willkie was fairly well known in public life by his articles, radio addresses, and interviews. In all these he expressed his somewhat idealistic opinions on national and international affairs. His star rose rapidly as a man to be reckoned with and listened to. As a result, "Willkie for President" and "Win with Willkie" clubs mushroomed all over the country without any real support from the professional politicians. They correctly estimated him as the kind of man who would be unresponsive to the pressure and persuasion

131

they hoped to use on the successful candidate.

Behind the Willkie boom were such "amateur" politicians as Russell Davenport and Oren Root, Jr., who conducted a well-organized businesslike pre-convention campaign. They enlisted the support of powerful publishers—Henry Luce was one of them—publicity and advertising directors, political idealists, and a smattering of big business. There wasn't a political boss or professional politician in the Willkie camp. It was a group which reminded me of the 1912 backers of Theodore Roosevelt and the Progressive party.

The Willkie band wagon rolled to Philadelphia with ever-increasing speed and assurance. At the convention, before the balloting started, Congressman Frank O. Horton, of Wyoming, and Governor Harold Stassen, of Minnesota, joined the Willkie camp. They were valuable recruits. Stassen, who was the keynoter of the convention, became Willkie's floor manager. Willkie himself campaigned vigorously among the delegates and won the backing of William A. White, editor of the Emporia *Gazette,* who put Kansas in the Willkie column. He wrote: "Never since Teddy Roosevelt have I known a man on whom I have pinned my faith as I have pinned it on Wendell Willkie."

Excitement ran high when the balloting started. Dewey led on the first ballot, with Taft second and Willkie third. Then Dewey began to lose ground, and Willkie overtook Taft. After the fourth ballot Willkie was considerably in the lead over the other two contenders. The packed galleries continued to chant "We want Willkie" and thousands of pro-Willkie messages poured in on the delegates.

On the fifth ballot, Willkie's lead had increased by a substantial margin, but not enough to put him across. Then, at the sixth ballot, came the convention's dramatic high

spot when all eyes were on Michigan and Pennsylvania. Michigan's delegates had been consistently for Vandenberg, while the Pennsylvania delegation was split between Governor Edward Martin, a favorite son, and Willkie. Finally, both states swung behind Willkie to give him the nomination, with the roar from the crowd shaking the rafters. The country had witnessed another political miracle.

The unusual and surprising thing about the Willkie nomination was that Willkie hadn't entered a single primary. He made no "deals" and he had no well-mapped-out, organized campaign to win votes. It was the efforts of the ardent amateurs, who were tired of the old-time politicians, and a swift but well-financed publicity build-up that won Willkie the nomination and flaunted tradition by routing the practical politicians and political bosses who had tried to win votes for Taft or Dewey.

The Republicans had adopted a weak platform which was called "a masterpiece of equivocation, evasion, ambiguity, and generalization." The plank on foreign policy straddled the real issues. Basically, during the campaign, Willkie and Roosevelt didn't differ much as to major policies. Willkie subscribed to most of the New Deal reforms, endorsed most of the recent social legislation, and even supported Roosevelt's foreign policy. His main issue was that he could improve on what was being done, and that Roosevelt was not indispensable. Rather than attacking policies, he attacked the New Deal administration. Willkie, whom that master of satire, Harold Ickes, called the "simple barefoot Wall Street lawyer," conducted a traditional campaign, traveling more than 30,000 miles and making 550 speeches. He even beat Bryan's historic barnstorming campaign of 1896. Willkie challenged Roosevelt to a series of debates, but through an intermediary Roosevelt stated that "he could not adjourn the Battle of Britain in order to ride the circuit with Willkie."

After pressure had been brought to bear on him by practical Republican politicians who knew all the tricks, Willkie changed his tactics. Toward the end of the contest he campaigned in the good old-fashioned way, aiming his shots directly at Roosevelt. The President made not more than five major speeches. It was an uninspiring campaign, with Roosevelt advocating some things in which he didn't believe and with Willkie indulging in unfamiliar campaign oratory some of which he later recanted. Both candidates asserted that they would keep the country out of war, while both realized that in all probability the United States would soon be in the war.

As a politician, Willkie can be considered a failure since he won only ten states in the 1940 election. But he will always be remembered for his honesty, his idealism, and his sincerity. He was one of the early proponents of the "one world" idea in international relations. As a result of his round-the-world trip in 1942 he wrote the best-selling book, *One World* in which he expressed his deep convictions about how men and nations could and should work and live together. After meeting him in September 1941, I wrote: "Wendell Willkie is one of America's most valuable citizens. He is intensely pro-American. He is a man of vision who knows we live in an integrated world in which we must now play a leading part." Looking back, I could have said much the same thing about Adlai Stevenson a few years later. He also flew around the world after being defeated for the presidency in 1952.

My last meeting with Wendell Willkie was not long before he died in 1944. Together with Mrs. Willkie, he was my guest at the River Club. He was not in good health and the eager crusading spirit against isolationism which had dominated our previous interviews was gone. His 1940 defeat, but more particularly the 1944 defeat in the Wisconsin primary which resulted in his decision not to try for the presidency a second time, had put a damper on his former ebullient spirits. It made me wonder whether we should not find some way to enable the country to utilize and care for men like Wendell Willkie who enter politics, not for what they can get, but for what they hope to give.

Wendell Willkie discusses his "One World" concept with H. V. Kaltenborn in 1943.

The most famous of all enlistment posters—by James Montgomery Flagg—appeared during World War I.

37.

Conscription in the United States

To millions of Americans the number 158 may recall an important day in Washington, D.C., and an eventful day in their own lives. The day was October 29, 1940. The number was the first one Henry L. Stimson, Secretary of War, drew from the big goldfish bowl. He thus set in motion the first peacetime program of compulsory military service in the history of the United States.

134

Blindfolded and in the presence of President Roosevelt and his cabinet, the Secretary of War used the same goldfish bowl that had been used for the 1917 draft in World War I. The drawing on that October day went on for seventeen hours with General Lewis B. Hershey, the Deputy Director of Selective Service, drawing the last number. At 125,000 registration places throughout the country 16,000,000 men had been registered two weeks before the drawing took place. Now they could be classified in the order in which they would be called upon to serve their country.

Congress passed the first peacetime Selective Training and Service Bill on September 16, 1940, when it became obvious that we might be drawn into the war. Right after Munich in 1938 at least one third of all Americans favored universal military training. By the spring of 1940 one out of every two favored it, and when the Germans took Paris in June 1940 two thirds of our people were in favor of prompt action to provide universal military training. The bill called for the registration of men between twenty-one and thirty-five for a one-year service period with the goal of 1,200,000 troops and 800,000 reserves. President Roosevelt extended the bill in 1941 and in 1942, when we were at war. Selective Service was placed under the War Manpower Commission headed by Paul V. McNutt.

Although the 1940 draft was the first ever enacted when the country was not actually at war, the idea of conscription was not new in our history. In 1778 George Washington told the Continental Congress that "Our greatest and only aid will be derived from drafting." In the war of 1812 volunteering failed to increase the size of the army and just as the war ended Congress was faced with the prospect of framing a draft law. In the War between the States, the Confederates began compulsory service almost at once. The North started to conscript men in 1862 when a draft act was passed. Unfortunately that law allowed for bounties and the hiring of substitutes. A man could buy his way out of service for $300, which naturally meant inequality of service. The draft riots in New York were so violent that soldiers had to be brought home from the front to quell the disturbances.

During the brief Spanish-American War the number of volunteers was far greater than the number of men needed. When we organized a company of volunteers in Merrill, Wisconsin, our chief concern was whether we would be incorporated in a Wisconsin regiment. All kinds of political pressure were used to secure the acceptance of local and state volunteer units. Regular army and state militia companies were usually included with the untrained volunteer units to form a regiment.

In World War I, the first registration, on June 5, 1917, produced a listing of 9,586,508 men between the ages of twenty-one and thirty inclusive. In 1918 the draft law changed the ages from eighteen to forty-five. Of the 24,234,021 men registered during 1917 and 1918, only 2,810,296 were called up for active duty. I was one of the 21,423,725 destined to remain uncalled. When I sought enlistment on the strength of my Spanish-American War experience, I was told that at my age—forty—my worth as war editor of the Brooklyn *Daily Eagle* was more important than anything I could do in uniform. I was unhappy, but not my wife.

The Selective Service Act of World War II expired on March 31, 1947. However, after the National Security Act had coordinated the Army, Navy, and Air Force into a single national military establishment under the Secretary of Defense, a new Selective Service Act was passed in 1948. It called for the registration of men between eighteen and twenty-five and provided for a twenty-one-month period of training.

On July 7, 1950, President Truman, as Commander in Chief, sent out a military order to 635,000 young Americans: volunteer or be drafted. It was the first step of man-

The first conscription drawing of World War I was made from this renowned fish bowl.

Secretary of War, Henry L. Stimson, drew in America's first peacetime conscription, 1940.

power mobilization in the move to build up the armed forces to full strength. Congress had set a top limit of 2,005,000 for the armed forces. At the time President Truman's order went out, the Army, Navy, Air Force, and Marines had only 1,370,000 men in uniform. Hence 635,000 men had the opportunity of volunteering or being drafted. Since then the draft law has again been extended. The starting age is eighteen and a half years under the latest extension.

There is every indication that this will pave the way for universal military training. This has long been advocated by our wisest civilian and military leaders. It is significant that following the Korean War our military appropriations mounted from more than $14,000,000,000 in 1950 to more than $46,000,000,000 in 1953. In a very real sense we have become a nation in arms. Wars past and the threat of wars to come absorb all but a small proportion of our national budget. In all probability this will continue to be true for many years to come. Since the end of the Korean War and with the development of more and more powerful atomic weapons the immediate threat of a world conflict has receded. Masses of infantry produced by conscription have become less important for defense than technicians trained in the use of modern instruments of warfare.

It is the laboratories and the scientific schools rather than the drill grounds that will produce the warriors of tomorrow. While communism continues to seek world conquest the free world cannot escape the sacrifices necessary to produce enough of tomorrow's trained scientific warriors to maintain control of the world's undersea and upper-air routes. The best we can expect to do is to develop the new wartime skills for peacetime use in the justified hope that this generation at least will not witness another major war.

136

38.

Churchill and Britain's "Finest Hour"

By June of 1940 Hitler had conquered much of Europe and Great Britain stood alone. The English Channel was the only barrier to Hitler's fast-moving legions. It was a grim picture, yet Churchill spoke of "their finest hour." For it was in those dark days of World War II that Winston Churchill's leadership was at its best. Just a few weeks earlier, on taking over the position of Prime Minister, he had made the historic address in which he told his countrymen that all he had to offer was "blood, sweat, and tears."

Then came the evacuation of Dunkirk. Some three quarters of the British Army on the Continent was rescued in a seemingly miraculous operation. But Dunkirk left the British armies devoid of weapons, tanks, and war matériel. That was when Americans began sending over hunting rifles for the British volunteers guarding the beaches.

The siege of Britain was on. The people displayed remarkable resolution in facing adversity. A British citizen army was created. Along the Channel coast there were barricades and defenses against the threatened Nazi invasion. "We will fight the enemy on the beaches, we will fight them in every village, every town, and every city. We will never give up. Shielded from above by the power and devotion of our airmen, we wait undismayed the impending assault." So Churchill declared, and so it was.

He also said: "We have become the sole champions now in arms to defend the world cause. We shall do our best to be worthy of

The successful British withdrawal from Dunkirk, a magnificent achievement amidst defeat.

this high honor. Let us, therefore, brace ourselves to our duties and so bear ourselves that, if the British Empire and its Commonwealth last for a thousand years, men will say, 'This was their finest hour.'"

That was the true voice of Britain in adversity. She stood alone expecting invasion. Hitler had accumulated a vast assortment of invasion craft in those Channel harbors which the Germans controlled. He even staged invasion rehearsals. But the British planes bombed the fleets and the ports and did much to knock out the German plan of invasion by water. It was said that Hitler prayerfully questioned Moses: "How did you ever get your people across the Red Sea?"

The German submarine blockade of Great

London withstood the savage bombings of Hitler's war machine.

Britain was increasingly effective, since the Germans had U-boats on the French coast and on up to Norway. The British Navy lacked destroyers until the United States traded fifty World War I four-stackers for leases on bases in the Caribbean.

It was on August 8, 1940, that Hermann Goering began his effort to seize control of the air over Great Britain by launching an all-out attack with the Luftwaffe. In the next ten days the Germans lost almost 700 aircraft, with the RAF bagging 185 in one day. Goering's air attack failed by a narrow margin. Small wonder that Winston Churchill said, "Never in the field of human conflict was so much owed by so many to so few" in his tribute to the RAF fighter pilots who prevented the Germans from gaining control of the air.

Then night bombing began. In November the historic city of Coventry was left smoldering in ruins. London and many other cities were subject to repeated attack. By the end of the year the Luftwaffe had killed 23,000 people and wounded 32,000. The worst bombings of the entire war occurred on the night of May 11 and 12, 1941, when about 300 German planes bombed London and 1,436 lives were lost. During that raid the Commons Chamber of Parliament was destroyed, the House of Lords was set on fire, and Westminster Abbey, Westminster Hall, Big Ben, and the British Museum were damaged.

In their final desperate effort to achieve victory the Nazis subjected London to one of the most remorseless attacks in all military history when they launched the robot V-1 and V-2 flying bombs. Those were Hitler's "secret weapons." The Germans were told they would win the war. The V-1 made a hissing and whistling noise as it approached, thus sounding its own warning. The V-2 was a rocket which weighed twelve tons and had a one-ton warhead. Because of its silent approach, it caused twice the casualties of the V-1. The significance of the V-2 was that it presaged the guided missile which many experts believe will become the decisive tactical atomic weapon of future wars.

My first experience with the V-1 was during

Prime Minister Winston Churchill sadly examines the devastation of Coventry Cathedral, October 1941.

my visit to the western front in Belgium and Holland. They kept me awake nights as they whistled overhead on their way to Antwerp.

At the time the Germans were launching the V-2's from Channel bases I was in London. This was in the autumn of 1944 when, after completing a tour of European battlefronts, I spent a few days in the British capital.

One night, as I was dining with Lord Beaverbrook, a distant powerful explosion shook the windows and dishes on the table. The dinner guests calmly continued their conversation as if nothing had happened. Then, a few moments later, Lord Beaverbrook casually commented: "That was another V-2. I wonder where it landed."

Being a good newspaperman himself and knowing what his American reporter guest would like to do, he suggested that I be permitted to open the window and look out. But I could see nothing, no glow or cloud in sight. But Lord Beaverbrook knew there would be something to see and he arranged for me to see it. Early the next morning a British Ministry of Information representative took me to

the spot where the "incident"—a typical British understatement—had occurred.

We sometimes think of the British as slow-moving, but there was nothing slow about the way they went into action when a V-1 or V-2 fell. Everything was already cleaned up around the huge hole covering an entire city block that had been destroyed by the V-2 explosion I had heard the evening before. The glass had been swept up from a large neighborhood, huge piles of stone and rubble blown out by the explosion had been cleared away, and ambulances had long ago carried away the three dead and twelve wounded (the block was largely made up of business buildings whose workers had gone home.)

But there was one waiting ambulance. It belonged to the Society for the Prevention of Cruelty to Animals. Half-a-dozen workers were still digging in the ruins in the hope of rescuing alive a stabled horse buried by the explosion. There was something peculiarly British about this humane concern for one animal at a time when human lives were being snuffed out by the thousands.

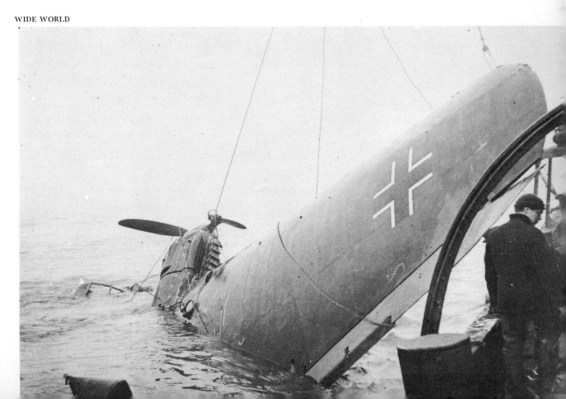

Many German planes never got through Britain's defenses. Here a German Heinkel III bomber shot down by the RAF off the coast is raised from its watery grave by a British patrol vessel.

39.

The Atlantic Charter

Early in August of 1941, just four months before the Pearl Harbor attack forced us into the war, German submarines were busily roaming the North Atlantic. The British battleship *Prince of Wales* was steaming westward and the United States cruiser *Augusta* northward on a common mission. Under the greatest secrecy, the two warships were headed for a rendezvous in Argentia Bay off the coast of Newfoundland. Then, on August 14, the three capitals of Washington, London, and Ottawa startled the world with a simultaneous announcement. It stated that President Roosevelt and Prime Minister Winston Churchill had met at sea to discuss the war and had agreed on an eight-point plan for world peace to follow the "final destruction of the Nazi tyranny." Morally, at least, it ranged the United States on the side of the nations at war with Hitler.

Thus the historic Atlantic Charter was born. Although the Charter was not a formal alliance between Great Britain and the United States nor a binding legal commitment, the joint declaration of principles formulated by the two leaders had profound repercussions. Briefly, the document which any nation opposing Nazi aggression could freely support pledged the United States and Great Britain to:

1. "Seek no aggrandizement, territorial or other."

2. Approve "no territorial changes that do not accord with the freely-expressed wishes of the people concerned."

3. "Respect the right of all peoples to choose the form of government under which they wish to live."

4. "Endeavor, with due respect for their existing obligations, to further the enjoyment of all States, great or small, victor or vanquished, of access, on equal terms, to the trade and raw material of the world. . . ."

5. "Bring about the fullest collaboration between all nations in the economic field. . . ."

6. Establish "a peace which will afford to all nations the means of dwelling in safety within their own boundaries and which will afford assurances that all men in all lands may live out their lives in freedom from fear and want. . . ."

7. Establish "a peace enabling all men to traverse the high seas and oceans without hindrance";

8. Work for "the abandonment of the use of force. . . . pending the establishment of a wider and permanent system of general security. . . ."

Here was an eight-point program, similar in some respects to the Fourteen Points peace program proclaimed by Woodrow Wilson during World War I which Germany at that time accepted as a basis for peace.

Some of the others aboard the cruiser and battleship were Lord Beaverbrook, British Minister of Supply; Admiral Sir Dudley Pound, First Sea Lord; Gen. Sir John G. Dill, Chief of the Imperial British Staff; Harry L. Hopkins, President Roosevelt's closest adviser; Under-Secretary of State Sumner Welles; Gen. George C. Marshall, United States Army Chief of Staff; W. Averell Harriman, lend-lease coordinator in London; Admiral Harold R. Stark, United States Chief of Naval Operations; Admiral Ernest J. King, commander of the United States Atlantic Fleet; Major General Henry H. Arnold, Chief of United States Army Air Forces.

The first night after the two ships reached their rendezvous all the American top brass and all the British top brass met at dinner on the *Augusta* to hear Churchill analyze the war situation. Churchill had met Roosevelt when Roosevelt was Assistant Secretary of the Navy in World War I, but Churchill had forgotten about that.

There were strong elements of drama and human interest in this meeting "at sea" which President Roosevelt, with his flair for the dramatic, had initiated. Certainly the idea of each head of government using a warship when the North Atlantic shipping lanes were being hunted by the Germans was unusual and daring. As to the timing of the meeting, it should be recalled that it took place between Hitler's attack on Russia in June 1941 and Japan's attack on Pearl Harbor six months later.

Churchill obviously hoped to get much from the meeting in the way of material aid. He had notified Dominion prime ministers that he expected momentous agreements which might require ratification. In this he was disappointed. The one thing he most hoped for was a common policy of resistance to Japanese aggression in which Russia and the Dominions would be asked to join. Roosevelt firmly refused to take any positive stand on that matter. The agreed declaration mentions only "the final destruction of the Nazi tyranny" without committing the United States to help bring it about.

Churchill also wanted to include in this Charter a reference to a new League of Nations. Roosevelt, haunted by the ghost of Woodrow Wilson, always conscious of the political effects he might produce, was afraid any such reference would merely antagonize the isolationists. It was Harry Hopkins who persuaded Roosevelt to accept the phrase in section eight of the Charter which reads, "...

the establishment of a wider and permanent system of general security." All of which meant the same thing as a League of Nations principle but without any unpolitic reference to the League.

The Atlantic Charter gave the war certain idealistic objectives, but it sent Churchill and his colleagues home empty-handed. They had expected much in immediate United States naval help but got, as one official said, "nothing but pious words." Robert Sherwood, in his book about Roosevelt and Hopkins, states: "To the officers of the British Government, the Atlantic Charter was not much more than a publicity handout." He might have added that Roosevelt loved such high-sounding declarations which included no specific commitments. This was shown later at Yalta, where the really important commitments were not publicized. Also, according to Sherwood, Churchill, at the Atlantic Charter meeting, found Roosevelt "a man of infinite subtlety and obscurity, an artful dodger who could not readily be pinned down." Roosevelt

President Roosevelt and Prime Minister Churchill met aboard the H.M.S. *Prince of Wales,* in August 1941, to draw up the Atlantic Charter.

found Churchill "stubborn, tenacious and pig-headed."

For his part, Churchill thought the biggest achievement of the Argentia meeting was the establishment of "warm and deep personal relation with our great friend."

In writing about the meeting, Harry Hopkins comments on Roosevelt's complete power to act, without so much as consulting his cabinet, while Churchill had to refer every proposed decision to his war cabinet in London. Even in the final draft of the Charter, the London war cabinet's suggestions were included. It is fair to speculate, in recalling what wartime Presidents Wilson and Roosevelt did during their independent foreign missions, whether some kind of home control would not have been better for the country. In the light of subsequent events even President Eisenhower's 1955 meeting with the Russians in Geneva may not stand up in history as a complete success. By long-distance negotiation Wilson, Roosevelt, and Eisenhower all achieved more satisfactory results than what they obtained by going abroad. Except for ceremonial visits, American presidents should remain at home.

Although many nations signed the Atlantic Charter and subscribed to its high ideals and principles, one of the chief effects was to stimulate the native politicians of North Africa, Burma, India, Ceylon, Malaya, Indo-China, and Indonesia to demand immediate independence. Neither Roosevelt nor Churchill foresaw this practical result of their meeting "at sea." As a matter of fact, Churchill had to tell the House of Commons: "We had in mind only the restoration of self-government to states under the Nazi yoke—not the evolution of self-government in regions which owe allegiance to the British Crown." Which shows that even the world's greatest statesman can be unpleasantly surprised by the unexpected results of his own actions.

40.

Pearl Harbor

"Yesterday, December 7, 1941—a date which will live in infamy—the United States of America was suddenly and deliberately attacked by naval and air forces of the Empire of Japan."

Those were President Roosevelt's sober opening words when he stood before the assembled Congress to ask for a declaration of war against Japan. "The United States," he continued, "was at peace with that nation, and, at the solicitation of Japan, was still in conversation with its government and its emperor looking toward the maintenance of peace in the Pacific. Indeed, one hour after the Japanese air squadrons had commenced bombing in Oahu, the Japanese Ambassador to the United States and his colleague delivered to the Secretary of State a formal reply to a recent American message . . . Japan has, therefore, undertaken a surprise offensive ex-

Pearl Harbor. December 7, 1941—"a date which will live in infamy."

A grim President Roosevelt asks Congress for a declaration of war against Japan on December 8, 1941.

tending throughout the Pacific area . . . I ask that the Congress declare that since the unprovoked and dastardly attack by Japan on Sunday, December 7, a state of war has existed between the United States and the Japanese Empire."

. . . "was at peace with that nation"? To all intents and purposes we were not at peace but in a state of cold war with Japan that fateful Sunday morning when the explosives dropped by Japanese bombers annihilated our fleet in Pearl Harbor and inflicted appalling losses on American naval power.

The war of nerves between Japan and the

The smiling diplomats. Kurusu (*left*) and Nomura (*right*) await Secretary of State Cordell Hull to begin talks about Far Eastern tensions. November 1941.

United States had been on for some time. With a message to the Emperor of Japan, President Roosevelt had assumed the initiative in trying to end the tension. But the Japanese military clique and the Army Cabinet were not waging a war of nerves. They had already launched a hot war, otherwise Pearl Harbor couldn't have occurred with negotiations still in progress in the American capital.

Japan had said "excuse it please" when our government asked for an explanation of troop movements to Indo-China. She gave as her reason the fear of invasion of French Indo-China by the unarmed Chinese people and implied that the only purpose of the Japanese in Indo-China was to defend that country against Chinese attack. In her polite note Japan added that the government of Vichy had consented to everything Japan wanted to do. So why did Britain and the United States continue to disturb the peace of the Far East?

In my Saturday-evening broadcast the night before Pearl Harbor I was commenting on the war of nerves between the United States and Japan. Regarding Japan's latest note and the question it raised, "Why did Britain and the United States continue to disturb the peace of the Far East?" I said that night, "That question was seriously asked today by General Suzuke, president of the planning board of Japan's war cabinet. He said, 'We Japanese are tensely watching whether Mr. Roosevelt and Mr. Churchill commit the epochal crime of further extending the world upheaval. Japan's patience would no longer be necessary in the event the countries hostile to peace in East Asia—countries whose identities are not absolutely clear—attempt to continue to increase disturbances in the Far East.'

"The doughty Japanese general said this to the East Asia Economic Council. Thereupon the Council obligingly issued a declaration in which it is said that regardless of how intensely hostile powers attempt to interfere, Japan will go ahead with the creation of a new order in East Asia." My broadcast continued:

"Various steps were taken in the Far East today to assert the new order whenever Japan's military leaders think the time has come to launch more disorder. At Singapore, British sailors have been recalled to their ships. In the Philippines the Cabinet took a number of emergency measures. NBC's Manila correspondent has just told us that ten fully-equipped divisions are ready for action. The United States has contined the dispatch of reinforcement to the Far East. Japan reports that the Russians are massing more troops on the border of Manchukuo which should help discourage Japan from getting the ABCD powers [American, British, Chinese, Dutch] on her back in the South Pacific.

"The United States Government is in a

difficult diplomatic position toward Japan. We know that her present army government is planning a new invasion from Indo-China. We know that this invasion, if unresisted, will soon reach the point where it threatens the safety of the Philippines and the security of American trade routes in the South Pacific over which we secure essential defense materials. Reports reaching officials here indicated a total of 125,000 Japanese troops were concentrated in Indo-China and that two large and heavily escorted Japanese convoys were steaming toward the Gulf of Siam.

"If we were a totalitarian government we would long ago have issued orders for a sudden surprise attack on Japan. Our navy would cut communications between Japan and her forces in Indo-China. Our air force would send a fleet of bombers to destroy Japan's industrial cities. At the same time, China would launch a vigorous offensive into Indo-China, while the Dutch and British fleets would join ours in sweeping up Japan's merchant marine. With that kind of a start it might not take long to finish the war. It was a surprise attack on the Russian fleet before war was declared that gave Japan a good start in 1904. But we are a democratic power which waits to be attacked. Which means that we must leave to Japan the great advantage of choosing her own time.

"Our State Department even refuses to admit that we have any understanding with our friends in the Far East. Australia announced today that eleventh-hour consultations had brought agreement on Pacific defense strategy in the event of Japanese aggression and that a joint declaration had been prepared. But the State Department insists it does not know of any joint declaration. Perhaps it is a memorandum and not a declaration. Anyhow, this administration is nobody's fool when it comes to naval matters and the first four letters of the alphabet will swing into action with one accord if, as, and when. But Japan must strike first."

And Japan did. Only a few hours later Japanese bombers were on their way to the unsuspecting Pearl Harbor naval base where the most elementary precautions against imminent attack had not been taken. Warnings were ignored, precautionary fleet dispersal was neglected, surprise was complete. Rarely in the history of warfare have so few accomplished so much damage against so many. No matter how you look at it or whom you blame it is one of the saddest chapters in American military history.

It happened that my regularly scheduled Sunday-afternoon broadcast began a few minutes after the first flash announcement of the Pearl Harbor attack. As a result thousands of radio listeners remember me as the man who first gave them the unhappy news that the United States was again at war.

41.

Broadcasting from Guadalcanal

The first step on the long, hard road to Tokyo was taken on August 7, 1942, when the United States Marines landed at Guadalcanal in the Solomon Islands. They seized the Japanese airfield and renamed it Henderson Field. The dramatic landing and the hard battles that followed when the Japanese sought to expel us from the island were a high point in the South Pacific campaign. Guadalcanal was

145

H. V. Kaltenborn broadcast from Guadacanal in 1943 before moving to Bougainville.

the key island in the Solomons group and the steppingstone for the drive to the north. The struggle for the island developed into a struggle for reinforcements. Our Marines held only a few square miles around the airfield. The Japanese held the rest of the island, lived in caves, and fought to the death. Repeatedly they attempted to land substantial reinforcements, but our final impressive victory in the naval battles around Guadalcanal put an end

to their efforts. After a six months' fight under what were for white men the almost intolerable conditions of jungle warfare, we finally forced the Japanese to evacuate Guadalcanal in February 1943.

In late November of that year it was my good fortune to be the first American correspondent to secure navy credentials for a flying round-trip visit to the South Pacific theater of war. Until then only permanently

Guadalcanal marked the beginning of the road back—1942.

attached war correspondents had been accredited. Through the cooperation of the Army Signal Corps I was able to make the first, and I believe the only, wartime network broadcast from Guadalcanal itself. Such radio "firsts" usually appear far more important to the radio fraternity than they do to the public. David Sarnoff's son was the Signal Corps operator who supervised the mechanical arrangements. With an inherited flare for the value of advertising he had painted a sign "Radio City Studios" which was hung in front of the tent housing the transmitter. The army censor wanted to know what I intended to say to the folks at home and this is what I wrote out:

"The first thing you realize about Guadalcanal is that it is no longer a combat area. It has become what is called a forward base. Just before leaving San Francisco I saw a film called *Guadalcanal Diary*. But this island is nothing like that any more. Yesterday I saw men pitching horseshoes, playing volley ball and badminton in well-built sanitary military camps. Henderson Field is now only one of a series. There is a network of air bases and 10,000-ton ships can dock at well-constructed piers. Many thousands of Seabees, engineers, infantrymen, and native labor battalions have created hundreds of miles of roads and a score of well-developed camp areas. . . . Eight months' work by American Army and Navy units can accomplish miracles in a small area. The thing to remember is that neither we, nor the Japanese, spread ourselves over the Solomons we control. We occupy a small area of beachland close to a harbor where it is possible to build an airfield. The rest of the island needs only to be watched. As I flew over the South Pacific from island to island, I gained a new conception of the meaning of modern war. Barren coral islands have been transformed into airfields, seaplane bases, and ship stations. Coral reefs have become runways. When we launch an operation down here it is so fully prepared that it is bound to succeed. We have already taught the Japs

INTERNATIONAL NEWS PHOTOS

Tarawa. The bloodiest, the costliest, the most heroic of Marine conquests in the Pacific.

U.S. Marines raise the American flag on Iwo Jima's bloody Mount Surabachi.

that once we set foot on any island they might as well get out, for they cannot hold it. . . . I have been promised permission to join our men at Empress Augusta Bay on Bougainville Island so that I may report to you on how they are faring. If war conditions permit, I will soon be back at this Guadalcanal microphone.

"I have spent the past two days with our troops on the front lines at Bougainville. I am the first radio reporter who was privileged to visit the beachhead we have established at Empress Augusta Bay. I can tell you definitely that while we control only some thirty square miles of our most northern outpost in the Solomons, we will never lose it. For we control the air over it and the sea around it and that is what counts in modern war. The Japanese can still bomb us there at night. And they do, nearly every night. They are all around us at Bougainville, but they will never surprise us. And very shortly we'll have another surprise for them. I saw the first airplanes that arrived on a fighter strip at Empress Augusta Bay.

"I watched that strip grow under my own eyes. A thousand workers were clearing away the jungle. Another thousand were using the

Bougainville, one of the Solomon Islands, provided another lesson in jungle warfare.

most modern machinery to build roads and taxiways. Hundreds more were driving bulldozers, scrapers, and rollers, evening out the large runways. And to top it off a hard working, nearly naked gang of Seabees were laying down the metal strips over which the Hell Divers and the Air Cobras will soon be rolling. I think this war in the Pacific is nine tenths the construction or destruction of airfields and only one tenth fighting. . . .

"The air trip from Guadalcanal to Bougainville is an experience. I made the first part of the trip as far as Munda in a four-engine bomber which the pilots on New Georgia fondly refer to as the beer truck. On one occasion it located a case of beer down in New Caledonia and actually delivered it at Munda.

"From New Georgia priority passengers for the combat area on Bougainville go by PYB —that's a battered old Catalina seaplane, workhorse of the South Pacific. She's a valiant old soul and carried a well-supplied machine gun to prove she can still fight. The Navy takes no chances. There are enemy concentrations on at least four points between Munda and Empress Augusta Bay . . . we have by-passed them, but all transport plane trips between Munda and our Bougainville beach-head require fighter cover. . . . I spent yesterday morning on the front lines at Bougainville learning how jungle positions are organized. I marveled at the skill with which our Army men and Marines have adapted themselves to jungle life. In a darkened tent within 300 yards of the front lines I sat with a hundred fighting men who were roaring with delight at a moving-picture comedy. Less than a quarter mile away I visited dugouts where keen-eyed machine gunners were on watch against surprise attack.

"Each day they kill or are killed. Yet alongside the beach guns they frolic in the surf or indulge in horseplay as though the enemy did not exist. The fighting American does not lose his sense of humor even when he faces death. . . . At night they let me board one of the famous high-speed PT boats that patrol the entrance to Augusta Bay to guard against surprise attack by sea. Imagine the beauty of a palm-fringed crescent shoreline, a moon-silvered sea, and in the background a golden glow from the cone of Bagana, the most dramatic volcano of the South Seas, dominating the center of Bougainville.

"It just does not seem possible that this can be war. The PT captain tells you that the flaming crater provides enemy pilots with a certain guide to our encampment. That moonlight always brings them. You notice three dark figures standing alongside three guns and straining through field glasses to see dark specks in the sky. The boat must stop instantly when they approach lest the white wake reveal our location. . . . An hour later they did come, but I was in a dugout on shore. When raids come every night they lose importance. We'll hold Empress Augusta . . . soon we'll move north again, ever closer to Tokyo."

But the home folks never heard these descriptive comments, and here's why. It had occurred to me that just after opening the broadcast I'd get a singing sergeant to voice a few bars of a then-popular song which expressed the fighting man's nostalgic feeling about home. So I called him in, he sang a few bars, and then I spoke my piece.

Soon after I finished, word reached us via San Francisco that New York had cut off the broadcast as soon as the sergeant began to sing. The music had not been cleared with the home office for copyright permission before it was put on the air. So there was no broadcast and this is the first publication of what was to have been a historic contribution to wartime radio.

42.

The Yalta Conference—1945

At the Yalta Conference, Russia certainly got the bacon. Many people are still vague about what actually took place at the secret meetings of February 1945, between Josef Stalin, Winston Churchill, and Franklin D. Roosevelt. Dead men tell no tales, and Roosevelt and Stalin are both gone. In his *Memoirs*, Churchill has told us much of the unhappy failures and disappointments of this Big Three session. Some of the Yalta Papers have been released by the State Department and we now know it was the important secret decisions between Stalin and Roosevelt that helped bring our troubles in the Far East. About the best that came out of Yalta was setting the place and date for the United Nations Conference in San Francisco. Even as our military and industrial might were winning the war, President Roosevelt's personal diplomatic intervention was losing the peace.

The ever-optimistic Roosevelt thought he could make a postwar friend out of Stalin by giving him everything he wanted as he had at the Teheran Conference in 1943. Stalin's biggest plum was Poland. According to James F. Byrnes, who was then War Mobilization Director, Roosevelt himself proposed the so-called solution of the Polish question and the formula by which it was to be accomplished. Eastern Poland went to Russia as Hitler and Stalin had agreed in 1939. Western Poland was put under the communist rule of the Soviet-created and Soviet-dominated Lublin Government. Poland was given part of German East Prussia.

150

The Polish Government in Exile in London, which the United States and Great Britain had recognized as the true government of Poland, called this Yalta agreement "the fifth partition of Poland." Stalin's almost complete victory on the Polish issue was the greatest tragedy of Yalta.

Stalin had to be appeased and paid, we are told, to make sure Russia would enter the war with Japan. In a series of secret agreements between Roosevelt and Stalin all the Soviet claims in the Far East were satisfied. Without China's being so much as consulted, communist Russia was brought into Manchuria, Port Arthur, Dairen, and North Korea. In addition she was given the Kurile Islands and southern Sakhalin which she had lost to Japan in 1904. Yet we positively know today, what some of our war leaders knew in 1945, that we had no need of Russia to help win the war.

Japan was beaten. General MacArthur had wired President Roosevelt outlining five separate unofficial Japanese requests for peace; Captain Zacharias, a navy expert on Japan, stated that Japan's readiness to surrender was known to the Navy before the Yalta Conference, and an Air Force general presented a report at Yalta which showed that Japan no longer had the capacity to resist. Japan had even asked Russia to mediate peace terms and Stalin had suppressed the request. But the ailing President Roosevelt was working only with his personally selected private advisers. He ignored the United States Senate as Wilson had ignored it at Versailles. Secretary of State Stettinius was urbane but lacked the stubborn honesty of Cordell Hull. When Harry Truman became president and James Byrnes secretary of state, they inherited the unrevealed Yalta decisions. Neither of them knew until months later what unhappy commitments had been made by the president who died so soon after making them.

In speaking of the secret agreement on the Far East, Churchill states in his book, "I must make it clear that though on behalf of Great Britain I joined in the agreement, neither I nor Eden took any part in making it. It was regarded as an American affair and was certainly of prime interest to their military operations. It was not for us to claim to shape it. Anyhow, we were not consulted but only asked to approve. This we did. In the United States there have been many reproaches about the concessions made to Soviet Russia. To us the problem was remote and secondary. It

The Big Three Picture at Yalta Finds a Place in the Archives

Prime Minister Winston Churchill, President Franklin D. Roosevelt and Premier Josef Stalin met at Yalta on the Crimean peninsula in 1945.

U.S. ARMY

would have been wrong for us to get in their way unless we had some very solid reason."

Just four days after the Yalta agreement was signed the results of this Crimean conference were debated on America's Town Meeting of the Air. William L. Shirer, Raymond Swing, Quincy Howe, and I were selected to discuss the decisions announced from Yalta. We all had the opportunity to state our opinions and discuss the issues with one another. After that we answered questions from the audience. Here are our summarizing observations as taken from the official recording published by Town Hall:

Shirer: "The decisions of the Crimean Conference are much wiser, much more farseeing, much more hopeful than we had any right to expect."

Raymond Swing: "Here is a convincing pledge that the Polish people themselves are to have free political expression. This is democratic vitality, not ruthless power politics."

Quincy Howe: "The Crimean Charter spells security for Russia, uncertainty for Britain, and warning for the United States. The United States has nothing to fear from a strong Russia. Quite the opposite, in fact."

My own comment was: "There will never be free elections in Poland or in Hungary or in Bulgaria before there have been free elections in the Soviet Union. . . . Secretary of State Byrnes tells us something significant about that magnificently phrased declaration on liberated Europe which thrilled all of us when we first read it. He says, 'President Roosevelt wrote it and Stalin and Churchill signed it.' I wish either Stalin or Churchill had written it and that Roosevelt had just signed it. I don't mean to be ironic, but I can't help remembering that at the end of the last war Clemenceau, the Tiger, said, 'Let me write the peace terms and Woodrow Wilson can have his League Covenant.' " At Yalta,

152

Roosevelt wrote the lofty phrases and Stalin took over the strategic places. Both Wilson and Roosevelt wanted peace but prepared the groundwork for future wars.

The unhappy results of the Yalta Conference were partly due to the fact that President Roosevelt was then a very sick man. This is borne out by Winston Churchill, who reports: "Upon arrival at the Crimea airfield, when the president was carried down the lift from the *Sacred Cow* he looked frail and ill." In another part he comments on the president "who seemed very tired" and after the conference was over "placid and frail."

Among the many critics of the Crimea Conference, William C. Bullitt, Roosevelt's one-time ambassador to Moscow, was among the most outspoken. He said bluntly: "No more unnecessary, disgraceful, and potentially disastrous document has ever been signed by a president of the United States." Bullitt also said that at Yalta Roosevelt was worn out and ill and found it difficult to formulate or express his thoughts, and adds, "Roosevelt was still determined to appease Stalin."

The Soviet intervention against Japan proved to be of no military benefit and was politically disastrous. During the Soviet occupation of Manchuria Russia looted $2,000,-000,000 worth of industrial equipment. Russia called the Chinese communist forces into Manchuria and turned huge stockpiles of Japanese armament over to the Reds. This was in direct violation of the treaty of friendship and alliance between Nationalist China and Russia which we forced Chiang Kai-shek to sign. Russia was pledged to give the Nationalists moral and military support. Instead, the Soviets gave both technical support and the tools of victory to the Chinese Reds. As a result one third of the world's population is now under communist control and the end is not in sight.

43.

Franklin D. Roosevelt Dies— Harry Truman Takes Over

The flash bulletin on my office teletype, announced by clattering bells, read: "Roosevelt dead." I ran down the corridor to the NBC newsroom studio and for hours stayed on the air reading bulletins and extemporizing comment on what this grave event would mean for us and all the war-torn world.

At one o'clock on April 12, 1945, President Franklin D. Roosevelt was sitting in front of the fireplace in his cottage at Warm Springs, Georgia. He was working on official papers while posing for Elizabeth Shumatoff, the portrait painter. Fifteen minutes later he fainted. About two and a half hours after that he died without regaining consciousness. At twelve minutes before six that evening the White House flashed the news to a shocked and stunned world. Less than two hours later Harry S. Truman had taken the oath of office in the Cabinet room in the White House and become the thirty-second president of the United States.

President Roosevelt was the seventh United States chief executive and the first Democrat to die in office, carrying on the happenstance that the man elected every twentieth year does so.

All news analysts, of course, did their best to interpret this grave event in the light of history. My first chance to recall historic parallels came in a broadcast scheduled for the morning of April 13. I pointed out that in the history of this country there has usually been a sharp contrast between presidents who died in office and their successors. "It would almost seem as though the natural law of action and reaction, of thesis and antithesis, dominated the presidential succession in the critical periods of our history. In my own lifetime I can recall the complete contrast in personality and point of view between the quiet self-effacing McKinley whose death brought to the White House the clamorous, assertive Theodore Roosevelt. That change came at the end of the Spanish-American War, which made America conscious of her world power at a time when we needed a strong president who could create a navy, a Panama Canal, and a belief in the concealed big stick that was to go with our soft speaking.

"Then came World War I and Woodrow Wilson. And when that was over Woodrow Wilson sacrificed his own life in a vain effort to persuade his people to underwrite the world role for America which he had accepted in Paris. This time the reaction was against further international adventure and the country voted for going back to normalcy with the inept Warren G. Harding. But normalcy did not return until the too-easy-going Harding had died in office to be succeeded by the ever-cautious Calvin Coolidge—another contrast in character and background.

"Now we are approaching the end of World War II. Once again the hand of death has been laid upon a great leader. And once again we face a great change and contrast. In many ways the man who is our president today is very different in competence and background from the man who yesterday passed to his well-earned peace.

"Franklin D. Roosevelt was born to the purple to be lord of the Hyde Park manor. All the advantages of wealth, the best in education that America affords—Groton and Harvard—important contacts, foreign travel and study, influential friends in high places, experience in high public office in state and nation

153

The caisson bearing the body of Franklin D. Roosevelt proceeds slowly along Constitution Avenue in Washington, D.C. as thousands mourn.

were all his. Harry S. Truman was born in a four-room cottage, a simple farmer's son. His public-school education ended with high school. With perseverance and sacrifice he managed to study law at night over a period of two years and prepare himself for practice. He earned his living at all kinds of little jobs, for his father was unable to pay for his education.

"During World War I, in which Franklin D. Roosevelt was Assistant Secretary of the Navy, Harry Truman had his first chance to display his talent and ability to get on with others. He became a captain of field artillery and led his battery through the Meuse-Argonne offensive. Franklin D. Roosevelt had a broad experience in government as state legislator, Assistant Secretary of the Navy, and

governor of New York before he became president. Harry Truman was elected directly to the Senate in 1934 and he has been vice-president for only a few weeks. But in 1922 President Truman was elected as one of three judges in Jackson County, Missouri. This gave him judicial experience and a respect for the law which will be apparent in the years to come. Just as Franklin D. Roosevelt was by instinct a passionate reformer, impatient of obstacles in securing needed change, Harry Truman, if we judge by his past, will be more eager to conserve the reforms of the past than to reach out for more innovations. His whole experience with money—of which he has never had much—and with friends of whom he has many should incline him to care and caution. Harry S. Truman promises that he

154

The nation wept.

On the day of the funeral at Hyde Park, Fala sits alone by the cornerstone of the Franklin D. Roosevelt Library.

will conserve what he has inherited from his great predecessor. Unless he changes much, he will not be inclined to sail uncharted seas."

It turned out that Harry Truman was more of an innovator than I had supposed. Once he had forgotten the "please-pray-for-me" humility with which he entered upon his high office he became cocky enough to fire General Mac-Arthur, to seize the steel mills when he had no authority to do so, to abuse a music critic who didn't like his daughter's singing, and to threaten to conscript striking railroad workers into the United States Army. Some of these things were done after he became president by popular mandate in 1948. But I cannot help wondering how different things might have been had Roosevelt outlived his fourth term.

Harry S. Truman takes the oath as President of the United States, April 12, 1945.

U.S. ARMY

The Normandy invasion. D-day, June 6, 1944, on Omaha Beach, American troops gained their first foothold on French soil.

44.

V-E Day and V-J Day in 1945

On the evening of Monday, May 7, 1945, I began my broadcast as follows: "In France they began a wild V-E celebration tonight. They are dancing in the streets of Paris and happy crowds jammed the boulevards. We began to celebrate V-E Day this morning. But since there can be no V-E Day until it is officially proclaimed, we found we were too early. Tomorrow will be the official Victory in Europe Day. At 9 A.M. Eastern War Time, President Truman and Prime Minister Churchill will make a simultaneous broadcast to the world."

At the same time I was making those statements on my NBC broadcast people all over the country were in a delirium of joy and celebrating with unrestrained jubilation. What difference did it make to them that the formal announcement had not been made? For them the war in Europe was over; Germany had surrendered.

The celebrations throughout the world were touched off that eventful Monday by an Associated Press correspondent's premature dispatch which broke an agreed release date. Edward Kennedy reported that Germany signed unconditional surrender terms in General Eisenhower's headquarters in a Reims schoolhouse at 2:41 that morning. The signers were General Eisenhower's Chief of Staff, General Walter Bedell Smith, for the Allies, and for the Germans, Colonel Gustav Jodl, Hitler's right-hand man on military affairs. At the signing Jodl asked to make a statement.

156

Paris was liberated in August 1944, though snipers remained to temper celebrations.

In April 1945, American reconnaissance troops linked up with units of the Russian Army on the Elbe River at Apollensdorf, Germany.

When the request was granted, he said only this: "With the signature of this document, the German people are delivered into Allied hands for better or worse."

There was a logical explanation for the confusion that surrounded the V-E Day announcement. At the time I explained it this way: "My guess is that the surrender of Germany took place exactly as reported from France by the chief of the Associated Press staff on the Western Front. The intention had been to make no formal announcement of the surrender until it could come simultaneously from Washington, London, and Moscow. But Kennedy got the information and by some miracle got it by the censors. Because it was accurate, it could not be denied. Because it was unofficial and unauthorized, it could not be confirmed. It was apparently impossible to get the Big Three governments to agree on an immediate V-E-Day proclamation. The British Government then apparently decided that the time had come to make some definite announcement and accordingly the British Information Service told the world that both Prime Minister Churchill and King George would speak tomorrow. Presumably the details of the German surrender will be announced by the Prime Minister and by the President of the United States at the same hour. In further confirmation of the fact that the war in Europe has officially come to an end, King George has sent a message to General Eisenhower asking him to convey a special message of congratulation to the British forces under his command. The fact that the war is considered over is emphasized in this message. King George says to the Allied Commander in Chief, 'To you was entrusted the task of annihilating the German armies. Under your wise leadership the Allied Expeditionary Forces have been brought to their goal of complete and crushing victory.'"

158

Not everybody was celebrating the V-E Day news. Fifty-four SHAEF correspondents immediately addressed a letter to General Eisenhower protesting the breaking of the agreed release date by the Associated Press and asserting they "have suffered the most disgraceful, deliberate, and unethical double-cross in the history of journalism." General Eisenhower then notified the AP executive director that Correspondent Kennedy was suspended because of "violation of SHAEF regulations and breach of confidence."

In announcing the German surrender and the official proclaiming of V-E Day on May 8, President Truman said, ". . . we must work to finish the war. Our victory is but half won. . . . When the last Japanese has surrendered unconditionally, then only will our fighting job be done." Prime Minister Churchill's statement was in his characteristic manner. ". . . we may now allow ourselves a brief period of rejoicing, but let us not forget for a moment the toils and efforts that lie ahead. Japan, with all her treachery and greed, remains unsubdued. The injuries she has inflicted against Great Britain, the United States, and other countries and her detestable cruelties call for justice and retribution. . . ."

The "justice and retribution" were not too long in coming. On the morning of Wednesday, August 29, 1945, the *Big Mo* steamed into Tokyo Bay under the command of Admiral William F. Halsey. At about the same time American airborne troops raised the American flag at Atsugi Airfield in Japan. Thus the stage was set for the formal surrender of Japan. The chief actors began arriving to play their parts. Admiral Chester W. Nimitz flew in from Guam. The next day General MacArthur established his headquarters in the new Grand Hotel in Yokohama. Upon arriving he said, "It has been a long, hard road. The surrender plan is going in accord-

German General Gustaf Jodl signs unconditional surrender terms in Reims, France.

General Douglas MacArthur signs the Japanese surrender document during formal ceremonies aboard the U.S.S. *Missouri* in Tokyo Bay, as Lieutenant General Jonathan Wainwright (*left*), hero of Bataan and Corregidor, looks on.

The most powerful force known to man—nuclear energy—was unleashed at Hiroshima and Nagasaki. It hastened the surrender of Japan.

AIR CORPS

ance with prearrangement. In all the outlying territories fighting has practically ceased and the enemy is preparing to capitulate."

Lieutenant General Jonathan M. Wainwright and British Lieutenant General Sir Archibald E. Percival also reached Yokohama. On his vessel in Tokyo Bay, Commander Harold E. Stassen, in charge of the evacuation of Allied prisoners, told newsmen that the stories told him by the released men indicated that they had lived under horrible conditions.

It was in a dramatic twenty-minute ceremony on the deck of the United States *Missouri* on Sunday, September 2, that the top Japanese political and military leaders signed the surrender terms. In contrast to the Japanese officials who wore uniforms and formal civilian attire and top hats, General Mac-

Arthur was casually dressed in army khaki trousers and shirt without a necktie. Right after the signing General MacArthur broadcast a brief speech in which he said: ". . . today the guns are silent. A great tragedy has ended. A great victory has been won. The skies no longer rain death—the seas bear only commerce—men everywhere walk upright in the sunlight. . . ."

Upon receipt of the word that the surrender papers had been signed—the news arrived in Washington on Saturday, September 1— President Truman proclaimed September 2 as V-J Day. This was the signal for the wild abandon that comes with victory celebrations. V-J Day brought to a climax the stirring events of the preceding weeks—the dropping of the first A-bomb on Hiroshima on August

160

The dimout and brownout were replaced by a flood of light in Times Square the night of May 8, 1945— V-E Day.

WIDE WORLD

6; Russia's declaration of war on defeated Japan two days later, and the A-bombing of Nagasaki on August 9, culminating in Japan's acceptance of the surrender terms five days later.

The day after V-J Day was Labor Day, and in my evening broadcast I said: "In a real sense, Labor Day this year is a peace day. It is the first full day of peace over large parts of Asia and the Pacific. Some Japanese surrenders preceded Labor Day; others are still to come. In China, where the war in the Far East began in 1937, formal peace will not be reestablished until later this week. It might not be a bad idea to settle on Labor Day of each year as the official peace day for World War II. Primarily, it was the workers who fought in the ranks and who did their part in the war plants who gave us peace. Peace Day might well coincide with Labor Day. . . .

"No previous Labor Day has ever seen this country or any other country at a higher pinnacle of power. For the second time in one generation this power has decided a world war. My one present doubt about my country is whether our people have developed a sense of world responsibility commensurate with our world power. It takes a long time for a nation to grow up to responsible world leadership . . . that is one more reason why, on this Labor Day, as we glory in the peace that is ours, we should pray for the long-range vision and the moral strength to face what is at once our stern task and our glorious opportunity." More than a decade later I can add truthfully and proudly: "We have not failed."

161

45.

Dramatic Ends of Hitler and Mussolini

Sic transit gloria—Hitler and Mussolini! They lived by the sword and they died by the sword. Such was the tenor of world thought in the spring of 1945. To those of us whose job it was to comment on the dramatic and momentous events in the final days of the European phase of World War II, the still unanswered question was: "What really happened to Hitler?"

On May 1 the Hamburg radio broadcast these two sentences: "It is announced that our Fuehrer Adolf Hitler fell for Germany this afternoon. He died at his post of commander in the Reich Chancellery fighting to his last breath against Bolshevism." Then followed the announcement by Grand Admiral Karl Doenitz, German Navy Chief and Hitler's associate, in which he proclaimed himself the new Fuehrer by Hitler's appointment.

With Germany collapsing and surrender inevitable, there was little reason to doubt that Hitler was dead. It was interesting to recall then that Adolf Hitler came into power at the same time as Franklin D. Roosevelt. Both men, together with Benito Mussolini, died at about the same time, one at the climax of victory, the other two at the climax of defeat.

I told my radio audience that I did not believe the Hamburg broadcast telling how Hitler died. "It is possible that Hitler was killed by a member of the Nazi party or by the Wehrmacht in preparation for surrender. We know that the Wehrmacht tried to kill him some months ago. The attempt failed and resulted in a purge. Many will not believe in

Hitler's death until they see his body. . . . Hitler may have died of Nazi-inflicted wounds. He may have been poisoned. He may have carried out his promise not to survive defeat and taken his own life. In any case he knew of his prospective death in time to provide for a successor whose only task is the liquidation of the Nazi regime. The Nazi party has already died or sent its remnants underground."

The Allied authorities expressed skepticism of the death announcement, stating that they would have to see the body before being convinced that it was not a Nazi trick. General Eisenhower wisely forestalled building up a legend about Hitler's death during the surrender negotiations. But in memory of Hitler, the Hamburg radio played music from Wagner's "The Twilight of the Gods" for half an hour before the official proclamation of Hitler's death by Admiral Doenitz himself that same afternoon.

Still the mystery remained. Where was the body? After Berlin fell to the Russians on May 2, they issued a bulletin which stated that Goebbels' deputy propaganda chief, Hans Fritzsche, made a deposition when captured in Berlin that Hitler and Goebbels committed suicide in the German capital. In Washington, President Truman said that he had received information from the best authority possible that Hitler was dead and that he personally believed it to be true.

But speculation continued. In June the Russians announced that a charred body they found in the ruined underground fortress beneath the chancellery was identified with "fair certainty" as that of Adolf Hitler by the teeth and other characteristics. They said that death had been due to poison.

It wasn't until November 1945 that the British echelon of the Allied Control Council in Berlin released a report based on all available evidence. This is the now generally accepted story of Hitler's death in all its drama. It created a world sensation and put an end to speculation. The report read, in part:

April 22. Hitler notified staff conference that war was lost and that he would remain in Berlin. Night of April 23–24. Hitler and Eva Braun married in small conference room in the Reich Chancellery bunker. A marriage feast was held in his suite. April 30. About 2:30 P.M. 200 liters of gasoline was ordered. About the same time Hitler and Eva Braun made their last appearance alive. They returned to their suites and Hitler shot himself while Eva Braun apparently took poison. Both bodies were then drenched with gasoline and burned outside the bunker until nothing was left.

A Counter-Intelligence unit of the United States Third Army found Hitler's "political testament" in a suitcase in the village of Tegernsee. It was made public on December 30, 1945, and in essence substantiated the British report.

The same day that brought us the news of Hitler's death also brought us the news that Benito Mussolini's body was buried in an unmarked grave in a potter's field near Milan. There was no mystery about Il Duce's death, no speculation whether he was dead or where his body was buried. Mussolini and his mistress, Clara Petacci, along with some of his followers, were caught on April 26, 1945. They were trying to escape from Como after they had been refused asylum in Switzerland. After a summary informal trial they were executed by Italian partisans near the little town of Dongo two days later. That night Mussolini's body and those executed with him were taken by van to Milan and dumped out into the Piazza Loretta where, the next day, crowds of angry Italians reviled the dead dictator and abused his body.

Later the bodies of Mussolini, of his mistress, Clara Petacci, and four others were strung up by their heels in front of a gasoline station where they hung several hours before being carted off to the morgue. I was in Rome

Adolf Hitler and his mistress, Eva Braun, relax in this candid study.

The bodies of Hitler and Eva Braun were cremated before this bunker in Berlin.

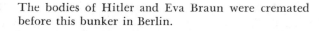

in March 1956, when Clara Petacci's family was permitted to conduct brief services over her disinterred body and consign it to a final resting place in a Rome cemetery.

Mussolini's death by execution marked the end of a dramatic quarter century for Italy. History makes the man as much as man makes history. But Mussolini, himself, more than most leaders, created the events of those unhappy years in which he strutted his hour upon the world stage.

It is difficult to be fair, even in death, to a man such as Mussolini, who was so much of a curse to his country and to all Europe. Yet, until he committed his aggression against Ethiopia and then sold out to Hitler, most Italians agree that he helped Italy. Apart from the suppression of free speech and the free press, the first fifteen years of Fascist administration set a new high for internal efficiency and accomplishment. As dictatorships go Mussolini's rule was relatively mild. Italy has retained a few aspects of Mussolini's corporate state because they provide an effective counterpart to socialism and communism.

Mussolini's assassination was a spontaneous expression of popular revenge. The fact that his mistress and leading associates died with him may well have been one of the more fortunate accidents of history. It satisfied the natural desire for revenge of those Italians who risked their lives to liberate their country. An order from the partisan prefect of Milan forbidding Mussolini's execution failed to arrive in time—he was to have received a more formal trial.

After summarizing the news of Mussolini's death I added, "If this dramatic mass execution helped satisfy the national popular Italian desire for revenge, if by this event Italy can avoid long-continued persecution of the many, many thousands whose chief crime under Fascism was that they obeyed its orders,

it may be of help to Italy and her long-suffering people. Thus, by the very fact of his inglorious death, Benito Mussolini may, in some slight measure, help atone for a national disaster for which he must bear the blame."

Benito Mussolini was an infinitely more attractive person than Adolf Hitler. I once interviewed both men in the same week and the contrast was impressed upon me. Mussolini was a cosmopolitan libertine, Hitler a provincial ascetic. For Mussolini, the extrovert, an interview was a welcome fencing match in which he was an expert. For Hitler, the introvert, it was unpleasant to meet anyone who disagreed with him and he compensated by delivering an oration to the interviewer. Mussolini lied brazenly with his tongue in his cheek. Hitler was foolish enough to believe his own lies. When Mussolini addressed the Roman crowd from the balcony of the Palazzo Venezia he was an actor. When Hitler spoke to a Nazi audience he became self-intoxicated. History played an ironic trick on mankind when it united two dictators so utterly diverse in a war of aggression that first destroyed Europe and then brought them both to a violent, unglorious end.

Vendetta. The mutilated bodies of Benito Mussolini and Claretta Petacci, his mistress, lie on a public square in Milan after being shot to death by Italian partisans.

U.S. ARMY

164

46.

United Nations Born as Polish Hopes Die

From April 25 to June 26, 1945, at a fifty-one-nation conference the United Nations was born. Those were eventful days in San Francisco. The United States and the Golden Gate city were hosts to representatives of the powers that had fought and won World War II. Many of the smaller countries that had remained neutral also participated. They were all assembled to form an international organization that would consolidate world peace.

Even as a veteran participant in international gatherings I felt it to be an impressive moment when the delegates gathered in the handsome San Francisco Opera House to stabilize the peace for which so much had been sacrificed for half a decade. After many weeks of discussion and some unfortunate but perhaps inevitable concessions to communist demands, President Truman addressed the closing conference and voiced his message of hope for permanent peace.

Behind the delegates were weeks of quarrels over procedure, diplomatic maneuvering in committees, and plenary sessions that revealed sharp differences. There were impressive speeches and much sincere effort to advance the cause of coexistence with communist states. Notable contributions to the success of the conference were made by such figures as Anthony Eden, Jan Smuts, Edward R. Stettinius, Joseph Paul-Boncour, Dr. V. K. Wellington Koo, Senator Arthur Vandenberg, and other western experts on foreign affairs.

Stalin, it must be remembered, was never

UNITED NATIONS

Secretary of State Stettinius signs the United Nations Charter for the United States while President Truman looks on.

enthusiastic about this conference. He even refused to send his foreign minister, Molotov, to San Francisco until after President Roosevelt's death and he was seeking favor with Roosevelt's successor. It was Molotov's successful demand for the big-power veto and his frequent insistence on consulting Moscow before making a decision that helped prolong the meeting.

It was on the sixty-third day of the parley that the climax was reached. The full conference finally approved the ten-thousand-word Charter. Then Viscount Halifax, the British Ambassador to the United States, who was presiding, declared the Charter unanimously adopted. The procession of signatories began with China's representative, Russia was second, and the United Kingdom third. The inviting powers were then followed by other countries in alphabetical order. The signing

165

Russia's Molotov, America's Stettinius, and England's Eden discuss a point in the United Nations Charter

ceremony went on for three hours. As host nation, the United States signed last, with President Truman looking on. After our delegation had signed the Charter, Secretary of State Stettinius in a brief speech emphasized the friendly spirit of a conference that had had many stormy sessions. The heads of the delegations formally expressed their appreciation to Secretary Stettinius for his work in "conducting the business of the conference."

In commenting on this final session, I told my radio listeners "If a formal pledge by fifty nations to maintain peace and security throughout the world means what it says, peace is assured. But whatever happens, the cause of world peace has been advanced."

What we witnessed at San Francisco during nine weeks in which the war in Europe was ending with a final orgy of destruction in Berlin, was a democratic meeting of the world's major and minor powers for a common purpose which was finally achieved. But as Secretary Stettinius rightly said as he signed the

166

document, it was not an end, but a beginning. The Charter was accepted, a new league for peace was born, and a war-weary world once again raised its head in hope.

At the signing ceremony many of us who had followed the League of Nations from birth to death could not help but think of Woodrow Wilson. It was his liberal ideas and his ideals for a world organization which were the spiritual parents of what was accomplished in San Francisco in 1945.

There were many significant high spots during the weeks I spent in San Francisco. One in particular stands out. The place was the ornate ballroom of the Hotel St. Francis. The occasion was one of the rare Russian news conferences. The speaker was V. M. Molotov, Soviet Secretary for Foreign Affairs, now displaced by a younger man. The question concerned Poland. At the very beginning of the conference word had come that the Russians had arrested the Polish non-communist leaders who had come out of hiding to work out a compromise Polish government with the Russians. Instead, they were imprisoned and the civilized world was outraged.

For obvious reasons Mr. Molotov did not like questions about Poland. Through his Russian interpreter he said, "It seems we can have no meeting without Polish questions. I will answer about Poland. The Polish question will be settled. We settled the Yugoslav question and we can settle the Polish question the same way. Does this answer your question?"

The press and radio correspondents laughed loudly and impolitely. It was our way of saying "No." We were much more interested in the immediate effect on the relations of the Big Three Powers of the arrest of sixteen Polish underground leaders than in the slow transformation of the Dumbarton Oaks agreement into a U.N. charter. We had expected

Mr. Molotov's press meeting—he was the last of the diplomats to grant one—to center on the Polish issue. We were disappointed at the Russian Foreign Secretary's refusal to deal with it in forthright fashion.

Yet we were grateful to Molotov for even exposing himself to the free press of the world. He was doing something that is rarely done in Russia. To be fair to Molotov he did answer some questions on world organization responsively and intelligently. Apart from the Polish issue some of his shrewd replies even won applause. There was no denying the high quality of the Molotov intellect. But each time I have met this old Bolshevik, who worked with Stalin for many more years than anyone now alive, I have been repelled by the man's ruthless indifference to any point of view but his own. If Stalin was a villain, so is Molotov. He supported Stalin's murderous decrees and helped execute them.

But returning to the Polish issue, it was Russia against the free world. It was the big country trespassing on the rights of the small country, just as the Nazi invasion of Poland had launched the world into war. The United Nations, ironically enough, were meeting at San Francisco to prevent something like that from happening again. And it was already happening!

The underlying cleavage between Russia and the West had even then become apparent. Winston Churchill had the Polish issue in mind when he said: "On the Continent of Europe we have yet to make sure that the words 'freedom,' 'democracy,' and 'liberation' are not distorted from their true meaning as we have understood them. There would be little use in punishing the Hitlerites for their crimes if law and justice did not rule and if totalitarian or police governments were to take the place of the German invaders."

Few of our administration leaders saw the situation as clearly. Averell Harriman, then our ambassador to the Soviet Union, came to San Francisco from Moscow to warn the Western delegations that Stalin was not a true ally. He cited the Kremlin's unwillingness to trust us or to work with us during the war years. He urged against further concessions to the Kremlin a whole year before his warnings were finally heeded. We deceived ourselves about Kremlin policies while the war was on and after it was over. At San Francisco we began to open our eyes to the truth and two years later we realized that the Soviet Union was our great potential enemy. As for the United Nations Charter, the Soviet Union has always regarded that document as a scrap of paper to be used or ignored.

No Time To Be Pernickety

47.

Nuremberg Trials and Executions

The great ten months' trial in Nuremberg ended in 1946. The world awaited the expected verdict from the four-nation court which included communist Russia's representatives. Twelve of the twenty-one Nazi defendants in this effort of the victors to apply formal courtroom procedure to the vanquished were sentenced to death by hanging; seven were given prison terms, and three were acquitted.

Thus ended a long, bloody road for the leading Nazi leaders. Their rise to absolute power had begun on the fateful day in January 1933 when Franz von Papen—ironically one of the men who was acquitted—induced the failing Von Hindenburg to appoint Adolf Hitler Reich Chancellor of Germany.

As retribution, this trial was not and never could have been a success. The sentencing to the gallows of Goering, the brutal corruptionist; of the adventurer Von Ribbentrop; of the murderer Kaltenbrunner; of Streicher, the Jew baiter; of Hans Frank who fired the German ovens in Poland—the execution of these men could never redeem the past. Real retribution for such crimes was not possible, and the balance of the past could be redressed only at the slow pace at which the curative powers of nature might operate.

The significant thing about the trials was that they sought to establish a new principle of international law, that aggressive war is the supreme crime. In an atomic age, as the American proposals to the United Nations show, there is a great need to place some limits on national sovereignty. In seeking to establish the new principle that making war is a crime against humanity and in imposing punishment for conspiracy to commit this crime, the four-power court abandoned a centuries-old principle. In the past it has always been held that legal punishment could not be meted out for acts committed under the guise of sovereign power. The men who were sentenced were being punished for just such acts.

A reason for Nuremberg: rows of bodies of dead inmates fill the yard of a Gestapo concentration camp near Nordhausen.

U.S. ARMY

Eight of the defendants at the great war-crimes trial in Nuremberg where for the first time individuals were held responsible for a nation's aggressive warfare. In box, *left to right,* first row: Goering, Hess, Von Ribbentrop, Keitel; second row: Doenitz, Raeder, Von Schirach, Sauckel.

The fact that in at least one instance this new international principle has been proclaimed as the law of the United Nations may —at least that is our hope—serve as a deterrent to those who might consider committing the crime of aggressive war in the future. But in the same way that there is disagreement as to whether capital punishment prevents crime there is a wide difference of opinion on the long-range effect of the Nuremberg trials.

Many believe that a speedy military court martial might have been more discriminating while satisfying the natural popular desire for vengeance on the Nazi leaders. Military men are particularly concerned that no general or admiral who happens to be on the losing side in a war should be held guilty of a crime because he was true to his oath of obedience to higher authority.

Sentence at Nuremberg was executed on

U.S. ARMY

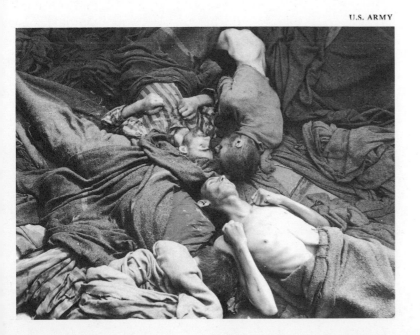

A reason for Nuremberg: starved bodies of Germans found dead in a freight car en route to Dachau.

October 16, 1946, when ten of those sentenced to death paid for their crimes on the gallows in the Nuremberg prison gymnasium. The executions were over in a matter of two hours, with only two of the three gallows erected in the gymnasium being used by Master Sergeant John C. Woods, of San Antonio, Texas, the hangman. The ten who had to mount thirteen steps to meet their doom were given the opportunity to make final statements before the noose was placed around their necks. After the executions were over, the bodies were cremated and "the ashes secretly dispersed" to prevent the remains from becoming a national shrine.

The dramatic climax of the Nuremberg trials was the fact that two hours before he was to have headed the death march, Hermann Wilhelm Goering, the boastful and ruthless Number 2 Nazi and commander of the Luftwaffe, committed suicide in his cell by taking potassium cyanide. How Goering obtained the glass cartridge containing the poison and how he managed to keep it and escape detection during the systematic daily search of his cell remain a mystery. The cyanide was contained in a small cartridge case similar to those found on other Nazis and like

Sequel to Nuremberg: Hermann Goering cheated the hangman with potassium cyanide.

U.S. ARMY

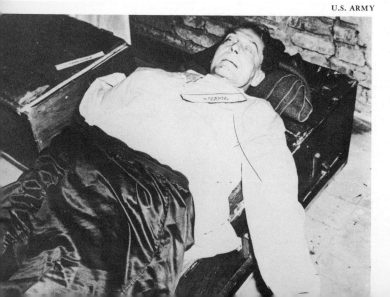

the one found on Goering when he was in Mondorf prison—he had that one hidden in a can of Nescafé.

Supreme Court Justice Jackson, chief prosecutor at the Nuremberg trials, had an optimistic interpretation of Goering's unexpected suicide. At the time, he said, the real significance of Goering's self-inflicted death lies in its effect on the German people. He believed that Goering was the only one of the Nuremberg defendants on whom a martyr myth might have been founded. Justice Jackson believed that Goering's suicide made it impossible to create such a myth. He said, "The gallows offered Goering the most effective platform from which to impress his sympathizers with the depth of his convictions and his selflessness for the cause. When he took his own life, he killed the myth of Nazi bravery and deep conviction." It was known that Goering repeatedly told his prison mates in the Nuremberg jail that the German people would some day dig up his bones and enshrine them in a marble mausoleum.

The judges in this first international war-crimes trial were Lord Chief Justice Sir Geoffrey Lawrence of Britain, presiding; Henri Donnedieu de Vabre, of France; Francis Biddle, of the United States, and General Iola T. Nikichenko, of Russia. Although one of the purposes for which the Allies went to war had been accomplished—punishing the Nazi ringleaders—there was mixed reaction all around the world. Legal minds in this country were especially outspoken, particularly in senatorial circles. Senators Vandenberg and Taft both condemned the results of the trials. Taft called them "an outrage against justice." In the legal sense, the late Ohio senator was probably right. But in the larger human sense much can be said in favor of punishing men who are responsible for so much bloodshed, cruelty, and corruption.

48.

Mahatma Gandhi
and Indian Independence

"One of the world's great leaders is dead. A fanatical assassin's bullet ended the selfless career of the man who did more than any other to bring political freedom to 400,000,000 Indians." Those were the opening words of my broadcast on January 30, 1948, just after the world was shocked by the news of Gandhi's violent death.

Gandhi was shot while walking with his grandnieces through the garden of Birla House in New Delhi to a place where he conducted a daily prayer meeting. A man, identified as Narayan Vinayak Gadse, editor of a newspaper in Poona, stepped in front of Gandhi, drew his attention by saluting in a gesture of prayer, and then fired three bullets into his body. He was dead within a half-hour.

Mohandas Karamchand Gandhi died a martyr to the cause for which he lived. Because he preached peace he was killed by a misguided fellow Hindu who believed in force. The man who lived for nonviolence died by violence. It was ironic that the champion of a free, united India and communal peace was killed less than two weeks after he had won an apparent triumph in the bloody strife between Hindus, Moslems, and Sikhs. He had ended the last of his many fasts only when the leaders of the three faiths pledged themselves to a seven-point guaranty of communal peace.

With a million people looking on, Gandhi's body was borne to the bank of the sacred Jumna River in Delhi for a traditional Hindu cremation ceremony. Two weeks later his

TRIANGLE

Mohandas Gandhi.

ashes were consigned to the Ganges in a ceremony in Allahabad attended by his close friend Prime Minister Jawaharlal Nehru.

One of the highlights of my world tour in 1947 was a visit with the seventy-eight-year old Mahatma. I had to choose between seeing Lord Mountbatten and the Indian leader Nehru in New Delhi or hurry to Calcutta to see Gandhi. I chose to see Gandhi and was one of the last American reporters to talk with him. He was then in Calcutta to restore peace between the Moslems and Hindus. In Calcutta each day, for more than a year, they had witnessed fratricidal murder. The moment Gandhi arrived there was peace.

When I saw him the villa which he occupied in the Moslem area of Calcutta was surrounded by a huge crowd of fanatical followers—Moslems mingled freely in the crowd. They were all shouting for Gandhi to make

171

an appearance. Weakened by his recent fast, Gandhi was lying on a mat covered with white cloth in one of the bare rooms of the old villa. He was surrounded by his secretaries and a few intimates. His granddaughter, who looked after his personal wants, was applying hot wet cloths to his fragile body. To look at him was to marvel that from this frail bit of humanity there could radiate a spiritual force that encompassed the world.

His head was bald. He had so few teeth I wondered at his perfect enunciation. His English was distinguished, yet he seemed the living embodiment of famine and poverty. It was hard to believe that this wizened, almost helpless human being was radiating greater personal influence than any other living man, that this was the man who had changed the face of India's destiny.

The room in which we were was ugly and bare. As we sat down on the floor near Gandhi, so we could hear his weak voice, the noise of the milling crowd outside rose to a deafening roar. We began our talk but the clamor increased to such an extent that slowly but painfully Gandhi was assisted to the window to show himself to the crowds. "Be at peace," he said in a weak voice. "Please be quiet and let me rest. Go to your homes and let each

Waders and boaters head toward the confluence of the Ganges and Jumna rivers to bathe in the sacred waters following the immersion of the ashes of Mohandas Gandhi. These were among the millions of mourners who saw the ashes of the assassinated leader carried from the railroad station for committal to the waters.

WIDE WORLD

one of you work for Hindu-Moslem unity. Let that be your prayer as it is mine."

Those nearest the window understood. The rest of the crowd renewed their clamor. Gandhi had told me that he had not wanted the division of India as it had been done. It was not the free, united India for which he struggled, for the division of India created too many problems. "Tell your fellow Americans," he said, "that our work is not done. We must have not only a free India, but a united, peaceful India."

When the news of Gandhi's assassination came, I could almost hear the cry of anguish that went up from the crowd when one of Gandhi's secretaries told them that their beloved Mahatma was dead. Gandhi was a strange mixture of spirituality and shrewdness in his unselfish personal and political leadership. If he had not had political genius as well as spiritual insight, he could never have become the great leader of his people. A British civil servant once told me that while most people thought of Gandhi as a saint who acted like a politician, he was really a politician who acted like a saint. My own feeling is that a man willing to sacrifice life itself to a great cause must be endowed with saintly qualities. He was, indeed, India's great soul as well as her great emancipator.

Politician or saint, Gandhi had within himself the qualities of true greatness and of true moral grandeur. Few men combined so much mind with so much heart. No man better deserved to have the blue-and-white flag of the United Nations lowered to half-mast in his honor. Even the great Christian martyrs would have moved aside to give him place. A great man died when those bullets killed Gandhi. India has good reason to cherish his memory. May his devoted followers continue to translate his spirit into the difficult task of governing a divided India.

UNITED NATIONS

WIDE WORLD

Israel joins the family of nations as its white and blue flag is unfurled at U.N. headquarters.

Prime Minister David Ben-Gurion signs the document in Tel-Aviv proclaiming the new Jewish state of Israel as Foreign Minister Moshe Sharett (*right*) looks on.

49.

The Birth of Israel

It was at midnight May 14, 1948, that the new Jewish state of Israel came into existence. Just eleven minutes later (it was 6:11 P.M. Eastern Daylight Time here) President Truman astounded the United Nations General Assembly and the world by recognizing the Jewish Republic. The United States thus became the first nation to acknowledge the existence of the new state as a legal national entity.

It was also just eleven minutes past midnight after the British mandate of Palestine ended that King Abdullah, of Trans-Jordan, signaled invasion of Palestine by five of the Arab League states. A few hours later the Egyptians began to bomb Tel Aviv, Israel's capital.

Such was the troubled birth of the first Jewish state in the Holy Land since the year A.D. 70 when Nero's Roman armies destroyed Jerusalem. The new state of Israel came into existence just as the United Nations General Assembly was in a special session to cope with the Arab-Jewish strife over the partition of Palestine. Since then, in and out of the United Nations, Palestine has been and still is the sore trouble spot of the Near East. Blood is still being shed in spite of continuing truce efforts.

On that highly dramatic occasion of Israel's birth, when the news tickers were working overtime to keep us informed, my evening broadcast was devoted to this historic event. I said: "Tonight the armies of five Arab nations are crossing the Palestine frontiers. Thirty thousand Arab soldiers are on the march. Egypt, Iraq, and Syria have declared martial law. Lebanon has proclaimed a state of emergency. Egypt has formally announced the entry of her army into Palestine. Troops

173

of the new Jewish army are said to be in control of the heart of Jerusalem. Arabs still control portions of the vital Tel Aviv road and heavy fighting continues. The Jews are said to have captured Acre. This is the northern seaport earmarked for the Arabs under the United Nations partition plan. . . . General Sir Alan Cunningham, British High Commissioner, turned his back on Palestine as he boarded ship at Haifa this morning, thus ending thirty years of British rule. Almost overnight Jewish hostility to Britain seems to have disappeared.

"Earlier today, in the three-story Tel Aviv museum in Palestine, Jewish Prime Minister David Ben-Gurion proclaimed the new state of Israel. An audience of 400 men and women wept in happiness. Tonight, in a surprise move that once again reverses our Palestine policy, President Truman recognized the new Jewish state.

"There will be immediate pressure that we allow the dispatch of arms and volunteers to permit the new state to defend itself against Arab attack, but this is a matter on which Congress will want to be consulted. Action on such an explosive issue is unlikely before adjournment. While our de-facto recognition says nothing about the boundaries of the new state, it must be assumed that they are those decreed by the United Nations Assembly, when it voted for partition. Great Britain is almost certain to follow our prompt action in recognizing the new Jewish state within a few hours.

"The Soviet Union will be disappointed. Russia expected to be the first great power to set up diplomatic relations with the new state. . . . For strife-torn Palestine this is an historic day. The mandate which the League of Nations granted to Great Britain has come to an inglorious end. Formal war between the newly proclaimed state and the surrounding Arab states has begun. This day also marks a series of unhappy and unnecessary defeats: A defeat for Britain because her mandate for Palestine ended in failure; a defeat for the United States because our prestige has been lowered by our shifting opportunist Palestine policy; a defeat for the United Nations because months of futile palaver have now ended in frustration. If any one nation has gained, it is the Soviet Union. By immediately recognizing the new Jewish state, it will seek both to gain favor with Zionists all over the world and to have the excuse to send its spies and saboteurs to go with its envoys to utilize this key position."

For more than thirty years I have made repeated visits to the ancient and troubled land of Palestine and the new state of Israel. I have talked with most of the Arab and Jewish leaders, including the Grand Mufti of Jerusalem and Chaim Weizmann, the father of Israel.

It is one of the great tragedies of our time

The old and the new, Israeli armored cars in the streets of biblical Beersheba after a smashing Israeli victory over the Egyptians—1948.

that disagreement between Jew and Arab continues. That great and generous spirit, Chaim Weizmann, who won from Lord Balfour the promise of a Jewish homeland, said to me in the twenties: "Arab and Jew can and must learn to live together."

But many difficulties, internal and external, have continued to surround the emergence of Israel. Only four months after the world's newest nation came into being Count Folke Bernadotte, who had been appointed by the United Nations as mediator in the Palestine dispute, was assassinated by Jewish fanatics. The rule of violence and the campaign of terror are still the order of the day.

Each time I return to Palestine I am more impressed with what the people of Israel have accomplished. In democratic methods of government, in the development of industry, in the application of science to agriculture, in the building of modern cities they have set new standards in the Near East. They are free to admit that they could not have done this without American help and that this help must continue for some time if they are to escape bankruptcy.

It would be much easier for them to meet current problems if they closed the doors to new immigrants while they absorb and integrate the hundreds of thousands of penniless Jews who have been welcomed during the past decade. But it is part of the Zionist creed that every Jew must be allowed to enter the Jewish homeland. They continue to pour in not only from the ghettos of Europe but from Asia and Africa. The humane and skillful way in which they are established and integrated into the economy from the day they land can teach the world a lesson on how to deal with immigrants.

In the Jewish-Arab controversy there have been grievous faults on both sides. The Arabs began it with their ill-fated military invasion of the new state. The Jews continued it by their refusal to cooperate in dealing with 800,000 hapless Arabs who were driven from or fled from their Palestine homes during the war. Britain and the United States found it difficult to agree on Palestine policy. Britain, because of her unhappy experience with Jewish terror during the period of the mandate, was inclined to lean toward the Arabs; the United States, because of the powerful political influence exerted by the Zionist partisans in this country, inclined toward the Jews.

Today the complete reliance of the NATO powers on Arabian oil has pushed us toward a more complete neutrality with heavy pressure calling for the delivery of more arms to Israel. As always when the Big Powers are at odds, the United Nations has been unable to enforce its rulings on Israeli boundaries in Jerusalem or elsewhere. Thus Jew and Arab go on wasting their substance on arms and their quarrel continues to imperil world peace.

Jerusalem itself—nonviolent—yet the heart of Arab-Jewish differences.

50.

Pope Pius XII

Pope Pius XII is aptly called the Pontiff of Peace. For years before he became Pope he devoted himself to the cause of peace in Europe and he continues to devote his energies to world peace. He could also be called the "Diplomatic Pope" or even the "Fighting Pope" because of the vigorous battle he continues to wage against communism.

He had been Papal Secretary of State before becoming Pope, and had also been what governments call an ambassador. He had a period of service as Papal Nuncio to Munich when, as Cardinal Pacelli, he was a firsthand witness of Hitler's methods and experienced Hitler's rise to power.

It was a fortuitous accident that the man who has always had such a deep feeling for the masses and who has worked so hard for peace should have been elevated to his eminent post just as World War II was made inevitable by the occupation of Czechoslovakia and Hitler's new demands on Poland. For it was on the afternoon of March 2, 1939, that a tiny wisp of white smoke emerged from the chimney of the Sistine Chapel to signify the election of a new Pope. The Cardinal Deacon, stepping to the balcony of St. Peter's, made the traditional proclamation to the throng below: "I bring you tidings of great joy. We have a new Pope." At the age of sixty-three Cardinal Pacelli became Pope Pius XII. Six months later Europe was at war.

During the talk I had with the Pope in November 1944, when I was in Europe doing broadcasts from various war fronts including Italy, he showed how keenly he was alive to the suffering of the people in war. He had ample opportunity to know about it at firsthand. When Rome was bombed during the Allied advance from southern Italy, he went into the streets and prayed with the people.

When I spoke of the importance of the Vatican's influence in maintaining the spirit of peace among the peoples of the world in wartime and suggested that the organization of world peace deserved frequent emphasis by the Vatican, he said, "You know I do speak frequently. Do you mean it could be helpful if I spoke even more often than I do?"

After my affirmative reply he again emphasized his firm belief that the problems engendered by hate and national antagonism could be softened and removed by the exercise of Christian charity. As to peace, he expressed his belief that mere diplomatic arrangements were not enough. Throughout our talk the Pope revealed himself not only as a great spiritual leader but a supreme diplomat with a practical appreciation of how to fight for his ideas.

At this time he was devoting many hours a day to public and private audiences, making a special effort to have some slight personal contact with every one of the many thousands of Allied soldiers who passed through Rome on their way to and from the fighting front. I witnessed several of these mass audiences and was much impressed with the patience and true human kindness he displayed. He mingled with those soldiers near the front of the chapel where he received them, blessed their rosaries, and smiled at them with what must have been real affection.

In talking with me the Pope spoke much more freely than one might expect. There was no reservation which I could detect but complete frankness. He revealed himself as a true cosmopolitan in mind and spirit. Pope Pius probably is more modern in some ways

Pope Pius XII.

than any of his predecessors. He has used the radio and television effectively and has traveled by airplane. He told me it was in the United States that he learned to enjoy flying, particularly when he found he could work en route.

When I first spoke with him our talk was in English, but since his German is much better than his English, we carried on our later conversations in German. His tall, lithe form is that of an athlete. His steps are quick and firm and his gestures graceful. When animated, his face presents a curious contrast of human kindliness and intellectual asceticism. When I saw him again in 1956, for what may have been the last time, it was to note with surprise how little age or his recent illness seemed to hamper him in mind or body.

This Pontiff of Peace has now become a militant leader against communism. I saw him in 1948 shortly after the defeat of the Communists in the Italian elections. It was obvious he had become a warrior against communism. Giuseppe de Vittorio, the leader of the communist trade unions, told me the election defeat of his party was due to two things. He said: "The result was a victory for the Marshall Plan and the Catholic Church." When I congratulated Pope Pius on the election results, he discounted their importance. "This was only a skirmish," he said. "We are far from having won a final victory. The struggle against communism has only begun and must be continued. Let us not underestimate communism. It is a patient and determined enemy. It would be a grave mistake to relax our vigilance."

To my question as to how the Catholic Church justified its entry into Italian politics he replied that the Church had not entered politics as such. Raising himself to his full height, he declared with great earnestness: "It is the mission of the Church to serve as the defender of the Faith. What we have done here in Italy is to defend the Faith against the destructive forces of communism."

His gestures, as he spoke these words, were those of a warrior. He was almost militant in manner. He raised his arms, doubled his fists, and flung them outward to emphasize the battle against communism. Then he said: "In the face of militant communism there can be no weakness, no appeasement—firmness is essential."

There was something comforting in the thought that this great spiritual leader was human enough to realize that more than prayer was necessary in the war against this dedicated enemy of the Christian faith. It was in this same spirit of holy anger that Christ chased the money-changers out of the temple. While Pope Pius XII lives his will be the most powerful voice against the evils of atheistic communism.

177

UNITED PRESS

"Taint the way I heerd it."

51.

The 1948 Election—
Everyone Was Wrong but Harry

On election night in 1948 I told the whole United States over the NBC network that President Truman didn't seem to be getting a majority of the popular vote (he didn't) and despite the early favorable returns would probably lose the election (he didn't). I lost—face.

My first contribution to the election of an American president was made in 1888 and that, too, was unsuccessful. At the time I was ten years old and an ardent Democrat. My father was a Democrat and that was enough to make me an enthusiastic supporter of Grover Cleveland for a second term. We boys didn't campaign on the issues because we didn't know enough about them. We just cam-

paigned. Whenever I could rally a few young Democrats in my block on Milwaukee's East Side, we would go stamping along the Jackson Street rattly wooden sidewalks of that day chanting at the top of our voices: "Four-four-four years more—Four-four-four years more." The louder the better. Those youngsters whose fathers were Republicans promptly marshaled their rival forces on the opposite side of the street for a chant which went like this: "Grover, Grover, Grover's term is over." When we got tired of chanting, which was none too soon for the neighbors, we'd forget partisanship and join in a game of prisoner's base. Looking back, I still think that those political chants were as good an argument as some people were subjected to in the 1948 Truman-Dewey campaign.

What I couldn't understand in 1888 was how Cleveland could get the most votes, as he did, and still lose the election. Just sixty years later I learned, to my sorrow, that Harry Truman could get less than half the popular vote and still win. Way back in 1888 I made up my mind that the electoral college system which defeated Cleveland was a bad system. I still hold the same opinion. If we must keep the outmoded electoral college, let us at least split the electoral votes in each state in proportion to the split in the popular vote. Thanks to our present outmoded electoral college system, we have already had thirteen minority presidents.

How wrong can you be in predicting the result of an election? It is still amazing to think how wrong everybody was in regard to 1948. That is, everybody but Harry Truman himself and a very few loyal Democrats. Shortly before the election, after Truman returned to Washington at the end of his barnstorming tour, public opinion, according to press and radio, was against him. Fifty of the nation's top political writers predicted unanimously that Dewey would win. Said Arthur Krock in the New York *Times,* "If the public opinion polls are correct, and they were never more unanimous or certain of their findings, President Truman is launched on a speaking campaign to persuade a majority of the American voters to change their minds toward him before November 2. . . . If expert political managers are right in their general belief that a majority opinion of this kind does not shift after early September . . . then Mr. Truman has no chance to achieve the great objective of his grueling journey."

This was the situation the day before the election. A betting commissioner called Dewey a 15 to 1 favorite; the Gallup Poll gave Dewey 49.5 per cent and Truman 44.5 per cent of the vote; Elmer Roper's Poll gave Dewey 52.2 per cent and Truman 37.1 per cent; of the New York papers, the *Times,* the *Herald Tribune,* the *Sun,* and the *Journal* predicted that the Dewey-Warren ticket would win and even gave the number of states the Republicans would carry.

Others went even further. *Life* magazine printed Dewey's picture on the cover with the caption, "The next President of the United States." The Chicago *Tribune* printed an edition with the heading "Dewey Defeats Truman." The Kiplinger *News Letter* from Washington stated "Dewey will be in for eight years—until 1957." The newspapers made curious reading the day after the election, since many columnists had written their daily contributions before the returns were in.

Along with all the other red faces at the time was my own, since I persisted over the air until shortly after midnight that Dewey would win. At any rate, my broadcast gave President Truman the opportunity to display his gift for mimicry and his sense of humor. At the electoral college dinner on January 20, 1949, Mr. Truman, according to the Associated Press dispatch, ". . . in white tie and tails last night at the electors' dinner pitched into H. V. Kaltenborn, the radio commentator. He gave an imitation of Mr. Kaltenborn's style and voice that rocked the electors with laughter."

Although I was not alone in being wrong in the election outcome, it seems he picked on me because he had tuned in on my broadcast election night while I was predicting his defeat. After writing the President a good-humored note about his successful imitation of my voice and manner, I received this reply:

Dear Mr. Kaltenborn:
I appreciated most highly your good letter of the twenty-sixth, and I assure you there was no malicious intent in the attempted take-off of election night—it was merely for a good time and a little enjoyment after a terrific campaign.
You were kind to write me as you did.
Sincerely yours,
Harry Truman

People still talk of the Truman-Dewey election upset whenever political predictions and forecasts are made. One good result of that experience has been to make everyone more cautious.

Of course, after the 1948 upset, almost everybody, including myself, had an explanation for the Truman victory and the failure of the "experts." James Reston, of the New York *Times,* in an unusually humble mood, wrote to his editor, "Before we in the newspaper business spend all of our time and energy analyzing Governor Dewey's failure in the election, maybe we ought to try to analyze our own failure. For that failure is almost as spectacular as the President's victory, and the quicker we admit it the better off we'll be." Much the same idea was expressed by *Time* magazine: "The press was morally guilty on

As Harry Truman and his daughter look on, H. V. Kaltenborn imitates H. S. T.'s imitation of H. V. K.'s 1948 election-night broadcast.

several counts. It was guilty of pride: it had assumed that it knew all the important facts —without sufficiently checking on them. It was guilty of laziness and wishful thinking; it had failed to do its own doorbell ringing and bush beating; it had delegated its journalist's job to the pollsters."

In 1948 everybody—or nearly everybody— was wrong but Harry Truman. He could revise a historic phrase to read: "I'd rather be right and President."

But personally, I still go along with polls and pollsters. They have learned a lot since 1948 and their worth today is better than it was then.

52.

The Berlin Air Lift—1948-49

Rolls-Royce delivery service to the world's biggest poorhouse! That was how the Berlin Air Lift was dubbed. No matter how costly— and it did cost about $100 a ton to fly supplies to starving Berlin—this Rolls-Royce delivery service which began on June 24, 1948, achieved the most spectacular single victory of the cold war. Actually, it turned out to be more. By its magnificent performance in sustaining the 2,000,000 residents of Berlin's blockaded area, the United States Air Force in cooperation with the British wrote a new and glorious chapter in the history of peacetime air power.

Russia violated her agreement to maintain Allied access to Berlin and isolated the city with a total road, rail, and canal blockade. She thought of this action as a shrewd diplomatic move which would force the Allies to give her control of the pre-war German capital. The Soviets had refused to consider a Western proposal for a four-power agreement for Berlin. They also insisted that Russian currency be used throughout the city. On June 23 the United States, Great Britain, and France inaugurated a currency reform in West Berlin to assist the population. The very next day Russia imposed her total blockade, cutting off Berlin from West Germany. The Berliners were thus cut off from normal communication with the West and faced the immediate prospect of a food and fuel famine. Existing supplies were only enough for a few days.

In a countermove to Russia's evil plan the Western powers, under United States leadership, proposed to break the blockade via the air route which was still open. Lieutenant General Curtis LeMay, commander of the United States Air Forces in Europe, was handed the huge problem of organizing an air lift that would supply 2,000,000 people with their natural needs.

It came to be known as Operation Vittles. Improvised in haste, it was sustained and made successful by the cooperative energy of British and American air power. During the air lift I made a point of seeing and reporting the fine cooperative effort that foiled the Soviet attempt to starve Berlin into submission. I began my study by making one of the regular air-lift flights from Frankfort to Berlin, riding with my wife, who loved the adventure, on top of ten tons of coal. It was thrilling to see the speed with which this plane and the unending line that followed were loaded and unloaded and the aircraft sent back to Frankfort at three-minute intervals.

It cost the American taxpayers a little more than $1,000 to carry this one load something over 600 miles.

Berlin is a city I know well, having returned to it for study, work, or pleasure many times since my first visit in 1900. It's been a crisis capital many times, but at the period of the air lift I found there all the excitement of siege and battle. For it was the air lift versus starvation.

Major General William H. Tunner, who had operated the lift over the Hump in China during the war, was in charge of Operation Vittles. For twenty-four hours a day, in good weather and bad, first the old C-47's, then the newer C-54's and later still a few available larger modern C-74's hummed overhead in a steady stream. Twenty planes an hour shuttled between airfields in the French, British, and United States zones to the Tempelhof and Gatow airfields. This is where we learned how much efficiency gain is provided by the use of larger as compared with smaller transport planes.

As soon as a plane rolled to a stop, army trucks backed up to unload the supplies. On the airfields at both ends of the lift was a continuous line of planes and trucks. While ground crews reloaded and serviced the planes, the pilots were briefed on weather conditions

West Berlin became a blockaded island behind the Iron Curtain in 1948 as a result of Russian transport restrictions imposed in hopes that all of Berlin would fall into Soviet hands.

The United States and Britain broke through the Iron Curtain by flying into Berlin thousands of tons of food and fuel, thereby making millions of friends the world over—not to speak of these young Berliners.

and the presence near the twenty-mile corridor of Russian Yaks which often buzzed the transports. Three of them closed in on our transport plane as we winged toward Berlin, then flew away. Their almost constant presence added to the nervous strain on our pilots. Perhaps that was their purpose.

The air lift's record day was on September 18, 1948—Air Force Day. It demonstrated a remarkable feat of disciplined flying. In weather so foul that instrument procedure was mandatory for eighteen out of the twenty-four hours, the task force flew 5,583 tons of supplies into Berlin in 652 flights. Operation Vittles meant business and was doing business. At the time I saw the lift in operation General Lucius D. Clay, the Military Governor in Germany, told me, "We must continue to supply Berlin. If we give up here, pressure on Vienna will be next and we'll gradually be pushed out of Germany."

About 5,000 men participated in the air lift, which lasted 321 days. All together, 277,264 flights were made jointly by the American and British crews. It cost 61 American lives and 22 British lives and pretty close to $200,000,000.

No one can estimate how many German lives were saved because of the air lift. But the grateful city of Berlin has erected an artistic monument in memory of the fliers who did the job.

Although the Western powers took the Berlin blockade issue to the United Nations Security Council in the autumn of 1948, that body was unable to relieve the blockade. The Russians, as was expected, vetoed every compromise proposal and even boycotted the U.N. discussions.

Then, with defeat a foregone conclusion, Russia called off the blockade. Her leaders must have realized they were beaten. They also realized the propaganda value of the air lift for the Western powers not only with regard to the Germans, but because of anti-Soviet reactions in many parts of the world.

On May 12, 1949, Operation Vittles ended, although the planes continued to fly for a few more months to amass stockpiles of supplies and thus make it impossible for the Russians again to catch Berlin unprepared for another siege. These supplies have been maintained. Since air-lift days there have been brief traffic stoppages on certain roads and canals leading to Berlin but nothing like a complete blockade. The late Ernst Reuter, valiant mayor of Berlin in air-lift days, assured me that the Russians would never try another complete blockade except in case of war.

The Berlin Air Lift proved that in dealing with the Kremlin it pays to take a firm stand. The blockade backfired on the Russians as had no previous maneuver. It was an expensive enterprise for us but taught us valuable lessons, for it helped us to develop a new concept of British-American air power. We learned that it is possible to move anything, anywhere, at any time via the air route. It demonstrated what could be done in the realm of logistics with vigorous cooperative effort.

This was aptly expressed in *Fortune* magazine: "It is no exaggeration to say that the lift in four months has taught American airmen more about the possibilities of mass movement of goods by air than they probably would have learned in a decade of normal development. In combination with the British, they have moved tonnage through the air on an ever-rising scale with a precision and economy that have confounded the skeptics and surprised many airmen."

53.

Union of South Africa

In 1948 the hands of the clock moved backward in the Union of South Africa. The Boer word *apartheid,* meaning race discrimination, expressed the new government policy. The election of 1948 had replaced General Jan Christiaan Smuts, the "grand old man of Africa," as Prime Minister. Dr. Daniel F. Malan, the anti-British Nationalist leader who succeeded him, had different ideas.

The new Nationalist Malan cabinet at once created more tensions and fears among the various racial groups. The problems of racial relations had always been important in South Africa where 3,000,000 whites face nearly 10,000,000 underprivileged nonwhites. There is also the rivalry of Boer and Briton which flared into war at the turn of the century and then nearly disappeared under the liberal Smuts administration only to return under his reactionary successors. Among the 3,000,000

whites, the 8,000,000 natives, the 300,000 Indians, and about 1,000,000 colored people of mixed blood relations today are far from satisfactory. Hatreds and apprehensions dominate all these groups.

It was Minister of Transport Sauer who was author of the sorry doctrine known as *apartheid* which has now become a major domestic issue. During my tour of the South African Union in 1949, when I talked with cabinet members and leaders of the Nationalist movement, Minister Sauer gave me this brief definition of his doctrine: "Whites and blacks must live in separate and self-sufficient areas. Complete separation of the races is not practical. We realize that it is necessary to compromise."

The Minister of Native Affairs Jansen expressed a more radical view of racial policy by saying, "We believe that the native should have a chance to rise. But he should have that chance only in his own institutions, completely separated from the whites. The black man is of a lower order of intellect. The thing to teach him is not book learning but trades."

Dr. Malan was harder to interview than his cabinet associates, but he gave me an interesting résumé of his Nationalist party doctrine which was, briefly, that the Nationalists believe that those who own the land are entitled to develop it and to control it. However, it was evident that what they needed most in South Africa was all the outside economic and financial help they could get. There was much interest in President Truman's Four-Point Program for undeveloped areas.

The ever-present question in connection with Africa's 160,000,000 natives is to what extent they are capable of self-government. In South Africa millions of natives have been detribalized to work in the mines, on the farms, or in the cities. They are separated from the traditional discipline of the tribe and the fam-

Two of the great leaders of the British Empire. Sir Winston Churchill and Field Marshal Jan Christiaan Smuts.

ily but are not permitted to participate in the white man's way of life. Many of them work on contracts that enable them to get home for a few weeks every year or two but their bachelor life in the compounds to which they are confined involves evil conditions. Even the family life of the native workers who occupy the improvised housing of native locations leaves much to be desired. Many must walk up to ten miles a day to get to and from work. Compared with most of the 160,000,000 African natives, even the poorest American Negroes live in luxury.

After my 1949 visit I summed up my observations in these words: "It is not always easy to assess the blame for the poor housing, the unfair and unnecessary racial discrimination, and the black man's low standard of living. The cities of the South African Union have grown up much like our own boom towns in the West. Only now they are beginning to supply the municipal services needed

184

by the whites. The blacks have just had to wait. The most unfortunate aspect of today's situation is the impossible *apartheid* policy of the new Nationalist government. My own conclusion is that while the present regime may continue to preach intolerance, it will continue to practice a large measure of tolerance. It is doing just that today. I spent time with a dozen government commissioners of native affairs serving under the Nationalist regime in various cities and native reservations. They all had a humane, generous, and farsighted attitude toward the native problem. My advice to anyone going to South Africa is this: 'Don't pay too much attention to what some people say. Observe closely what most people do.' "

In discussing the Four-Point Program with General Smuts, he said that if he had $1,-000,000,000 to spend in Africa he would use it to promote health—human health, animal health, and the health of the land. South Africa is in desperate need of leaders such as the late General Smuts with his humane approach, his practical genius, and his superb gift of leadership. He accomplished so much good that it was unfortunate he didn't live longer to do more. General Smuts was a farmer who loved solitude and outdoor life. He was a modern Cincinnatus. Like that Roman consul, he led his people to victory in war and then went back to his "farm."

Africa is, as he suggested, a huge underpopulated area with vast, varied, and untouched resources. But it is not a land of milk and honey. It is a continent of extremes. Desert and jungle, drought and flood, gold and starvation. Opportunities are everywhere, but so are difficulties. While the spirit of man delights in challenge, the Dark Continent will have the same lure that peopled our America and made it great.

Dr. Malan.

"Black Sash" women, carrying a black-draped book representing the South African Constitution, march through Cape Town in silent protest against the government's plan to take Negro voters off the common electoral vote.

54.

1950—Year of Decision and Indecision

"I am talking to you tonight about what our country is up against and what we are going to do about it. Our homes, our nation, all the things we believe in are in great danger. ... Because of all these things I have been talking to you about I will issue a proclamation tomorrow morning declaring that a national emergency exists. ... The American people have always met danger with courage and determination. I am confident we will do that now, and with God's help we shall keep our freedom."

If you were listening to President Truman on the radio on December 15, 1950, that is how you heard him begin and end his speech telling the people about his decision to declare a national emergency because of the North Korean and Chinese attack on South Korea.

Many people have called 1950 the year of decision. They are right—it was a momentous year of many decisions. Yet, in some ways, it was also a year of indecision. Looking back over 1950's events and administration action or reaction it seems to prove that the American people have sometimes been ahead of their leaders. It did not take the proclamation of a national emergency to make us sense the danger created for us by aggressive communism. As we look back now on the events of 1950, it appears that our government *reacted* to events but rarely *anticipated* them. We seemed to have lost the vigorous initiative in world leadership which we developed with the Berlin Air Lift, the Marshall Plan, and the Atlantic Pact. Some courageous decisions

were made, but, by and large, indecision was the keynote.

As the year 1950 opened President Truman had concluded that we should abandon the defeated Chiang Kai-shek. He said we would take no military action, direct or indirect, to help this Chinese Nationalist leader whom we had supported during the war and the half decade that followed. The President stated, "The United States will not pursue a course which will lead to involvement in the civil conflict in China." Secretary of State Acheson also came out definitely against further commitment to Nationalist China. On January 12 he said, "The United States must keep hands off Asia except where its economic guidance is invited." That was great news for the Chinese Communists. They seized American property, jailed our consular officials, and took over our consular offices in Peking.

After the Russo-Chinese pact was signed in Moscow, firmly establishing the alliance between Communist Mao Tse-tung and Communist Joseph Stalin, Truman and his advisers became a bit more concerned about the state of things in the Far East. But Truman cautioned against "the vain hope of finding a quick and easy solution to world problems." He decided against the proposals by Senators McMahon and Tydings to go to Moscow for talks on a big global four-point program to win over Russia.

At this time the Russians were spending about 25 per cent of their national income on their armed forces. We were spending barely 6 per cent, yet Truman said that our defenses were in better shape than ever before in time of peace. He denied that military economies instituted by Defense Secretary Johnson had lessened our defensive power.

Military experts were less confident about our military situation. General Eisenhower said in March, "America has already disarmed to the extent, in some directions even beyond the extent, that I could possibly advise." General Bradley, Chief of Staff, told congressional leaders that new tension was building up throughout the world. Yet at a news conference in early May, President Truman said he saw no reason to fear that the cold war was about to turn into a shooting war. He promised to reduce the defense budget, called the Marshall Plan our main weapon against Russia, and indicated that we would soon pull our soldiers out of Japan.

On June 1 President Truman decided to ask Congress for increased military aid for Europe. Sternly he said, "The threat of aggression casts its shadow upon every quarter of the globe." But just a little later he told his press conference, "The world seems closer to peace than at any time in the last five years." He added that he disagreed with the Gallup Poll which indicated that most Americans expected war within five years.

It was only a couple of weeks after these remarks by Truman that the North Koreans, on June 25, completely surprised us as they crossed the 38th Parallel on aggression bent. The cold war became hot. It was then President Truman made the most forthright and important decision of his administration. He ordered our air and sea forces to give the South Korean troops cover and support. He instructed the Seventh Fleet to "prevent any attack on Formosa." He also asked Chiang Kai-shek to stop his provocative bombardment of the Chinese mainland. This was a "police action," he said, and insisted we were not at war. He explained it this way: "A bunch of bandits has attacked the Republic of Korea. We are trying to suppress this bandit raid. . . ."

The United Nations (it was our good fortune that Russia had temporarily withdrawn from the council) endorsed our action and

Truman Shows Them How to Run the Course

MR. LOW ON AGGRESSION IN KOREA

"Honest, Mister, there's nobody here but us Koreans."

American soldiers surrender to Chinese people's "volunteers" in Korea.

EASTFOTO

thus became an effective instrument against aggression in North Korea. But American forces bore the brunt of the campaigns in Korea. It was some time later before the token forces provided by some fifteen other U.N. members arrived at the front.

We all know now that the bandit raid turned out to be something more than that. The President soon ordered American ground troops into action and slowly, but only slowly, began to mobilize the country for war. In mid-July, as our forces were being driven down the Korean peninsula, the President declared, "We must realize that the engagement in Korea will be costly and may not be short. We must prepare against the possibility that other crises may arise elsewhere...." The President's speech to the nation on July 25 was a plan for defense, but it was not a compelling call to arms. He no longer called the Korean action a police action, but he did not call it a war. The attack on South Korea was "raw aggression." He said, "The free nations face a world-wide threat. It must be met with

a world-wide defense. The free world has made it clear through the United Nations that lawless aggression will be met with force. This is the significance of Korea."

But if the free world was to make good on the promise to meet aggression with sufficient force, there should have been a good deal more action than was seen in Washington during the summer of 1950. The proposals by Bernard Baruch for strict controls over the economy were rejected. Even in August the President was still hoping that all-out mobilization would not be necessary. He decided against rigid formulas and seemed satisfied with the standby controls that Congress had given him. By the end of September the North Koreans appeared completely routed and Washington relaxed. The Administration decided to make appeasing overtures to the Chinese Communist leader Mao Tse-tung, with the President reiterating that we had no designs on Formosa. Truman expressed his hope that "the people of China will not be misled or forced into fighting against the United Na-

A grief-stricken American infantry-man whose buddy has been killed in action is comforted by another soldier.

U.S. ARMY

tions and against the American people who have been and still are their friends."

When Red China did enter the war late in 1950 the Administration was faced with what General MacArthur rightly called a new war which required fateful decisions. How were we to meet the numerically greatly superior forces of Chinese Communists with the limited number of American and U.N. troops at hand? Would we acknowledge that Red China was at war with us and draw the necessary military conclusions? We temporized. The United States continued to mobilize its strength at a slow pace. A real war was being fought even as we refused to admit that we were at war with a major power.

However the decisions and indecisions of 1950 may be judged, the Korean War was the most distant, the most unsatisfactory, and the most costly in which we have ever engaged. It is also the only war we deliberately refused to win. The net result of our three-year effort in Korea was that our prestige reached a new low ebb throughout Asia.

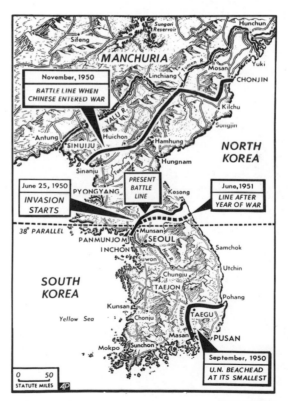

WIDE WORLD

This map, prepared as the Korean War entered its fourth year, shows the highlights of the war up to June 25, 1953. For the preceding two years most of the fighting went on in the narrow area between the June 1951 line and the line marked *Present Battle Line*.

55.

President Truman Dismisses a Cabinet Member and a General

President Truman called reporters to the White House on September 20, 1946, to tell them he had fired Henry A. Wallace. He said he had asked the Secretary of Commerce to resign because of a "fundamental conflict of views on foreign policy." Wallace, the last holdover of the original Roosevelt cabinet, wrote to the President, "As you requested, here is my resignation. I shall continue to fight for peace. I am sure you will join me in that great endeavor."

The "fundamental conflict" was brought to a climax by a Wallace speech at a big New York City rally on September 12. The meeting was sponsored by two left-wing organizations, the National Citizens Political Action Committee and the Independent Citizens Committee of the Arts, Sciences and Professions. Before the pro-communist audience they provided, Secretary Wallace delivered his now-famous "two-worlds" speech.

Among other things, he warned against a "get tough with Russia" policy, stating "the tougher we get, the tougher Russia will get."

A flood tide of criticism at home and abroad followed this Wallace speech. Secretary of State Byrnes was attending the 1946 Paris Peace meeting and there waging a "get tough with Russia" policy. The Republicans joyfully attacked President Truman for having two directly opposed policies for dealing with the aggressive actions of the Soviet Union. They accused him of "betraying Byrnes" by endorsing an "ease-up-on-Russia" policy, since he had approved the Wallace speech. Truman

190

had also made the surprising statement, "I think it [the Wallace speech] is in line with Secretary Byrnes' policies." When he faced mounting opposition from all quarters—even from within his own official family and from Democratic congressmen—Truman issued one of his numerous "statements of clarification." In this he said there had been no change in our foreign policy and that he supported Wallace's right to make the speech. Then he added this phrase which flatly contradicted what he had said before, "I did not intend to indicate that I approved the Wallace speech as constituting a statement of the foreign policy of this country." Truman, with his usual cheerful, carefree attitude under such conditions, called it a "natural misunderstanding." What it really meant was that he had read the speech carelessly and had failed to realize that it was in direct conflict with the Truman-Byrnes policy.

After conferring with Secretary Wallace at the White House for two and a half hours on September 18, the President announced that the Secretary of Commerce would not resign from the Cabinet and that Wallace would "make no public statements or speeches" until the Paris Peace Conference ended. Two days later Henry Wallace was out. President Truman then told the country: "No member in the Executive branch . . . will make any public statement as to foreign policy which is in conflict with our established foreign policy."

Here was an instance where a Cabinet member was in direct conflict with the most important single aspect of national foreign policy and voiced that conflict publicly at a meeting ·organized by opponents of that policy. The firing of Wallace thus became inevitable and it is no credit to Truman that he took so long to realize it.

Now we come to a dismissal that was as unjustified as the Wallace action was inevitable. It concerned a matter of military opinion where the expert on the spot who had proved his competence on many previous occasions was exercising his mature judgment in an area where his knowledge far exceeded that of anyone in Washington.

Not quite five years after the Wallace ouster, President Truman created a worldwide sensation with this second historic firing. On April 11, 1951, the President, as Commander in Chief, dismissed General of the Army Douglas MacArthur from his four United Nations, Allied and United States commands in the Far East. The five-star general and one of our all-time military heroes was ousted because of his persistent demand for a more vigorous and effective war against Red China. President Truman and the United Nations were unwilling to undertake a real effort to win the Korean War because of their wholly unjustified fear that this might persuade Soviet Russia to enter openly (as she had entered secretly) into the Korean War. The White House charged and MacArthur denied that he had time and again violated orders not to make public statements favoring a more vigorous reaction to Red China's entry into the war. We continued to ignore Red China's active participation and handicapped our forces by confining all military action to North Korea.

It was on the last day of the President's sixth year in the White House that his press secretary, Joseph Short, gave out this presidential statement: "With deep regret I have concluded that General of the Army Douglas MacArthur is unable to give his wholehearted support to the policies of the United States Government and of the United Nations in matters pertaining to his official duties. In view of the specific responsibilities imposed upon me . . . I have decided I must make a

The outgoing mailbox on Henry A. Wallace's desk forms a fitting setting for the ousted Secretary of Commerce.

change of command in the Far East . . . I repeat my regret at the necessity for the action I feel compelled to take in this case."

General MacArthur's dismissal was gratifying to the United Nations countries which were only supporting the Korean War halfheartedly and were terrified at the mere thought of a general war in Asia. But in this country, the curt dismissal of a great national hero touched off one of the most bitter and violent controversies in our history. The repercussions are still being felt. The arguments and the reappraisals still go on. When the startling news broke, more than a quarter million telegrams poured in on the White House and Congress, most of them protesting the ouster. The Republicans again pounced on Truman and quickly moved to have MacArthur come home and tell his side of the case before Congress. In some quarters there was foolish talk of impeaching the President and forcing the dismissal of Secretary of State

191

President Truman and General MacArthur appeared to be in complete agreement during their Wake Island meeting in 1950.

The dismissed General returns to the U.S. from the Far East and receives a royal welcome in San Francisco.

Acheson and Defense Secretary George Marshall. Impeachment talk was nothing more than hysteria, but it was indicative of public feeling.

General MacArthur's dismissal was probably the second most sensational firing of a top military figure. Not since President Lincoln relieved his first Civil War commander, General George B. McClellan, had anything like this occurred. While the Truman-MacArthur controversy had been simmering for some time before the momentous decision, it might never have reached a climax with the President had it not been for a letter which seemed to enter the area of politics. That is an area where Harry Truman is particularly sensitive. The general had written a letter to Congressman Joseph W. Martin, then Republican minority leader in the House. Mr. Martin made the letter public for political advantage and so bears some personal responsibility for what happened. Publication of this letter brought the showdown. MacArthur told Martin he believed in a second front against Red China, using available Chinese Nationalist

troops. He stated, in effect, that all-out war on Asia's Reds was Europe's only salvation. There was no indication in the letter that General MacArthur expected it to be published.

In my news analysis over the air on the evening of the dramatic firing I discussed President Truman's statement of policy in regard to the Korean War and his brief comments on General MacArthur's dismissal. In conclusion, I said: "It is not often that the removal of one man by the President of the United States excites such violent reaction all over the world. Summing up in a single word the effect produced in world capitals, it might be said that Tokyo weeps; Peking sneers; Paris approves; Moscow cheers; London wonders; Seoul regrets, and Washington divides."

Practically all those who approved the President's decisive action justify it on the ground that in a democracy civilian authority must dominate the military in peace and war. We can accept that truth and still conclude that Truman's action was unjustified and the manner of it inexcusable. Democracies have

192

often found it difficult to restrain or silence successful generals. General Eisenhower put it this way: "When you put on a uniform there are certain inhibitions you accept." But if General Eisenhower had been less anxious to conciliate Russia in the closing weeks of the war we might have avoided communist domination of Berlin and so large a part of eastern Germany. And has General Eisenhower ever approved of General MacArthur's dismissal?

President Truman was right when he dismissed Wallace, wrong when he dismissed MacArthur. Because of that dismissal we failed, for the first time in our history, to win a war. Moreover, we also gave communism a favorable truce whose terms have not been kept. We paved the way for a further communist victory in Indo-China. We enhanced communist prestige throughout Asia and helped consolidate communist control of China. It was a series of fateful steps some of whose unhappy consequences still lie in the future.

56.

NATO Meets
at Lisbon—February, 1952

At first the Russians called it "an aggressive ogre." Actually, NATO, which came into being on April 4, 1949, after nine months of talk, was a defensive organization. Its purpose was to check Soviet aggression and serve as a realistic implement of the United Nations. The Kremlin had prevented the creation of the United Nations Armed Force provided in the Charter.

The North Atlantic Treaty Organization— to give NATO its full name—put the Soviet Union squarely on notice that invasion of any one of the twelve European founder nations (since its formation Greece and Turkey have joined) would be resisted by all twelve. Although it was organized as a defense organization with military strength pooled from various nations, it appears now that the scope of NATO will be broadened to offset Russia's new policy of economic penetration and political infiltration.

When the NATO Council met in Lisbon in February 1952 I flew to Portugal to cover the sessions. It was the ninth Council meeting since the organization came into being three years before. Broadcasting from Lisbon, I said: "The first thing you realize when you attend a conference of this kind is how hard it is for free nations to work together. Experienced foreign ministers such as Anthony Eden, Dean Acheson, and Robert Schuman, of France, know what needs to be done. But to get it done is quite another matter. When a dictator decides that something should be done, he does it first and explains later. When a democratic foreign minister agrees with his colleagues that they must all sacrifice some small amount of immediate national interest to serve the long-range cause of world peace, he must go through a whole series of steps before he can commit his country. He must get the approval of his prime minister or his president. He must secure the backing of public opinion and through that public opinion he must secure the approval of the national legislature.

"Foreign Minister Schuman, of France, came to an agreement with Chancellor Adenauer, of Germany, on various subjects when they conferred on them in London. But it was not until the French Chamber of Deputies had approved their compromise decisions

193

NATO meets in Lisbon—1952.

that the Big Three were able to go to Lisbon for the North Atlantic Treaty Council meeting. And the meeting had to be postponed for three days until they had agreed. Yesterday Secretary of State Acheson, Foreign Minister Eden, and Foreign Minister Schuman hailed completion of the project for a supra-national European army. Germany will make next to the largest man-power contribution to that army. In return the Occupation Statute will end when the Treaty creating that army has been ratified.

"France's Foreign Minister pointed out what it means when a country like France gives up its own national army. Mr. Eden emphasized the importance of the return of Germany to a united Europe and praised Mr. Schuman's contribution to that end. Mr. Acheson warned of problems still ahead but saw what has already been done as the end of a long road.

"Now that a real European Defense Community has been created, NATO is much more of a reality than I had supposed before seeing it in action here. Here was united Europe. Military leaders pointed out what

194

needs to be done, foreign ministers worked out the practical political agreements, and the ministers of finance, including the ever-important United States Secretary of the Treasury, figured out how the mountainous cost of common defense is to be met. The experts say it will total $225,000,000,000 over the next three years. . . ."

The Big Powers at the Lisbon Conference were eager to wind it up as quickly as possible. Eden had important issues to settle with Iran and Egypt. Dean Acheson had to get home to lay his plans on foreign aid before a reluctant Congress. Robert Schuman knew that a French Government majority of only forty on such a decisive issue as German rearmament meant that his foreign policy lacked strong support.

The small powers of NATO objected to being hurried through the conference. They had more time, or at least were willing to take more time, to get their points of view heard by their big brothers in NATO. Here is the way Foreign Minister Schuman expressed it to me: "The small powers are very sensitive about any time pressure. They don't want to be pushed around. When we try to hurry things, they resent it. Which means that this meeting will run into next week."

The debates and decisions of the meeting were all behind closed doors. You don't tell a potential enemy just how you are going to defend yourself against him. All the speakers at the opening session emphasized that the purpose of NATO was the preservation of peace—peace through strength was the theme. If Russia had any spies at the public meeting they must have reported that not a word was uttered which the Soviet Union could take amiss. Because the work of defense must be kept secret, the security regulations surrounding the gathering were more strict than those at most international meetings.

The reception to the delegates, dignitaries, and newsmen at the gorgeous presidential palace the night after the conference opened was an event to be remembered. The grand staircase was lined with a double file of handsomely uniformed guardsmen, their drawn swords flashing in the light from crystal chandeliers. We passed by huge bowls of camellias and orchid sprays as we moved through a dozen beautifully furnished anterooms whose walls were hung with old masters. Finally we came to the big reception hall where President Lopez, of Portugal, wearing his general's uniform, headed the reception line, flanked by members of his cabinet.

The President and his wife actually shook hands with more than a thousand guests who moved on into an even larger banquet hall. There a huge center table and a half-a-dozen side tables were laden with every kind of delicacy. Waiters in ancient court uniforms, resurrected from heaven knows where, kept a thousand glasses well filled with Portugal's best wines. France is the only other country that could have rivaled this show put on by the little Republic of Portugal for its distin-guished and undistinguished guests. It was a noble and expensive effort.

The man who really rules Portugal, Premier Salazar, generally referred to as a benevolent dictator, was not present. He kept himself in the background throughout the meeting. When I applied for an interview word came back that he would be happy to see me but only when the conference was over. I did have an interesting talk with Portugal's Foreign Minister. He took the opportunity to stress the importance of getting Spain into NATO. "Her power is so much greater than ours," he said. "There is no natural boundary between us and from the military point of view we must act together. Jointly we are a powerful military unit whereas Portugal alone can add little to NATO's strength."

That was said in 1952. Since then the United States has recognized Spain's strategic importance by completing air and naval bases on Spanish soil. These have even larger importance since the Western position in North Africa has grown less secure. Today our Spanish bases are more important than those we built so hurriedly and expensively in Morocco.

President Truman displays the North Atlantic Treaty after signing it in July 1949.

In one of the Lisbon broadcasts I described NATO's new flag which symbolized peace through strength. It featured a shield symbolizing defense which stood out from a background of blue waves. Originally these were supposed to be the waves of the North Atlantic, but since Italy also faces the Adriatic and since Greece and Turkey, who had just become the thirteenth and fourteenth members, are on the Mediterranean, the blue waves behind the shield have a broader significance. The theme of peace through strength is directly symbolized by a sword and an olive branch. The Kremlin can choose which it wishes to seize. . . .

My final words from Lisbon were these: "The free world can only hope to save peace by closer union and further strengthening its armed power. That means sacrifices must be made by all concerned. The need for more sacrifice by all powers is the first lesson of this Lisbon meeting."

57.

Premier Mossadegh—Iran—Oil

"Your sacrifice today has saved my country. I wish I had been killed instead of so many innocent persons." Those were the dramatic words Dr. Mohammed Mossadegh addressed to the cheering Iranian Nationalists who marched to his home in the summer of 1952. He had just been recalled as Premier after three days of rioting in which 500 people were killed. Ex-Premier Ghavam, who had held office for only two days and then went to jail, escaped from Teheran to avoid being murdered by Nationalist fanatics. The Iranian extremists who wanted no compromise on the oil issue with Britain were once more in control.

A year later, in 1953, Mossadegh was arrested for treason and rebellion when he attempted to lead a revolt against the Shah of Iran. He was sentenced to three years in solitary confinement because the Shah, asking that mercy be shown, intervened against the prosecutor's demand for the death sentence.

Recalling an interview with Mossadegh when I was in Iran during the summer of 1951, I predicted at the time of his return to power that unless a market could be found for Iranian oil, the country faced complete bankruptcy. Knowing the internal conditions Mossadegh would have to face, I realized that the Premier was not going to have a happy time for the balance of his premiership. He most certainly did not, and the country suffered because this stubborn fanatic retained power too long.

Mossadegh himself brought on the entire disastrous and unnecessary Iranian oil crisis when he became Premier in 1951. Oil was the key problem throughout the Middle East, the big issue in international relations. Great Britain's somewhat reactionary Anglo-Persian Oil Company operated the oil wells and huge refineries which were Iran's chief source of income. Soviet Russia was casting covetous eyes on the undeveloped oil resources in northern Iran. The United Nations had frustrated an earlier Russian effort to control them. A series of historic council sessions at Hunter College in New York City did much to persuade Russia to withdraw from northern Iran while it helped establish the prestige of the new international organization.

Mossadegh's Nationalists were aided by the

Weepy Mohammed Mossadegh forced 1952's Iranian oil crisis. A year later he was jailed for treason and rebellion after attempting to lead a revolt against the Shah.

Communists who had infiltrated the country. Mossadegh nationalized the oil industry over strong British protests. Iran broke her contracts with the Anglo-Iranian Oil Company and confiscated British property without compensation. The British evacuated the oil industry personnel in October 1951. All negotiations failed. The loss of oil revenue soon left Iran in a precarious economic position. Mossadegh brought his country to the verge of ruin and revolt.

To talk with Mossadegh, as I did during this period, was to become convinced that this aging fanatic would see his country ruined before he would agree to any reasonable settlement with the British. He was a super-nationalist with the conviction that every Britisher was a selfish exploiter of Iran's natural resources with whom no loyal Iranian could do business. I gave it as my opinion that there could never be peace so long as Mossadegh remained in control.

To get to see Mossadegh I had to go through heavy police cordons in the streets that led to his home, before the gate, in the courtyard, and even outside his bedroom. There, on a small iron bed, hunched up wearing a gray flannel robe, he looked like a cadaverous ascetic. Actually, our talk was not an interview in the customary sense, but a conversation in which, as he said, "We won't talk about oil." The exchange went like this:

"Can Iran get along without foreign help?"

"A country must rule itself on the basis of nationalism."

"But must it confiscate foreign property?"

"Foreign exploiters take not only our national resources, but they exercise powerful political pressure."

"But didn't you sign a contract with the Anglo-Iranian Oil Company?"

"The oil company officials influenced our government for selfish purposes."

"But didn't the British develop your oil resources?"

"We are a poor country, and the natural resources belong to the people."

"But the British have a legal contract with

197

Oil—the cause of tension in the Middle East.

the government which you have broken."

"We must not be led astray by external formalities. We must look to the truth of things."

"But you will sacrifice aid from the United States if your government violates its agreements with foreigners."

"You have only given us $500,000, which is nothing."

"But we've offered you a $25,000,000 loan."

"That isn't enough and you are also trying to tell us what we must do with the money."

When Mossadegh spoke of revolution and that "empty stomachs make people desperate," I reminded him that he had cut off cash income for Iran by confiscating the oil properties. His answer was, "We did that only because we want to control our own resources."

When I asked him if there was any message for the American people, he replied, "Tell them it is only the truth that counts. They must not be misled by external appearances. Hold to the truth!"

Iran—a contrast of the old and the new. The Abadan oil refinery and an ancient coastal craft.

That was fine advice if you could agree on what is true.

After the three-year oil battle that bankrupted Iran, unseated Mossadegh, and ruptured the relations between Iran and Great Britain, Iran and Western oil companies finally reached an agreement in August 1954 to reactivate the frozen Iran oil industry. Iran had failed in a long series of efforts to sell her oil to foreign countries. Lack of tankers and fear of British reprisals held off would-be buyers.

The United States played a major role as final mediator in the British-Iranian negotiations. To Herbert C. Hoover, Jr., then a State Department oil consultant, must go much of the credit for bringing about a settlement. He conferred patiently with both sides during the protracted negotiations. In recognition of his successful efforts and his evident talent for international relations, President Eisenhower made him Under-secretary of State.

58.

Eisenhower Elected—1952

"The verdict is in. It remains to appraise what happened and why. The people have spoken and they have spoken with a loud voice."

Those were the opening remarks of my broadcast on Wednesday, November 5, 1952, the day after election. Another presidential election year has rolled around since that time, but it seems like yesterday that I was commenting on the size and particularly the manner of the Eisenhower victory that surprised foreign more than domestic observers, including those pollsters who had gone wrong in 1948 and in 1952, who didn't dare predict what their polls implied.

In my analysis of the 1952 election I assumed the American people felt it was "time for a change," but they did not vote blindly. Never before in a national election had there been such a crossing of party lines. The careful selection of individual candidates indicated that voting the straight ticket was becoming obsolete. Millions of Democrats voted for Republican Eisenhower but picked Democratic congressmen. Thousands of Republicans voted for Democrat Stevenson and picked Republican governors and senators. The voters throughout the country chose individuals often regardless of party. In Massachusetts, for instance, they picked Republican Eisenhower but rejected Republican Senator Henry Cabot Lodge, Eisenhower's chief sponsor. Lodge lost to the young Democrat John Kennedy, who made a particular appeal to women voters. Then the same voters rejected Democratic Governor Paul Dever, the windy political orator, and elected the much more able Republican Christian Herter as their state executive. Ohio went easily for Eisenhower and returned John Bricker to the Senate. But the Ohioans decided they wanted a Democrat as governor and rejected Charles Taft's bid in favor of able and experienced Governor Frank Lausche. The late Senator Robert Taft's campaigning was successful for Eisenhower, but not for his own brother. In New York City the Democratic candidate for senator, a boss-picked political hack, ran half a million votes behind Stevenson.

These mixed choices and the new voter independence of party and party bosses were good signs. It takes more thought and more discrimination to vote a split ticket than to vote straight. It indicates that coat-tail riding is going to be a little less easy.

HARRIS & EWING

The Eisenhowers meet the Trumans at the White House before the swearing-in ceremonies.

President Eisenhower takes the oath of office.

HARRIS & EWING

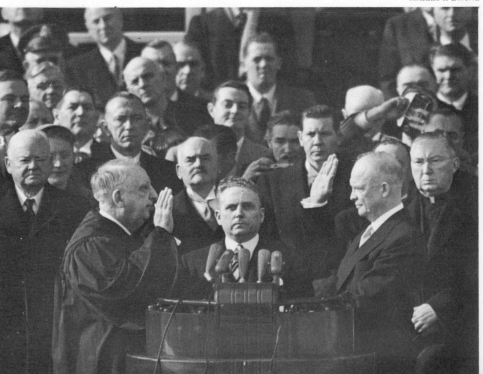

Other 1952 election results were equally striking. The American electorate gave General Eisenhower a great popular mandate, a sweeping personal victory. The electoral vote was 442 to 89. Both the Republican and Democratic presidential candidates received the highest popular vote for a winner and loser in United States history. Of special significance was the disappearance of the solid Democratic South, this time for a better reason than in 1928. Tennessee, Virginia, Florida, and Texas all went Republican. At the time I said, "Let us hope that the solid South is gone for good and all. Voters below Mason and Dixon's line are sick of voting for one party just because of an outworn tradition and the accident of geography. The solid South should disappear, and if it does, it may well rank as one of General Eisenhower's most important contributions."

This beneficent change in the South actually began at the Republican convention in 1952 when some of the corrupt southern "do-nothing" Republican party bosses were tossed out and overruled by the younger enthusiastic supporters of the General. So the 1952 Republican victories in the South, and in the border states, may prove a landmark in our political history. In 1928 the Republicans first broke the solid South, but the liquor issue and Al Smith's religion were partly responsible for Republican success that year. In 1952 the high Republican vote in the South meant a genuine break with the old tradition. The two-party system was making its way in the South. Most of us can agree that the presence of two great parties in every state of the Union is an essential element of the democratic process.

For me, the fascination of a presidential election lies in trying to appraise and interpret what happened; to seek to explain why our citizens voted as they did. In 1952 the

Now Let's Get One of the Whole Family Together

© 1952 NEW YORK HERALD TRIBUNE INC.

voters even turned their backs on their own president when he tried to frighten them with the worst speeches of the campaign. The demogogic political oratory which helped make Harry Truman a minority president in 1948 had lost most of its appeal by 1952. The American people administered a stern rebuke to Truman for the low level of his whistle-stop harangues. He surely shared the blame for Stevenson's defeat just as he shared the credit for his own election four years earlier.

But with all his guttersniping talk, Harry Truman is a fine American at heart. The day after election he promised full support to Eisenhower and his administration and in-

201

vited the General to the White House to discuss the problems that lay ahead. "Such a meeting," he said, "would make it plain to the world that our people are united in the struggle for freedom and peace."

He called on the American people to support our government in the measures that were necessary to achieve peace in the world even though the way would be long and hard. As I commented after I heard Truman's announcement, "What a happy contrast with his predecessor (F.D.R.) who, for four months in 1932 and 1933, rejected the slightest measure of cooperation with outgoing President Hoover and thus helped precipitate and aggravate the bank panic that worsened the existing depression and delayed recovery."

59.

The Death of Stalin

"Stalin is dead. Hail Malenkov." It was the startling news from Moscow that enabled me to make this announcement on March 6, 1953. Premier Josef Stalin died in his apartment in the Kremlin on March 5. The world had not known of his illness until the day before, when the Moscow radio announced that Stalin had suffered a brain hemorrhage on the night of March 1. Many people believed he had already died or been killed and that by announcing his serious illness the Moscow Government was preparing the Soviet population for the news of his death.

At the same time Stalin's death was made public the Moscow radio stated that Georgi Malenkov, the fifty-one-year-old Stalin disciple, had taken over the government of the Soviet Union as well as direction of the all-powerful communist party. To avoid any break in the continuity of power and to handicap the expected propaganda efforts of the free world to exploit Stalin's death, the Kremlin leaders announced Stalin's successor in record time. Less than a day after the death of the despot who had ruled for twenty-nine years Moscow radio gave us the new lineup in the Russian Government. The question of the immediate succession to Stalin was settled.

In my evening analysis of the dramatic news that came from Moscow I said "The real succession, if there is to be one, will be decided by the struggle behind the scenes that has now begun. In a dictatorship, ruled by terror and intrigue, no man is permanently safe. All but one of Stalin's early companions in power disappeared long ago. Most were murdered or executed. Trotsky was exiled and then murdered. Perhaps their experience will serve as a warning to Malenkov's associates in the new hierarchy. The four most influential and best-known men in Russia, after Malenkov, were appointed vice premiers—Viacheslav M. Molotov, who has been in the position under Stalin; Lavrenti Beria, chief of the Soviet Secret Police; Marshal Nikolai Bulganin and Lazar Kaganovich, an old-time Bolshevik. . . .

"Malenkov, Russia's new leader, is busy making plans for one of the greatest funerals of all time. Stalin is almost certain to be buried in or near the Lenin mausoleum in Red Square. All motor traffic was suspended in the streets of central Moscow today. This was done so that Moscow's millions could make their way to the great Trade Union Hall where Stalin lies in state. They came to see the body in clear view, clad in a marshal's uniform with a single decoration. The orders and

Thousands of floral wreaths cover Stalin's casket in Red Square.

The body of Josef Stalin lies in state.

The new rulers of Russia, Bulganin (*left*) and Khrushchev (*right*) visited London in April, 1956. Standing between them is the Lord Mayor of London.

medals of the seventy-three-year-old leader of the Soviets were displayed on red silk cushions. The catafalque was banked in flowers and uniformed men of all the armed forces served as a guard of honor. Orchestras played soft dirges and works by Stalin's favorite composers, Tschaikovsky and Glinka. All the leading members of the Communist party, the Presidium, and the Cabinet, wearing mourning brassards, stood solemn vigil around the bier, succeeding one another every few minutes. The era of Stalin has ended. A new era begins."

To me Stalin's death inevitably brought back memories. I last saw Josef Stalin at one of the big Red Square parades in the thirties. He was on a platform built on the front of the squat structure that houses Lenin's tomb. I was on an adjoining stand that accommodated foreign dignitaries, so I was about as close to the Soviet dictator as ordinary mortals ever get. Stalin never sought to create any particular impression when he appeared in public. He was not an instinctive actor though he

knew well how to dissemble. His was a squat, rather unimpressive figure. That day he was natural and unaffected. He talked with whom he pleased, occasionally walked about, saluted clumsily with a curiously awkward wiggle of his fingers. He exchanged jokes with his associates and had neither the appearance nor the attitude of a man who was the world's most powerful dictator.

But among the many thousands of young men and women who streamed past Lenin's tomb that afternoon—it was the annual "physical culture" parade—there was not one whose eyes did not seek out the stocky figure with the visored cap that stood near the center of the first row, between Molotov and the bearded President Kalinin. This brief glimpse of their leader was for them reward enough for weeks of drill and many weary hours of waiting, marching, and parading.

A dead Lenin and a living Stalin were then receiving the blind devotion once accorded to the far-famed Moscow virgin whose shrine and statue were located at the entrance of the

204

Red Square. When I first began my visits to Moscow in the middle twenties you would always find men and women kneeling in the street to pay their devotion to the virgin oblivious to the inscription on the wall above their heads: "Religion is the opium of the people." Since then Stalin worship has largely replaced religious worship, at least in public. When Stalin died, the inevitable question was raised, "What will replace Stalin worship?"

The answer is that it has not been replaced. Stalin's immediate successor, Malenkov, was soon replaced by Bulganin. He decided with his associates that too many men must die before any one man could replace Stalin. Hence the safety and well-being of all Kremlin leaders would be promoted if committee rule succeeded one-man rule. Today—no man can tell what tomorrow may bring in a communist state—a Kremlin oligarchy has replaced the Stalin autocracy.

This has softened Russian foreign policy and made the Soviet Union somewhat more accessible for trade and travel. It has not changed the fundamental communist aim of world domination, but it constitutes an admission that the achievement of this aim must be relegated to the distant future, and that it cannot now be achieved by force of arms. For some time to come propaganda and penetration will replace militant aggression. The free world will find it more difficult to maintain its unity and its preparedness in the face of milder communist tactics. But the new Kremlin attitude has also helped to develop a more militant spirit of independence in the Soviet Union and in the satellites. On the whole the West has grown stronger since Stalin died.

The more recent revelations by Khrushchev, Communist party leader, that Stalin was a new incarnation of Ivan the Terrible has brought widespread negative reaction from communist leaders in satellite countries and the free world. It has lowered the prestige of the present Kremlin leaders both in and out of Russia. The chain of reaction which has just begun may imperil the position of men like Bulganin, Khrushchev, Molotov, and Malenkov who worked with and for Stalin and helped execute the nefarious actions for which they now condemn him. We may be at the beginning of one of those bloody internal crises which mark the history of every dictatorship.

60.

Elizabeth II Becomes Queen

"There is a noble motto borne by many of my ancestors, 'I serve.' I declare before you all that my whole life, whether it be long or short, shall be devoted to your service. God help me to make good my vow, and God bless all of you who are willing to share it."

It was this noble pledge and the way it has been carried out that have endeared Queen Elizabeth II to the British people. She addressed these words to all the peoples of the British Commonwealth and Empire. The occasion was her twenty-first birthday on April 21, 1947, when, as Princess Elizabeth, she was on a royal tour of Africa with her parents, King George VI and Queen Elizabeth. A little less than five years later Princess Elizabeth was again in Africa, this time with her handsome husband, Prince Philip, Duke of Edinburgh. It was there she received news of the death of King George VI on February 6, 1952. The

The Queen arrives from Kenya where she received news of the death of her father, King George VI. Awaiting her are from *right to left:* Prime Minister Churchill, Mr. Attlee, Mr. Eden, Lord Woolton.

Churchill cited history to show that Queen Elizabeth II's reign might bring an era of prosperity for Britain. "Famous have been the reigns of our queens. Some of the greatest periods in our history have unfolded under their scepters," he said. For the first time in history England had three living queens, Elizabeth II, Queen Mother Elizabeth, and Queen Grandmother Mary.

The pomp and ceremony that go with a king's death and a young queen's accession attracted the fascinated attention of the entire world. In commenting on the historic events then taking place in London the day after the saddened young queen had returned from Africa, I remarked, "The colorful medieval pageantry now taking place in London seems to satisfy a human need which the more sober ceremonies of modern democratic government cannot supply. Golden trumpets sounded in London to summon its citizens to hear the proclamation which declared Elizabeth II Queen of the Realm. In a huge crimson and gilt banqueting hall which has seen British kings come and go from the days of Henry VIII, father of the first Elizabeth, young Elizabeth took the oath today. In a firm, clear tone she told the Privy Council, 'I pray that God will help me discharge worthily this heavy task that has been laid upon me so early in my life.'

"Three thousand people gathered outside the palace for the first reading of the proclamation by Sir George Bellow, Garter King of Arms. He was dressed in elaborate cloth of gold worked with the royal coat of arms over a suit of velvet. Other members of the royal entourage stood by also dressed in ancient gold-braided costumes. Then a formal procession of carriages drove to different spots in London where the proclamation was read again. They were accompanied by the Household Cavalry. . . . The new Queen is now at

event that saddened the entire British Commonwealth and the world at large had made her a Queen. The Princess and her consort had just left London a few days before and were enjoying a holiday at an East Africa hunting lodge.

"The King is dead, long live the Queen," was what the formally attired royal herald proclaimed throughout London in one of the traditional ceremonies connected with the British monarchy. A new Elizabethan era was thus launched. Elizabeth became the sixth woman to rule Britain, not counting Lady Jane Grey's fourteen-day reign in 1553 after which she was beheaded. In paying tribute to the dead King, Prime Minister Winston

The Coronation of Queen Elizabeth II.

Queen Elizabeth II.

Sandringham, the royal family's country home where her father's body lies in state. Next week the casket will lie in state in Westminster Hall near where so many of England's great leaders and public figures lie buried. The new Queen went immediately to the great bedchamber in which her father lay in his favorite uniform as Admiral of the Fleet. She stood alone for an hour in the gathering gloom of a winter's twilight until her husband came quietly to her side and took her hand. Then she followed her father's coffin as the estate gamekeepers wheeled it 300 yards through the darkness to the fifteenth-century Church of St. Mary Magdalene, where the royal family worship.

"There is tremendous interest in every detail of the funeral and accession, not only in Britain, but also in this country. It is a curious paradox that the popularity of the British royal family has never been so high as today—when its real power has never been so low. . . . But today press and radio, television and mov-

ing pictures in both England and America vie with one another in paying tribute to the late King. Pictures and life stories of young Queen Elizabeth are being read with eager interest all over the world."

Almost a year and a half passed before world interest in British royalty was to rise to new heights with Elizabeth II's coronation on June 2, 1953. It was one of the mightiest spectacles of the century, with all the age-old colorful pageantry and tradition of monarchy and the highly significant two-and-a-half hour crowning ceremony in venerable Westminster Abbey. Millions of Britons and visitors from all parts of the world crowded London streets for long hours to pay homage to the Queen. Seldom in history has there been such an aura of sheer romance and dramatic impact surrounding any momentous event—a twenty-seven-year-old queen, a veritable fairy-tale prince for a consort, two children, Prince Charles and Princess Anne, who would be next in line of succession to the throne. The eyes of the world were justifiably fastened on the gilded four-ton state coach as it swept out of Buckingham Palace, accompanied by thousands of Commonwealth troops, as it bore the Queen and Prince Philip to the Abbey.

For weeks the coronation had been headlined in every paper in the country. Millions of Americans were just as fascinated with the stories and pictures about the royal family and the coronation as their British cousins. When the great day finally came, there was a transatlantic race to see which television network would show the first films of the event to the eagerly waiting American public. As was eminently fitting, the British Broadcasting Company won the race. The kinescope recordings flown to Montreal via Goose Bay, Labrador, in jet planes, went on the air in New York City seven and a half hours after leaving London via the Canadian Broadcasting Corporation and the ABC network here. NBC and CBS, whose specially chartered planes were delayed, failed in the race to be the first on the air with TV coronation films.

The Queen was crowned—what next for Britain? That question concerned many minds on the day after the gay and colorful coronation. Would Britain again be able to return to what was known as "the spacious times of great Elizabeth?" I told my radio audience that we Americans would like to think Britain could enjoy another marvelous Elizabethan age. For good or ill, the English-speaking world to which we belong must live and stand together. The fact cannot be obscured that as between the free world and the slave world the English-speaking peoples have a common purpose and perhaps a common destiny. The coronation ceremonies in London make us remember our common loyalty to a great tradition of democratic government and to those spiritual values in which we find a common source of strength.

61.

Marshal Tito and the Soviet Union

The men and events of yesterday often provide the headlines of today and tomorrow. Marshal Tito was very much in the news nine years ago when he made his historic break with Russia. In 1956 he again made headlines with his reconciliation visit to the Soviet Union. But this only came after Premier Bulganin and Party Chief Khrushchev visited Marshal Tito to apologize for one of the late Premier Stalin's many mistakes.

It does seem like yesterday that the Russian radio broadcasters were telling Yugoslavia's communist neighbors that Marshal Tito was planning aggression against them. Then the anti-Yugoslav broadcasts from Moscow and from the satellite capitals took up a new line. They emphasized the weakness of the Yugoslav army, its lack of morale, and its inadequate equipment. "The time is not far off when the treacherous Tito gang will be overcome by the shameful fate of dishonest hirelings of imperialist reaction." This was Molotov's dire prediction on the occasion of Stalin's birthday in 1949. When Tito visited Moscow in 1956 Molotov was previously removed from his post as foreign minister as a gesture of good will.

In 1950, when I visited Yugoslavia, the conflict between Tito and the Cominform commanded much attention. Yugoslavia was then a focal point in the cold war. With Stalin at the helm in Moscow any incident might have provoked armed intervention by Russia, Rumania, Hungary, Bulgaria or all of them combined. Yugoslavia's break from the Moscow

Marshal Tito reviews a tank contingent during the May Day Parade—1954.

camp had evolved into bitter conflict between the two governments. Tito's defiant attitude was a heavy blow to Soviet prestige in eastern Europe and a serious obstacle to further Soviet penetration. Thanks largely to American aid and Tito's break with Stalin, Greece had been kept outside of the Iron Curtain. Tito's withdrawal of support for the communist-inspired Greek guerrillas caused Moscow to denounce Tito as "an enemy of the Soviet and an agent of foreign imperialist circles."

When I met Ambassador Delcoigne of Belgium in Yugoslavia he told me that the "Big Boy," as Tito was called in diplomatic circles, was most happy to see the United States and western Europe speeding up rearmament, because Tito insisted that force was the only thing the Kremlin would respect. While Yugoslavia moved away willingly enough from Russia, she was moving only slowly and carefully toward capitalist United States.

The leaders in Yugoslavia—Tito, Kardelj, Djilas, Piyade, Bebler, and other lesser lights —were all fanatical Communists, yet realized they had copied too much concentration of power from Russia. They were developing their own ideas, such as the organization of workers councils in every industrial plant. They felt the Russian system did not give individual plants sufficient autonomy. Tito told me that bureaucracy and centralization were the two great enemies of Socialist success. He was fighting both. In the Zagreb area the number of executive commissioners had just been reduced from 435 to 86. As one leader expressed it, "It is the spirit with which people fight for their independence that counts. In this respect, Yugoslavia is strong. We are working out our own experiment which is subject to change. The trouble with the Russians is they think they have the one and only successful system and they want to impose it on everyone else."

Tito impressed me as a true Yugoslav patriot. He had risked his life for his country many times as a guerrilla fighter and was ready to risk it again. He also suggested that, as a dictator, he could be ruthless and arbitrary. In my lengthy interview with him he talked like a cautious statesman. He was dressed neatly in a light tropical-weave suit with a conservative necktie. But he wore a ring with

210

President Tito and his wife went to Moscow in 1956 after Khrushchev and Bulganin had patched up differences on their visit to Belgrade.

SOVFOTO

an enormous solitaire diamond. He chain-smoked cigarettes using a curious perpendicular holder. Affable and smiling throughout the interview, he proved a generous host by offering his guests wine, beer, vermouth, absinthe, and coffee.

I told him that Americans were disappointed by his refusal to join us in opposing North Korean aggression. He replied, "We must be extremely careful not to provoke Russia. We are in a delicate position and must not provide any excuse for an attack on us. But we are definitely opposed to any kind of aggression and are loyal members of the United Nations. If there is any aggression against Yugoslavia we will make an immediate appeal to the United Nations. But we anticipate no aggression from Russia or from our neighbor states in the East. Frontier incidents have been exaggerated."

On the matter of neighborly relations, Marshal Tito went on: "We tried to re-establish diplomatic relations with Greece. We sent an envoy to Athens, but they sent none to Belgrade so we recalled ours. The Greeks keep agitating the Macedonian ques-tion through their Macedonian minority. We have established a Macedonian state within Yugoslavia. There's no sound reason for creating difficulties between Greece and Yugoslavia on this issue."

Tito had relaxed police controls in Yugoslavia and I asked if he expected to relax them still more. He replied that there is no theoretical or practical reason why a Socialist state must be a police state and that he hoped to demonstrate this truth in his country. In regard to his belief in the co-existence of communism and capitalism I quoted Lenin's statement that one must destroy the other. The Marshal remarked: "You exaggerate the meaning of what Lenin did say. The two systems have lived together and can continue to do so. We do not propose to export communism. We are also willing to accept help from capitalism. We have received several small loans from the United States, but we can use additional credits to great advantage. We have mines rich in copper, lead, and manganese. You need these minerals and we would like to sell them to you. But we need up-to-date mining machinery to get them out of the ground.

211

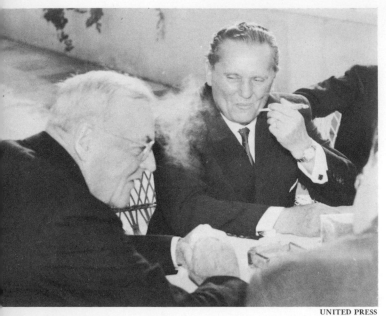

Secretary of State Dulles meets with Marshal Tito in 1955 to discuss the world situation.

62.

Supreme Court Decision on Racial Segregation in Schools—1954

One of the most significant domestic events of our time was the Supreme Court ruling of May 17, 1954, outlawing segregation in public schools. The "separate-but-equal schools" doctrine which had been in effect since 1896 was declared unconstitutional.

This dramatic unanimous decision, read by Chief Justice Earl Warren, set off a chain of reactions that will echo and re-echo for years to come. The opinion affected seventeen states with compulsory public-school segregation and four states with "permissive" school segregation.

Loudest in their denunciation of the ruling were the five states of the deep South. The viewpoints ranged all along the line from Governor Herman Talmadge's boastful threat that his fellow Georgians would "fight to manage their own affairs" to a pledge of full compliance with the ruling by Harold R. Fatzer, Attorney General of Kansas. Governor Talmadge voiced the irresponsible and demagogic charge that the Supreme Court had "reduced our Constitution to a mere scrap of paper and lowered itself to the level of common politics." Less vituperative, Governor James F. Byrnes, of South Carolina, stated he was "shocked to learn that the Court has reversed itself," while Senator Harry Byrd, of Virginia, denounced the decision as a "most serious blow to states' rights."

Senator James O. Eastland, of Mississippi, was reckless enough to predict "the South will not abide by or obey this legislative decision by a political court." Seven months after the

However, there is a definite limit to what we can accept on credit. We must be able to pay back what we borrow. We do not propose to mortgage our future or to sacrifice our independence."

Tito insisted that Russia was an aggressor state that followed neither Marx nor Lenin. "They haven't got communism," he said, "they've got state capitalism."

Much has happened since 1950. The Soviet Union is relatively weaker while Yugoslavia has become stronger. Stalin is dead and has been pulled down from his high pedestal. Tito and Stalin's successors have had a love feast and patched up their differences. The Yugoslav dictator insists that his friendly relations with the West remain unchanged. We are not so sure.

212

"AN APPLE FOR THE TEACHER"
By Anne Mergen in the Miami Daily News

"PUTTING IT DOWN IN BLACK AND WHITE"
By Grover Page in the Louisville Courier-Journal

WIDE WORLD

Supreme Court's decision was handed down, the voters in Mississippi, by a majority of about two to one, approved a state constitutional amendment to permit the abolition of public schools if there were no other way to avoid racial segregation of school children. The governors of all the southern states also met in a special conference to discuss the possible methods of delaying or avoiding compliance with the ruling.

Most excessive and most unnecessary in the chain of negative reactions was the trouble in Milford, Delaware. There white students boycotted classes after eleven Negroes had been enrolled in the high school. The board of

education which had authorized the enrollment was weak enough to resign and through the efforts of Governor J. Caleb a new board was formed which dropped the Negro students.

In contrast to the reaction in the South, the outlawing of school segregation was loudly lauded in other parts of the country and by western European newspapers. The National Association for the Advancement of Colored People said the decision gave the "lie" to communist propaganda that Negroes were denied equal rights in the United States.

The person who probably made the most sense about the ruling was one of the great

213

A segregated Negro school in Georgia.

Clinton, Tennessee, 1956. The Supreme Court decision was not popular.

Negro leaders of the day, Dr. Ralph J. Bunche. He predicted that segregation and discrimination would be "completely broken" in the United States by 1963. Addressing the closing session of the National Association for the Advancement of Colored People's Convention in Dallas, Texas, on July 4, 1954, he advised Negroes to indulge in no "boasting, gloating, or vindictiveness" but to trust in the "good hearts and fairness of the American people." He said, "This is the time to serve our country's best interests even more than our own."

Only time will tell how soon the great social change will be completely realized. Four months after the Supreme Court decision, segregation ended in Washington, D.C., fulfilling President Eisenhower's hope that Washington would set the pattern for the rest of the country. Although there was some boycotting of schools by white students, the boycott ended within a month. Desegregation is working in the national capital as it is in Baltimore and other large cities of mixed population. By the end of January 1955 racial segregation of white and Negro students ended entirely without incident in St. Louis' public high schools and later in the elementary schools. There was much further progress throughout 1956.

In the die-hard states there is still resistance to integration with a variety of incidents. In October 1955, the Supreme Court ordered Alabama University to admit a Negro student, Autherine Lucy. However, her admittance and attendance at classes in February 1956 touched off some rock and egg throwing by the segregationists at the university. About 1,000 individuals, largely students, took part in the demonstration. Miss Lucy was suspended for "her own safety," to be followed by indictments and lawsuits which attracted national and even international attention. Miss Lucy finally renounced her ambition to obtain an education at Alabama University.

One unfortunate reaction to the Supreme Court decision came from a group of national legislators in the spring of 1956. On March 11 nineteen senators and seventy-seven congressmen issued a manifesto denouncing the United States Supreme Court's public-school desegregation on legal grounds. Naturally, the group represented the rebellious southern bloc.

One enlightening effort to have the question of desegregation understood and to show how the Supreme Court's ruling was functioning was a survey made early this year by the New York *Times*. The *Times* sent a corps of reporters throughout the South and to border states to observe firsthand what was taking place. According to the findings, Alabama, Georgia, Mississippi, South Carolina, and Virginia were "resisting" the decision that racial segregation be abolished. The states of Florida, Louisiana, North Carolina, Tennessee, and Texas were divided or delaying compliance with the decision. Delaware, the District of Columbia, Kentucky, Maryland, Missouri, Oklahoma, and West Virginia were "integrating" with most encouraging results.

Generally, the survey found, white southerners seemed more troubled, confused, and resentful, rather than rebellious. And the southern Negroes likewise seem to be troubled and rebellious. White spokesmen speak of staving off integration for twenty to twenty-five years which strongly indicates eventual integration in all areas.

My first contact with the Negro problem came in 1898 when my Spanish War regiment was sent to Camp Shipp, outside of Anniston, Alabama, for training purposes. I had seen few Negroes and few southerners and soon learned to like them both. This helped me understand why segregation had come to be accepted by both races and why it would take

215

A revival of the dread Ku Klux Klan threatened as hooded Klansmen gathered in Montgomery, Alabama.

WIDE WORLD

time to work out full equality before the law.

When riots developed between members of a white Kentucky and a colored Alabama regiment, both stationed in Camp Shipp, my Company F of the Fourth Wisconsin Volunteers was called out for riot duty in the city of Anniston. For the first time I realized how a few hotheads could fan latent racial antagonisms into open violence. Ever since I have been in favor of the middle way which is now so ably championed by southerners such as William Faulkner and Negroes such as Dr. Bunche.

The extremists who preach illegal resistance or immediate compulsory compliance are doing a disservice to both races. It required a generation after the Fifteenth Amendment was passed before the courts could set aside the many devices used to block Negro suffrage. Today a large and growing segment of southern Negroes are able to vote and do vote. It will take time to do away with some of the devices which southern states will develop to prevent desegregation. There must be steady progress in implementing the Supreme Court decision. But it will be better to let fair-minded southerners direct that progress in their own way than to exacerbate the problem by hot-headed northern insistence on immediate compliance.

216

Index

218